Readings in Values Clarification

Readings in Values Clarification

Howard Kirschenbaum
Sidney B. Simon

Winston Press
Minneapolis

Winston Press, Inc.
25 Groveland Terrace
Minneapolis, MN 55403

Distributed in Canada by
Holt, Rinehart and Winston of Canada, Limited
55 Horner Avenue
Toronto, Ontario
M8Z 4X6
Canada

Acknowledgments

Grateful acknowledgment is given for permission to reprint the following excerpts from copyrighted materials:

"Song of the Open Road" by Ogden Nash. From *Verses from 1929 On* by Ogden Nash. Copyright 1932, by Ogden Nash. Used by permission of Little, Brown and Co.

"A Caution to Everybody" by Ogden Nash. From *The Private Dining Room & Other New Verses* by Ogden Nash. Copyright 1950, by Ogden Nash. Used by permission of Little, Brown and Co.

"Plenty of Rein" by Clair Roskam. From *The Seeking Years* edited by John M. Gunn. Copyright 1959. Used by permission of The Bethany Press.

"A Conservationist's Lament" and "The Technologist's Reply" by Kenneth Boulding. From *Man's Role in Changing the Face of the Earth*, edited by William L. Thomas, Jr. Copyright 1956 by the University of Chicago Press. Used with permission.

From "Self-Concepts of the Socially Disadvantaged" by Travis L. Hawk. *The Elementary School Journal*, January 1967. Used by permission of the University of Chicago Press.

From The New York Times. © 1972 by The New York Times Company. Reprinted by permission.

From "Observer" column by Russell Baker, January 5, 1965. © 1965 by The New York Times Company. Reprinted by permission.

"Merry-Go-Round" by Langston Hughes. Copyright 1942 by Langston Hughes, and renewed 1970 by Arna Bontemps and George Huston Bass. Reprinted from *Selected Poems*, by Langston Hughes, by permission of Alfred A. Knopf, Inc.

From "Protestor, Police & Politicians" by Jesse Unruh. Copyright 1970 by Saturday Review Co. First appeared in *Saturday Review*, February 21, 1970. Used with permission.

Contents

Readings in Values Clarification

Values Clarification and Other Perspectives

INTRODUCTION

The fields of philosophy and religion have for centuries been concerned with the area of values. More recently, the modern professions — sociology, anthropology, psychology, and others — have also taken a great interest in this realm. The wide-spread focus on the values domain has caused a similar spread in the locus of value education. Traditionally, training in values was left to the home and the church. But in recent times, as the family and religious institutions have had an increasingly small influence on the values of youth, there has been a gradual movement to involve the schools in the difficult task of values education.

In our society, families and organized religions will not allow the school to usurp their role and teach a particular set of values. Therefore, modern values education as it has evolved in the schools has, for the most part, emphasized the teaching of a *process* of valuing, rather than any one value or value system.

Values clarification, stemming from the pioneer work of Louis Raths, is one approach to teaching a process of valuing — in schools, in homes, or in any setting where values issues may be present. In this section, the Harmin, Simon, and Kirschenbaum articles, "Values" and "Values and the Futures Movement in Education," present an overview of the values-clarification approach.

The Holt article, "The Values We Teach in Schools" takes a look at some of the specific values which seem to be present or absent in the schools and in society. The author's analysis leads him to the conclusion that we, as educators, must face squarely the value confusion and contradictions of our times and that we must help young people learn to make choices and to act upon their values.

The next several articles step back from the values-clarification perspective and look at some other approaches to valuing. While values clarification treats the valuing process as having three aspects — the affective, the cognitive, and the active — the Phenix and Kohlberg articles fall in the long tradition of viewing valuing as primarily a cognitive task.*

*For much more background on and examples of cognitive approaches to value development, we would recommend *Values Education, 41st Yearbook: Rationale, Strategies and Procedures*, by Jerrold R. Coombs et al. Lawrence E. Metcalf, ed. (Washington, D.C.: National Council for the Social Studies, 1971).

Nevertheless, their thinking, research, and teaching approach seem, for the most part, consistent with values clarification in that they urge students to examine alternatives and consequences and encourage them to reach their own decisions, morals, and values. In a short interview, Kohlberg and Simon exchange their views on how each other's work relates to his own.

The Rogers article, as opposed to the Kohlberg and Phenix essays, views valuing as primarily an emotional process with incidental rational overlays. Rogers attempts to trace the relationship between the child's developing values and his self-concept and poses the stimulating suggestion that the valuing process in people leads, in the end, to some common and constructive human values. Rokeach, taking a different tack, explores the relationship between certain cognitive valuing exercises and changes in the students' behavior— their actions. Those interested in values clarification might consider whether Rokeach's approach comes closer to clarifying or manipulating the students' values.

The section ends with the Kirschenbaum essay, "Beyond Values Clarification," which offers some criticism of the traditional values-clarification theory and argues that values clarification should be integrated with the other approaches to humanistic education. It goes on to suggest how that might be done.

Values

by Merrill Harmin and Sidney B. Simon

INTRODUCTION

There is good reason to wonder if our schools have sufficiently helped students with value development. We see young people with substantial knowledge who do not know what to do with that knowledge. We see others who chronically react in a negative and unthinking way to almost everything in their surroundings. In general, we see many students who are confused about what their values are or should be.

Given the condition of the world, such value confusion is quite understandable. The contrasts and changes that surround all of us today are dramatic.

Look at these social realities, for example: Support for the arts is hard to come by. Educated men insist that our leaders twist the truth for their own purposes. The crime rate goes up and up. Roaming mobs face riot-trained police. And American soldiers in foreign lands are accused of rounding up old men, women, and children and shooting them.

At the same time there is new concern for the plight of the American Indian, the elderly, and the slum dweller. People no longer look aside as the air, streams, and lakes become polluted. The courts strengthen the individual's freedom of speech. The rich are asked to pay more taxes; there is new support for the poor. And people are wondering aloud if America is on the right track.

One can see how it is difficult for students to relate to this inconsistent world. Traditional values are not accepted the way they used to be; some students plainly reject them. But many students cannot seem to find replacements for traditional values. The result is often an absence of values. Students are unsure of what to do with the knowledge they find in school. Some are not sure that knowledge has any use at all. And some seem to confuse knowledge with wisdom and adopt a life-style of either chronic conformity or impulsive rebellion.[1]

More precisely, a value problem is indicated for a student if, in the absence of a prior emotional disturbance, he finds it very difficult to face typical life situations and to make choices and decisions. Or if he typically makes choices without the awareness that some alternatives may be more worthy than others. Or if he does not behave in ways that are consistent with his choices and preferences—that is, if there is a gap between his creeds and his deeds.

WHAT TEACHERS CAN DO ABOUT VALUES

There are other ways of characterizing value problems among youth.[2] But however one sees value problems, the question of what, if anything, teachers can do remains. That is the subject of this article. What alternatives are open to a teacher who would help students with value development? We will address that question by listing several of the more common approaches to values and commenting briefly on each. There is no assumption that the list is exhaustive or that any one approach should be used exclusively. For example, although the authors favor the last approach introduced, we would use other approaches in certain circumstances, as we note in our concluding remarks.

Teachers have three main alternatives in dealing with value development. One alternative is to do nothing about such development. Another is to transmit a pre-existing set of values to students. A third is to help students find their own values.

DOING NOTHING ABOUT VALUES

Some teachers choose the first alternative because they
believe that values are the domain of the family and religious
institutions. Others choose it because, practically, they
do not know what to do. Some educators choose to do nothing
about value development because they are trained for and
are interested in teaching only subject matter. A few
educators believe that values come from trial-and-error
interaction with life, and that there is nothing a school can
do other than provide an array of useful experiences and
encourage students to use those experiences the best
way they can.

But the reality of schooling is that it is impossible to do
nothing.[3] When a teacher says that it is important to master
a lesson to get good grades to get into college to get a good job
to earn a good salary, he is obviously promoting several
values — a work ethic, a future orientation, and materialism,
to name a few.

When a textbook constantly pairs communism with
autocracy and capitalism with democracy, values are clearly
suggested. And when schools simply talk about safety, good
manners, and good health, they are usually trying to promote
these values. Thus, it is unreal to say that schools should do
nothing about values. The question is, should they continue
to work at values the way they currently do?

There is a special problem facing those who would leave
the teaching of values to the family or to religious institutions.
Most parents probably do not know how to impart values,
and most religious institutions have only minimal impact on
the values of youth.[4] One could, of course, argue that these
institutions should learn to be more effective. Until that
happens, however, it is unlikely that parents or religious
institutions will change the way young people perceive and
deal with values.

TRANSMITTING VALUES

Some educators who are concerned with the state of youth's
values believe that we must work more effectively to transmit
the values we know are right, desirable, and good. They
assume that such values are known, at least in part, and

that the task of the educator is to learn better ways of passing those values along to students.

Two general problems face such educators: being certain that their values really are universally right, desirable, and good; and finding ways to transmit them. The problem of value certainty is beyond the scope of this article, but it is dealt with in a book by Abraham Maslow.[5] The question of transmittal is considered below in a discussion of six common approaches to transmitting values: the model approach, the reward-and-punishment approach, the explanatory approach, the nagging approach, the manipulation approach, and the transmittal liberal arts approach.

The Model Approach

Some people who assume that what is right and wrong can be identified and communicated to others believe that one should model desirable values. Such people try to behave in ways that reflect the values they want to transmit.

There is much evidence that modeling has a strong influence on children's behavior. If we assume that one absorbs values as one absorbs behavior patterns, we can say that modeling affects children's values as well as their behavior.

There is a parallel between modeling and what is sometimes called imprinting. Thus some experiences, especially those repeatedly or strongly presented to a susceptible subject, are deeply imprinted in the growing organism.[6]

The most serious problem for the modeling approach to value development is that, in our complex society, conflicting models exist for almost every value one could name. A parent or teacher could model hard work, for example, but a friend or television star or storybook character might present the opposite model. The modeling approach by itself provides no means of helping youngsters deal with the conflicting and inconsistent models that they are almost certain to perceive in a world drawn closer and closer together by modern communication devices.

The modeling approach is also weak in dealing with values that are only imperfectly reflected in public behavior. It is difficult to model certain very personal values and internal phenomena, such as aspirations, faith, or loyalty.

The Reward-and-Punishment Approach

Some educators believe that one does not so much influence values as shape behavior. In the reward-and-punishment approach, the teacher or parent first identifies desirable behavior and then, by judicious rewards, encouragement, and the like, encourages the repetition of that behavior. Thus one might reward punctuality, reflective thinking, and kindness and ignore their opposites.[7]

Sometimes teachers try to develop certain value habits by giving students materials or activities that channel behavior in desired ways. For example, a teacher might give students round pencils and tilted desks to encourage the habit of tidiness; the built-in penalty for a pencil left carelessly on a desk is a pencil rolling away.

However, proponents of this approach have the problem of explaining how it can influence internal operations of humans, operations below the observable behavior level. One can shape much behavior, but can one shape feelings and thought processes?

A somewhat different problem is that humans are not completely malleable. Humans have certain innate and early-learned drives and limitations. They have their own individual processes of thought and evaluation, drives for activity and power, and needs for self-expression. How does the notion that adults can shape children's behavior come to terms with children's internal powers and inclinations? What happens if there is a conflict between the two?[8]

The Explanatory Approach

Some educators propose that children be provided explanations such as the following for values that are to be promoted:

"If you do not wait your turn, people will not be happy to have you in their groups."

"If we steal from one another, we will all be insecure about our property."

"If we didn't have rules, aggressive people might take advantage of others."

"If you do that, your conscience may bother you."

The explanatory approach to value development is obviously useful; many students appreciate knowing the reason for existing standards and adult beliefs. Moreover, it is likely that children will more deeply accept those standards and beliefs that are supported by understandable reasons.

Unfortunately, almost all explanation is bound to be incomplete and to rest on prior assumptions, which are seldom explained. "If you do not wait your turn, people will not be happy to have you in their groups" — the assumption here is that it is valuable to have people want you in their groups. One could explain this by saying that if people do not want you, you will be cut off from much human support. But then one may ask why it is valuable to have a lot of human support. "One will feel lonely," the reply might be. "Why is it valuable not to feel lonely?" one might ask, in an endless series of questions.

There is another problem with the explanatory approach. Values presumably influence an individual's decisions, and many decisions we face involve a conflict between two or more desirable elements. Knowing why honesty and politeness are both worthy does not often help us when we are faced with the choice of being either dishonest or impolite.

The Nagging Approach

Less recommended than practiced is what we call the nagging approach. Educators employing this approach frequently remind students what is right and wrong and what is expected of them without attending to whether or not the students understand the reasons for those standards. Often this approach is based on the assumption that values emerge from authority: "We are in charge here, and we know what is best." Although such educators sometimes praise compliance, they more often punish and complain about deviations from accepted standards.

The problems with this method are obvious. Students are more annoyed than educated by this negative approach, and there is the real possibility that educators using it will find themselves disaffiliated from and "tuned out" by their students.

The Manipulation Approach

The manipulation approach is also less often recommended than practiced. Educators use it when they manipulate the

environment or the experiences to which students are
exposed so as to favor certain value outcomes.

One manipulatory approach is to withhold knowledge of
alternatives from students. Students might not be told about
the alternative of telling the truth *sometimes*, or of the
alternative of conducting a campaign of persuasion to
change a school's policy. Students might then assume that
the choices are between complete truthfulness and complete
untruthfulness, or between acquiescence and revolution.
Teachers probably influence student values more than is
usually appreciated merely by restricting the alternatives
that enter students' awareness.

Another way of manipulating situations is to distort the
consequences of certain actions. When a teacher suggests to
a student that he cannot hope to be happy in life unless he
graduates from high school, he is distorting reality in favor
of a value that he wants to promote. Many educators are
quick to paint rosy pictures of things they favor and dark
pictures of things they disfavor.

A third manipulatory approach is to restrict a student's
experiences in ways that have value consequences. Some
persons prevent racial integration and thus sustain racial
myths. Others restrict the books students read — not because
they want to protect students from emotionally difficult
experiences but because they want to insulate them from
sympathetic accounts of certain value positions.

In a sense, it is even manipulatory for teachers to fail to
raise controversial issues in school, for that perpetuates the
status quo. Forces for change do not have a fair chance. Thus,
schools that do not raise such issues as the role of women
in society, the problems of minority groups, and the forms
of real political power in the country might be accused of
manipulating values.

The manipulation approach has several disadvantages.
It is uncomfortable for those who believe that man's rational
processes need to be fully utilized. And it runs counter to
current trends in society, as more people are being exposed
to more ideas through increased communications. It is
increasingly difficult to keep ideas away from students, to
sustain distorted consequences, and to limit student
experiences.

The Transmittal Liberal Arts Approach

Some educators believe that right values exist and will be revealed to those who are immersed in what is often called the liberal arts. These right values, these basic goods, might not be the ones currently accepted, it is asserted, but they do exist and will most likely be found by those who study man's thoughts and accomplishments with an open mind. Educators who take this position, called the transmittal liberal arts approach, want students to read widely, think deeply, and experience broadly. They trust that life experiences and thoughtful study provide a route to absolute goods and values.

However, because values are complex and because man's thoughts and accomplishments are both abundant and complicated, it is difficult to recommend that the average student rely upon this approach. It takes substantial mental stamina and ability and much time and energy to travel this road. While the study of our cultural heritage can be defended on other grounds, we would not expect it to be sufficient for value education.

CLARIFYING VALUES

The two approaches outlined below are not based upon the assumption that absolute goods exist and can be known. They view values as relative, personal, and situational. The main task of these approaches is not to identify and transmit the "right" values, but to help a student clarify his own values so he can obtain the values that best suit him and his environment; so he can adjust himself to a changing world; and so he can play an intelligent role in influencing the way the world changes.

Proponents of these approaches have at least two problems. First, they must learn methods whereby, without promoting particular values, they can help students obtain values that will work for them and for those around them. Second, they must devise methods of controlling behavior so that, while students are in the process of developing values, they and others are protected against destructive behaviors. The usual solution here is to have behavior rules that are not defended as values, but merely as devices for protecting individuals and groups against pressures from others.

The Clarifying Liberal Arts Approach

The clarifying liberal arts approach is similar to the transmittal liberal arts approach; both utilize the records of man's thoughts and accomplishments. But the purpose of the clarifying liberal arts approach is different: It is aimed at exposing students to the best in the culture so that a student may find the best values for himself and his environment, not so that he may discover the "right" values for all times. In the clarifying liberal arts approach, students read widely, think deeply, and experience broadly—not to find universal values, but to find themselves.

Unfortunately, it is probably not much easier to use all of culture to find oneself than it is to use it to find eternal truths. Our cultural heritage is too broad, too complex, and too inconsistent to expect the average student to grasp it and relate it to his life and times with any degree of comfort and comprehension.

The Value Skills Approach

Another approach holds that the problem is not so much helping a student find values as it is helping him learn skills to continue the value-clarifying approach throughout his life and to apply his values in ways that are personally and socially useful. Proponents of this value skills approach often note that the world is changing rapidly and recommend that we provide students with skills to change values as the world changes and as students become more knowledgeable. Noting that it is easy to mouth creeds and not perform the accompanying deeds, they recommend that we teach how to apply values in real situations, so that behavior reflects value thinking.

Pragmatic philosophers after Dewey[9] have favored developing in students an experimental attitude toward life. They believe that value questions should be treated like other questions, with thoughtful consideration of alternatives and consequences, both social and personal. They assert that moral issues are as susceptible to rational processes as are other issues. Persons who take this position believe that, just as one learns critical thinking skills, so one learns value skills. They often favor in schools a nonmoralizing examination of current real-life issues; this is sometimes called the problems approach and is usually used not in place of academic study, but in addition to it.[10]

Some children's readers have been built around value issues and are meant to encourage value thinking.[11] And some curriculum approaches have been built in this style. In this connection, special note should be made of the work of Donald W. Oliver and James P. Shaver.[12] They have identified specific skills useful for dealing with political controversy, especially the ethical problems that arise out of such controversy. Measuring instruments for those skills are also identified.

In general, the purposes of these approaches are to sensitize children to value issues, to give them experiences in thinking critically about such issues, to give them opportunities to share perceptions with others and learn cooperative problem-solving skills, and to help them learn to apply value skills in their own lives.

Some educators approach value skills from a psychological perspective. Many so-called humanistic psychologists, such as Carl Rogers, say that if a person is put into a supportive social environment and encouraged to tune into his feelings and the feelings of others, and if he is taught communication skills that minimize communication distortion, he will naturally tend to make wise judgments and will use experience to correct judgments that are unwise.[13] Such psychologists place a good deal of trust in man's internal evaluation mechanisms and in the ability of groups who share data to arrive at wise decisions. A key implication is that teachers should be helped to become more honest, warm, and empathetic.

A more comprehensive methodology, built on the positions of the pragmatic philosophers and humanistic psychologists, has identified seven broad value skills and has gathered a series of classroom techniques to help students learn those skills. The skills are: 1) seeking alternatives when faced with a choice; 2) looking ahead to probable consequences before choosing; 3) making choices on one's own, without depending on others; 4) being aware of one's own preferences and valuations; 5) being willing to affirm one's choices and preferences publicly; 6) acting in ways that are consistent with choices and preferences; and 7) acting in those ways repeatedly, with a pattern to one's life. Those skills and the exercises to develop them are presented by Louis E. Raths, Merrill Harmin, and Sidney B. Simon in *Values and Teaching*.

There are, however, problems with this approach, too. When one focuses upon processes of valuing and not upon the values themselves, one is faced with the problem of what to do with students whose processes are faulty, or who for other reasons (sometimes emotional pressures) come to adopt values that are, for them or for others, counterproductive.

There is the additional problem of knowing which skills best prepare persons to clarify and revise values. Could it be that those who advocate a particular list of skills are saying that they have found a new set of universal values (which happen to be in the form of processes rather than products)?

CONCLUSION

Research on the effectiveness of the various approaches to values is lacking. Researchers to date have not agreed on goals for value education, especially on the balance between value indoctrination and value clarification. They need better measuring instruments, especially to distinguish values expressed on paper-and-pencil tests from values woven into behavior.

We conclude from what sketchy research does exist, and on the basis of rather consistent observations of young people's difficulties with values, that value confusion is growing in the United States. Teachers can help students avoid substantial drift and ambivalence by giving them value-clarifying experiences. A combination of the clarifying liberal arts approach and the value skills approach is probably best. The former provides data often useful for making choices, and the latter provides a climate and experiences for practicing value choice-making.

Models are also useful, but not as prescriptions of behavior to be emulated. They are useful as illustrations of what a life *can* be, not what a life *should* be. Students should be helped to examine models critically and to consider what is recommended by them, and not be led to believe that they should try to plan their existence as an imitation of the models.

Explanations are likewise useful if they inform a student's thinking, not if they are delivered as the last word on a value. When a teacher explains why he supports a certain value, he is being honest and open and responsive to students' needs to know. Explanations, as long as they are offered as personal or consensual statements of positions and not as dogma, encourage rational processes and thus develop value skills.

No matter what approach to values one takes, there will be some students who will behave in ways that contradict the teacher's, the school's, or the society's values. These students must be taught that there are limits to accepted behavior. But they should not be led to believe that they must accept the values upon which those limits are based. Thus a student should be told that we cannot accept his disturbing the work of others, even though we can accept the fact that his disturbing behavior is motivated by a strongly held value. Of course, we also believe that this position is relative; sometimes the value that the student is defending is more important than the disturbance he is causing (as many felt was the case with the black sit-ins at southern lunch counters a few years ago). The point here is that one may view values as situational and personal without believing that society should be lawless or chaotic. Indeed, observations of children who have learned to be rationally self-disciplined suggest that values-clarification approaches, based as they are on individual responsibility, are more likely to produce lawful and orderly environments than are approaches for transmitting values, which too often leave students feeling confused and valueless.

NOTES

1. Louis E. Raths, Merrill Harmin, and Sidney B. Simon, *Values and Teaching* (Columbus, Ohio: Charles E. Merrill Publishing Co., 1966).
2. Crane Brinton, *A History of Western Morals* (New York: Harcourt Brace Jovanovich, Inc., 1959); Jacob W. Getzels, "A Stable Identity in a World of Shifting Values," *Educational Leadership* 14, no. 4 (January 1957): 237-240.
3. Gunnar Myrdal, *Objectivity in Social Research* (New York: Pantheon Books, Inc., 1969).
4. Lawrence Kohlberg, "Development of Moral Character and Moral Ideology," *Review of Developmental Research*, ed. Martin L. Hoffman (New York: Russell Sage Foundation, 1964).

5. Abraham H. Maslow, ed., *New Knowledge in Human Values* (New York: Harper & Row, Publishers, 1959).

6. Philip H. Gray, "The Theory and Evidence of Imprinting in Human Infants," *Journal of Psychology* 46 (1958): 155-166.

7. Israel Goldiamond, "Moral Behavior: A Functional Analysis," *Readings in Psychology Today* (Del Mar, Cal.: CRM Books, 1969).

8. Joseph R. Royce, "Metaphoric Knowledge and Humanistic Psychology," *Challenges of Humanistic Psychology*, ed. James F. T. Bugental (New York: McGraw-Hill Book Co., 1967), pp. 21-28.

9. John Dewey, *Experience and Education* (New York: The Macmillan Co., 1938).

10. Maurice P. Hunt and Lawrence Metcalf, *Teaching High School Social Studies* (New York: Harper & Row, Publishers, 1968).

11. V. Clyde Arnspiger, James A. Brill, and W. Ray Rucker, *The Human Values Series* (Austin, Tex.: Steck-Vaughn Co., 1967).

12. Donald W. Oliver and James P. Shaver, *Teaching Public Issues in the High School* (Boston: Houghton Mifflin Company, 1966).

13. Carl R. Rogers, *Freedom to Learn* (Columbus, Ohio: Charles E. Merrill Publishing Co., 1969).

Values and the Futures Movement in Education

by Howard Kirschenbaum and Sidney B. Simon

Reprinted with permission from Alvin Toffler, editor of *Learning for Tomorrow*. New York: Random House, 1973.

Unless one believes that the future is inevitable—that we have absolutely no control over our private and public destinies—the study of the future must include not merely possible and probable futures, but *preferable* futures. This is why the broad movement aimed at shifting education into the future tense also brings with it a heightened concern with values.

Of course, a concern with values is not entirely new in education. What is new is the way in which this concern must express itself. In the past, we taught values, or tried to. Yet simply "teaching values" cannot and will not suffice for the future.

The child of today confronts many more choices than did the child of yesterday. He is surrounded by a bewildering array of alternatives. Modern society has made him less provincial and more sophisticated, but the complexity of these times has made the act of choosing infinitely more difficult.

Areas of confusion and conflict abound: politics, religion, love and sex, family, friends, drugs, materialism, race, work, aging and death, leisure time, school, and health. Each area demands decisions that yesterday's children were rarely called upon to make.

"Should I try marijuana? From everything I've seen and heard it seems less harmful than alcohol."

"Should we live together before getting married? Maybe the present staggering divorce rate would be lower if more of our parents had done some experimenting."

"Why bother going to college or staying in school? I think I could get myself a better education on my own."

"Why bother even voting? The only thing that seems to bring about change these days is taking to the streets, maybe even violently."

"What's the point of work at all? I see so many adults slaving their lives away—for what? They don't seem very happy."

Although the content of the questions sometimes varies over generations, it is not new that young people are asking questions. Children and youth have always wondered about themselves, their future, and their society. Consciously or not, they have always fought to develop values by which to live.

And, traditionally, the educators of the society—the parents, the schools, and the churches—have most often taken a common approach toward helping young people develop values and toward answering the value questions that young people raise.

We call this approach *moralizing*, although it has also been known as inculcation, imposition, indoctrination, and in its most extreme form, brainwashing. Moralizing is the direct or indirect transfer of a set of values from one person or group to another person or group. Sometimes moralizing is very direct and coercive; sometimes it is gentle and barely noticeable. In all cases it is based on a common assumption. "From my (our) experience, I (we) have come to believe that a certain set of beliefs and behaviors is better than another set of beliefs and behaviors. Therefore, rather than have you go through the pain of discovering this for yourself, and rather than risk the chance that you might come up with a different set of values, I shall do my best to convince you that my (our) set of values is the most desirable for you."

In a world in which the future bore a close resemblance to the past, moralizing was a relatively effective means of transmitting or "teaching" values. Educators, for the most part, agreed with parents on what values children should hold. Children were taught what to believe and how to act, and with rare exceptions, accepted these moralizations without serious question. Why should they question? The adults seemed in agreement, and there were few or no impinging forces to make them doubt their elders' wisdom.

Why Moralizing Doesn't Work

But consider the child of today. From every side he is bombarded with different, and often contradictory, sets of values. His parents offer one set of moralizations (communications on what to believe and how to behave) and often *two* sets, because the male-female roles have altered so dramatically that the woman need not agree with all her husband's values. His school teachers might have an entirely different set of values which are urged upon the child. And different teachers have different values—whether the issue be Vietnam, homework, competition, freedom, or gum-chewing. Organized religions offer still another set of moralizations, and as almost any newspaper or magazine will show, religious groups too are confused about their values. The communications media—television, Hollywood, radio, magazines and newspapers—literally bombard the growing person with all sorts of stimuli and inputs about what to believe, how to behave, what kind of language to use, how to dress, what type of life style to follow, and even how to avoid growing old. Always there is the implicit message: This is how you should think and act if you are going to get ahead, be successful, impress your superiors, and have sex appeal. Then there is the peer group, one of the most influential moralizing forces. "If you want to belong and be accepted, *here's* what you think and how you act." Add to these forces the political leaders, the youth movement leaders, folk and rock heroes, sports figures, each adding to the confusion with a new set of moralizations, and you have the dilemma of the child of today.

Any *one* of these moralizations might be very wise or very foolish, helpful or harmful, moral or immoral. But who's to say? Certainly not the young person, who, caught in the crossfire, can barely make sense out of any of it.

We have tried to teach values. But in a world of confusion and conflict about values, this is not enough. No matter how sincere we may be in our desire to help, all we leave the young person with is one more input, one more moralizing message, which goes into his overloaded computer to be processed along with others.

Hopefully, it gets processed. More likely the principle of "might makes right" applies to the confused person's valuing process. Whichever set of moralizations are most recent or most often repeated are the ones that dominate his thinking and behavior. He has all the inputs rolling around upstairs, but his values are entirely situational, and the locus of control is outside himself. If the peer group is most persuasive at a given time, it is these values he will draw upon. In the presence of authority, it is the authority's values that dominate. At no time is the young person in control of his own decisions. His values are not his own. They are the introjections of numerous moralizations which are undifferentiated to the individual. His lack of clarity about values often is manifested in apathetic, flighty, overconforming, and overdissenting behavior.

If moralizing has not prepared young people (many of whom are now adults) to sort out the value confusion of the *present*, then moralizing certainly will not help young people learn to cope with the future. Change is so rapid, and new alternatives arise so quickly in every area of life-choice that no one set of specific beliefs and behaviors could possibly answer all the choice situations of the future. Nor can our moralizings take the form of general guidelines and be expected to do the jobs. Values like "honesty," "religion," and "patriotism" may be beautiful ideas, but they simply do not answer specific dilemmas in which people find themselves. Taking the last example alone, one does not need Socrates to remind him that patriotism has a debatable definition and that "patriotic" citizens not long ago spent a decade both dying in Vietnam and protesting the war at home.

The shortcomings of moralizing have become increasingly apparent to educators concerned about teaching for the future. Talk to parents and religious leaders. Talk to any teacher with twenty years or more of experience, and they will tell the same story. "These kids just aren't the same as when I started teaching. It used to be the teacher's word was gospel. The children listened. They respected age and experience. But not now. Now they think they know more than you do. You can't tell them anything..." Depending on whom you talk to, the passing of the old days is looked upon with regret or with a feeling of "good-riddance." But the result is the same: kids just don't seem to be buying what the moralizers are selling anymore. They've got to discover it for themselves.

Laissez-Faire in the Classroom

The growing awareness of this reality has led many educators to eschew moralizing and adapt a *laissez-faire approach* toward values. Their response goes something like this: "No one set of values I teach or impose can solve the dilemmas of the unknown future. Ultimately people must develop their own values if the values are to work for them. Thus, I will give the young people I come in contact with the freedom to go their own way, make their own discoveries, and find their own answers. This is what they seem to be asking for. It's *their* world, in a way; they're the ones who will save it if anyone will. I'd better get out of the way and let them go to it." This approach is particularly attractive in public schools, which serve diverse populations with diverse values and would rather do nothing about values than offend a segment of the community by "teaching" the "wrong" values. Subject matter, after all, is a lot less controversial than what the students are going to do with their lives and how they will cope with their futures in a changing world. So the adult steps aside and avoids dealing with values altogether.

Yet, what has changed? The young person is *still* bombarded by most of the same stimuli and inputs. From everyone, save the one or two people in his life who have moved to the laissez-faire approach, there are still the pressures and forces urging him to believe this and to do that. The problem is slightly less than before, with one or two inputs removed, but is still there. He still has to process all the inputs, to select the best and eliminate the worst of all that he is being told to believe and to do.

Most of the people we have known—children, youth, or adults—don't really want to be left alone to solve all of life's dilemmas and problems unaided. When faced with a perplexing choice situation or some kind of doubt or problem, it is comforting to go to a friend and know that there will be

an empathetic listener who by his concern and questioning
can help one regain his confidence and achieve clarity
sufficient to guide his own course into the future. Learning
to guide one's life is a skill. There is a valuing process by
which we sort out all this stimuli around and within us. We
don't help our young people learn that process by ignoring
the problem.

Modeling

Not wanting to either moralize or ignore the problem,
educators have tried a third approach to transmit values to
young people, that of *modeling*. "If the direct inculcation of
values doesn't seem to work anymore, and if a laissez-faire
approach just leaves you floundering in what you might very
well perceive as a lack of concern on my part, then I will try
living a set of values. If I can be a model of an adult who
seems to know where he's going and is deriving satisfaction
from living, then surely my example will be seen and
respected, and young people will try to emulate me in many
ways and adopt many of my values."

This approach has some merit, insofar as it recognizes
that living by one's values is absolutely essential when
working with young people. They have no patience with
hypocrisy and will not tolerate adults whose lives are fraught
with contradiction yet who seem so complacent. The modeling
approach also has merit in that it offers a *concrete* alternative
for young people to consider. Vague words about high ideals
rarely communicate with the strength and clarity of a living
example (a reality most colleges of education have yet to
learn). We believe that teachers need to sacrifice some of
their neutrality and "objectivity" and become real human
beings to the students—human beings with feelings, goals,
values, and contradictions they are willing to reveal and
discuss, just as they would like their students to do.

But, for all its merits, modeling has the same major
drawback as moralizing. *There are so many models.* Parents,
teachers, religious leaders, peers, sports figures, movie,
television, and recording stars all present different models to
emulate. The young person still has to go through a
sophisticated choosing process if he is to wisely sort out the
best and worst from the various models.

If moralizing, laissez-faire, and modeling do not teach
young people a process for sorting out and making sense of all

the inputs and alternatives they have been exposed to, and will be increasingly exposed to in the future, how *will they* learn the process? Does the future hold any promise?

The Clarification of Values

In recent years, there have been many exciting developments in the field of "humanistic education." This movement is attempting to teach young people the intrapersonal and interpersonal skills they will need to deal with the values conflicts and decisions of the future.

The humanistic education movement has many branches. For example: "values clarification;" "education of self" at the University of Massachusetts; the Philadelphia Public Schools Affective Education Project; achievement motivation training; the "magic circle" exercises of the Human Development Institute; Parent and Teacher Effectiveness Training; the open classroom, etc.

The different branches of the movement have had different emphases; but they all contribute, to varying degrees, to teaching the same process of values clarification. Louis Raths once defined a "value" (as opposed to an attitude, belief, feeling, goal, etc.) as an area of our lives which meets seven criteria.[1] We think of his criteria as the seven valuing processes which all branches of the humanistic education movement seem to be teaching. If we want to prepare our children to meet the unknown challenges of the future, to be able to guide their lives through all the difficult values choices ahead, then we must consciously and deliberately go about teaching at least the following seven processes of valuing.

Prizing

1. *Prizing and Cherishing.* We need to find ways to help young people discover what is important *to them*, to learn to set priorities, and to know what they are for or against. So much of our education forces us to deny our feelings and to distrust our inner experience. Valuing is not only a cognitive process. Education has to include the affective realm too. The future will hold many surprises. Unless people are capable of tuning in to their own feelings, they will be ill-equipped to make the decisions that the future calls for.

2. *Publicly Affirming.* One way we show our values is to stand up for what we believe, to voice our opinions, to publicly affirm our position. Education can encourage this, rather

than creating an atmosphere in which we keep our important thoughts and feelings to ourselves. As trust builds and self-disclosure increases, so does self-understanding, creativity, and productivity. Public affirmation is essential for democracy. Groups increase their efficiency in decision making as more information, supplied by the members, gets thrown out on the table. To deal with the personal and societal decisions of the future, we need people who have learned to publicly affirm their values.

Choosing

We make choices all the time, thereby indicating preferences or values. But the choices which the future will call for demand more than glib, whimsical, or conforming choices. Education must teach a process of choosing.

3. *Choosing from Alternatives.* Many people take the first choice or the first good choice that comes along. "This is the way I was taught, so this is the way I teach." "We've always handled our Christmas present-giving this way. You mean there are alternatives?" "Everybody in my circle of friends smokes pot on Saturday night. What else is there to do?" The future will offer us new alternatives for our personal lives and for the society. Whether we embrace each alternative as it comes along, or whether we take our time and choose from several alternatives, could mean the difference between enormous disappointment and waste or more effective decisions.

4. *Choosing after Considering Consequences.* This valuing process goes hand in hand with the former process. It is essential that we teach young people to examine the *consequences* of the alternatives under consideration and thus illumine the pros and cons. For example, the future will undoubtedly legitimize many different patterns of dating, mating, and marriage. This is already happening. An important part of valuing in this area would be to consider seriously the consequences of each alternative before making a choice, and not just gravitate toward the alternative that seems most attractive at first glance. This holds true in every area, whether it is marriage, ecology, economics, or religion. We cannot predict the future or all the outcomes of our decisions. But by proceeding with eyes open, having weighed the pros and cons of the various alternatives, our

chances for good decisions are increased.

5. *Choosing Freely.* Everyone wants his children, when they grow up, to be able to guide their lives as mature, responsible citizens. Yet, at every turn of their education, most young people's choices are so prescribed and limited that they never have the chance to learn to guide their lives until they are thrown in the water and told to swim. By that time, it is often too late. The problem is compounded by a marking and grading system which literally destroys opportunities for free choice.[2] We need to create environments in which young people can make choices—about their beliefs, about their behaviors, and about the course of their own education—in which they have the opportunity to look at alternatives, weigh consequences, make *their own* choice, look at the actual consequences, and then go through the whole process again. There is no shortcut. We can't teach people to make responsible choices unless they are given the chance to make real choices. All else is to impose values, which simply will not help them deal with the future.

Acting

6. *Acting.* Acting is a valuing process. We have limited time, money, and energy. How we spend our time, money, and energy reveals what we value. Students are continually formulating beliefs, goals, and ideals. As a part of their education, they should be encouraged to *act* on these beliefs, goals, and ideals. As the barrier between the school and the outside "real" world breaks down, students can become increasingly involved in community work, in helping relationships, and in other experiences that encourage personal growth and value development. Many adults rarely get (or make) the chance to act on their beliefs, to achieve their goals, or to actualize their potential. An education that encourages action, as well as contemplation, will help create a future in which men will increasingly close the gap between what they say and what they do, between what they want and what they achieve.

7. *Acting with a Pattern, Repetition, and Consistency.* This valuing process is an extension of the previous one. As we become clearer about our values, we begin to develop patterns of actions and to repeat our most valued activities. In addition, we eliminate those behaviors that are contradictory

to our most cherished values. Young people can be helped to examine the present patterns in their lives. While the unexamined life may or may not be worth living, it is certainly true that until we begin to examine the present patterns in our lives, we rarely move in directions that enable us to achieve our most prized and cherished goals and aspirations—our preferable futures.

We envision a future in which young people are very much in touch with their own inner experience, continue to go through an intelligent choosing process, act on their beliefs, and do something about their goals. Whether they are making a decision for their own personal lives or for the community they are a part of, their valuing process will help them to sort out the available information, to make a decision that is truly their own (rather than an introjection of authority or peer pressure), and to act with commitment on that decision.

Values as Process

We are suggesting that what has happened with subject matter education must now happen with values education. Traditionally, subject matter has been regarded as a fixed body of knowledge which all people needed to know. Shakespeare, the parts of speech, quadratic equations, the major products of Argentina, and the parts of the digestive system were treated as the ends of education. More recently, we have realized, that in a world in which the amount of knowledge increases geometrically, and in which no one can keep pace with it, we need to change our emphasis from *what* to learn to *how* to learn. The new curriculum projects have emphasized the *processes* of the discipline, the ways in which the historian or the scientist goes about investigating his subject. The shift has been from content to process. Learning how to learn has become more important than the specific facts and concepts learned.

A similar change of orientation must take place with respect to values. The process of *how to develop values*—that is, the processes of prizing, choosing, and acting—must receive increasing emphasis in the curriculum and in the home. Slavishly adhering to outdated methods of values education will render educators and parents as obsolete and irrelevant as the subject matter teachers who continue to say,

"Repetitive drill and rote memorization of facts worked for me, didn't they? Well, then, I don't see why they won't work for the kids today."

What would a school look like if the educators did accept the need for teaching a values-clarifying process to young people and tried to implement it on a practical basis? Current experience in the utilization of humanistic education approaches in schools suggests that implementation takes place on any or all of three levels: 1) by incorporating humanistic education approaches into presently existing courses; 2) by creating new courses with a specific focus on some aspect of humanistic education; 3) by reorganizing the whole school, or major parts of it, to allow for humanistic approaches.

The first level of involvement usually occurs when one or more teachers from a given school attend a workshop on one of the humanistic education approaches. The individual teachers then return with a desire or commitment to "humanize" their own classrooms, that is, to incorporate methods and materials which deal with the real values and identify concerns of their students, to help them become clearer about who they are, where they want to go, and how they are getting there. This could apply equally to elementary and secondary or college teaching. Many of the humanistic approaches have numerous methods or strategies for accomplishing these goals.[3] To the extent that one teacher can be successful in such an enormous undertaking, her students develop some practice and skill in using the valuing process in their own lives and are, therefore, more prepared to deal with the concerns, conflicts, and choices they will meet in the future.

When several teachers from a given school or system, or when a key administrator is committed to implementing humanistic approaches in the school, a common result is the establishment of specific elective courses. Students, usually with parental permission, elect to take a course in "values clarification" or "controversial issues" or "education of self" or "communications" or "urban studies" or "family living" or "human relations." The course titles are as varied as the orientation of the teacher, the interests of the students, and the political realities of the school and community. What each course has in common, though, is not its humanistic *content* (Is the study of the reproductive system any more "human" than the digestive system?), but its emphasis on the *processes* of valuing, communication, self-understanding, and so on.

Frequently, consultants are called in to help schools establish such courses and to work with the teachers at the beginning. Many schools are introducing courses of this type. Doing so gives students and teachers an attractive option, and can be extremely valuable to them in the years ahead. Yet, this type of implementation has its drawbacks. Since only a limited number of students can take these specialized elective courses, the other teachers often say, "Well, I don't have to do anything about preparing them to make values decisions in the future. We have a course on that." Another drawback is that course offerings of this nature tend to be faddish. When humanistic education is "in," or when some students, teachers, or community groups are exerting pressure for educational change, it is often convenient to create a course merely to satisfy the demand for change. This takes the pressure off the school, and if, a few years later, the course is eliminated, it rarely creates much of a stir.

A few schools have gone further in their attempts to make education a training ground for the future. They have made major school-wide changes toward humanistic process education. One method has been to create a "school-within-a-school," sometimes called parallel schools. Somewhat similar to the elective courses, but on a broader scale, students can choose between the traditionally run school and the parallel school. The latter organizes its whole curriculum around humanistic approaches, even in the traditional subject areas. The parallel school often moves away from traditional grading and marking systems which tend to prevent young people from developing their own values.

Another approach to school-wide humanistic change is to organize the whole school according to the open classroom model. In this case, the total school, and the community, too, are seen as environments rich in educational resources. Students take the major responsibility for guiding their education through that environment. Teachers serve as facilitators, making their skills and knowledge available to help students move toward their own learning goals.[4,5] Such a school is in many ways like real life in which people must take responsibility for their own directions, but can share resources with each other and can call on help when needed. In this laboratory setting, students gradually learn the valuing skills and the learning skills that will serve them throughout their lives.

One of the most daring proposals for a school-wide curricular reorganization along humanistic lines comes from Gerald Weinstein and Mario Fantini.[6] They suggest that the school day be divided into three equal time segments. During the first third of the day, the time would be spent learning the fundamental skills and areas of knowledge which now take up most of the day, in most schools. (This, in itself, is a challenging assertion: that students don't need nearly as much of the traditional curriculum as we think they do, and that what is really essential for them—the skills of communication and calculation and the basic facts a member of this society needs to know—could be telescoped into one third of the normal day.) The second third of the time would be open for the students to choose any areas they wanted to learn more about. Many students would spend their time with arts, crafts, music, and sports—skills and pastimes that could last them all their lives. Others might want to work with teachers in the academic subject areas in greater depth. The final third of the day is devoted to "education of the self." During this time, all students are involved in activities and discussions which help them become clearer about who they are, how they view themselves, what their values are, what goals they are setting for themselves, how they are achieving their goals, and so on. Here it is possible to examine not only personal goals, but preferable futures for the community and society as a whole. In this segment, students are actually studying themselves; they are the subject matter. And they are learning the process of self-understanding, values clarification, and communication that will continue to serve them twenty and forty years hence, when predictably, the world will be very different.

No one can predict the values that will emerge from an ongoing valuing process. No doubt, many of our most cherished values are worth maintaining and will be maintained for years to come. Yet other values, whether privately held or shared by the society, will fall by the wayside. Young people who have internalized an ongoing valuing process will make mistakes, just as their teachers made mistakes. But behind the process is a faith in man; that if we can recognize, accept, and express our own feelings, if we can consider alternatives and consequences and make our own choices, and if we can actualize our beliefs and goals with repeated and consistent action, our decisions will lead us toward a future we can cope with and control. It is when we deny our feelings and hide them from others, when we accept the first alternatives and don't look ahead to consequences, when we allow others to make our value choices for us, when we do not act on our beliefs and ideals, *then* we relinquish control over our futures and find ourselves floundering in a world and a body we do not understand.

Unfortunately, this latter alternative describes the future for all too many individuals. Yet such a grim future need not be. As educators, we want to continue to model the values *we* believe in. But, most important, we now have the insight and skills to begin designing learning environments in which young people learn a *process* for clarifying and developing their own values. Only in this way can we turn preferable futures into probable futures.

NOTES

1. Louis E. Raths, Merrill Harmin, and Sidney B. Simon, *Values and Teaching* (Columbus, Ohio: Charles Merrill Publishing Co., 1966).
2. Howard Kirschenbaum, Sidney B. Simon, and Rodney W. Napier, *WAD-JA-GET? The Grading Game in American Education* (New York: Hart Publishing Company, Inc., 1971).
3. Sidney B. Simon, Leland W. Howe, and Howard Kirschenbaum, *Values Clarification: A Handbook of Practical Strategies for Teachers and Students* (New York: Hart Publishing Company, Inc., 1972).
4. Herbert Kohl, *The Open Classroom* (New York: Random House, Inc., 1970).
5. Carl R. Rogers, *Freedom to Learn* (Columbus, Ohio: Charles Merrill Publishing Co., 1969).
6. Gerald Weinstein and Mario D. Fantini, *Making Urban Schools Work* (New York: Holt, Rinehart and Winston, Inc., 1968).

The Values We Teach in School

An Interview with John Holt

Reprinted from the September 1969 issue of *Teacher* magazine with permission of the publisher. This article is copyrighted. © 1969 by Macmillan Professional Magazines, Inc. All rights reserved.

"Our schools preach a humanistic kind of philosophy, but they tend to practice something quite different. There's a certain amount of doffing of the hat to things like *sharing* and *kindness* and *making choices*. But these ideals, principles, values – whatever you want to call them – don't really penetrate into the classroom.

"In class, the children are judged all the time. They're told to sit still, be quiet and courteous, do what they're told to do when they're told to do it. And that's exactly what most of them do. They've gotten the real message of our schools: *You're worthless. You can't be trusted. You're incompetent to do anything. You've got to let other people manage your life for you or you'll make a terrible mess of it.*

"Generally speaking, the restrictions on the school child's life are more stringent than those of a maximum security prison...."

John Holt sits leaning back in an old swivel chair near the window of his cluttered, fourth-floor downtown Boston office. There's a convention in town and brass bands pass stridently on the street below. Holt's phone rings almost constantly. For some unknown reason a cannon is fired every now and then.

You've shut the window and turned off the roaring floor fan to shut out the noise. It is sweltering. But John Holt, a little grayer than you had expected him, a little heavier, looks cool. You've asked him about the values we teach in school. Which values are actually taught. How they're taught. What they mean to the children.

"There's an awful lot of talk in the early grades about sharing, about cooperativeness, about democratic values. Every morning we start off with liberty and justice for all. But there's a kind of dissonance in this. Because, with all our talk of these ideals, we continually set the children at each other's throats. We make them compete for approval — approval of the school and the teacher. And this is really a zero-sum game for them because they've found out that whenever one person wins in school, somebody else loses. The child who shines in class, usually shines at the expense of somebody else.

"The whole set-up of the class tells the children that they are expected to enter into a kind of cutthroat competition with each other. If they're asked to share, it's not the things they're most eager to share — their knowledge, their feelings, their work. Sharing their feelings is called *acting out*. Sharing their ideas is called *cheating*."

You're very hard on teachers. But are you fair? What about the values taught in, say, group discussions? Aren't the children being helped to learn about a real democratic ideal — the importance of people coming together and asking questions and exchanging views and coming to conclusions?

"That's another place where there's dissonance. Look at the teacher's manuals. Over and over again you'll see the direction: 'Have a discussion and bring out the following points.'

"Most teachers — I include myself; it's true of me in some respects — most teachers think of a discussion as a thing during which points are brought out. And even in these so-called discussions, the teacher usually talks more than all the children put together.

"That kind of discussion never moves into the things the kids themselves are really interested in. Teachers constantly talk about keeping the discussion on the track. Or keeping to the point. *Whose* track? *Whose* point? The teacher's. Always."

Isn't bringing out certain points and keeping things on the track part of the teacher's job? Isn't that what at least in part she has been hired to do?

"I'll buy that as a reason for her doing what she does. All I say is, it makes a mockery out of what we're talking about— values. It makes expressing what you really feel impossible."

Why is that important?

"Expressing what you feel is the only way in which you learn to use language well. I'm amazed—no, mildly horrified— to find out how kids who are extraordinarily articulate in a conventional school discussion often find it very difficult to talk about anything meaningful to them outside the school. They have misused language so glibly in the classroom that they've grown to distrust it.

"I think the effect of this is very serious. It has led to the don't-trust-anyone-over-thirty notion—a kind of credibility gap between young and old. And this is dangerous. Society is held together by trust. Erosion of trust, whether between young and old or black and white, is really bad.

"Distrust of all words arises from the young person's sense that he has been made to use words dishonestly. This is foolish, perhaps, but understandable. And it has a very serious consequence. A person who believes that there's no such thing as honest verbal communication has been turned off to the whole symbolism of life. We never meant to accomplish that in our schools."

Surely this wasn't accomplished by the schools alone?

"Of course not. There are probably similar dissonances at home. Take the child who is told to be truthful and then asked to tell someone who calls on the telephone that Mommy isn't home. That child quickly sees the dissonance between what people say and what they do.

"And there's the whole society we live in. I recall very vividly coming to a fifth grade a number of years ago, just about the time the big Boston police scandal erupted. Some TV cameramen had set up in a room overlooking a bookie joint and took pictures of uniformed policemen getting payoffs. The story hit the national newspapers and TV.

"Well, I—simple innocent that I was, still in the process of unlearning what I had read in my civics texts—was horrified by this. My fifth-graders took it for granted. *They* knew policemen took bribes. But I was surprised."

"Isn't it too much to go against, this current of valuelessness

in the schools, among parents, in city officials such as the police? Can teachers do anything about this?

"A lot of teachers ask that. And, of course, it's very difficult. What we have to do is try to be authentic human beings. It's hard to do. But we have to try."

What do you mean by authentic?

"Authenticity is *not pretending*. Not pretending anger, for example—teachers use simulated anger as a disciplinary threat. They pretend to be upset or angry about something when they really aren't.

"Another kind of pretend is disapproval: *Nice people don't say (or do) that kind of thing.* Or approval or affection can be pretend. What I call the honey-dearie routine.

"Then there's the unauthentic *control* of anger. The prevailing orthodoxy, at least in 'nice' schools, is that you show only 'nice' feelings. And so teachers—those complicated, passionate, sensitive people—just don't come across the way they really are. And that's not being authentic."

*Should we really try to be authentic all the time? What about those days when everything seems to be wrong and the least little thing will make you blow up? The anger may be authentic. But is it "pretend" to try **to control it?***

"You can still be authentic—honest, if you will—about it. On days like that I go into the class and say, 'Boy, I had a bad night's sleep or I feel down in the dumps or I feel lousy...so you better watch it. The stuff I ordinarily wouldn't mind is liable to bug the heck out of me right now. So take it easy. Watch it.'

"This is perfectly fair, reasonable advice. The kids understand it, and they're liable to be very accommodating.

"So, after a few hours I'm beginning to feel all right so I tell the kids, and they say, 'Good, now we can be ourselves again.' "

How do you react when children turn around and get mad at you?

"I had a student once who used to tell me he hated school. Now in a repressive school he'd have been punished. And in a 'nice' school he would have been talked out of it: 'You don't really mean that! Oh, no, you don't really hate school!'

"I think punishing a kid for, or trying to talk him out of, his honest feelings is a really bad thing to do. I used to tell this particular child: 'The law says you have to go to school; it doesn't say you have to like it.' The other kids would usually laugh and there'd be some flicker from the kid himself.

"Or, suppose he said he hated *me*. I'd say, 'You have to go to school. You don't have to like the teacher.' Or, 'What are you trying to do? Hurt my feelings?' And the kid would usually laugh or say, 'Yeah,' depending on how he felt.

"Now, there is something very sick and unauthentic about the way a lot of 'nice' schools deal with this sort of thing. So many teachers hear a kid say he hates school or he hates the teacher and their response is, 'Oh, we must talk that out!'

"Children don't want to spend all their time talking about their feelings. What they want to do is express a feeling and then go on to something else. They don't want to spend a half-hour explaining to some adult why they're angry — especially when the implication in the teacher's concern is that to be angry is to have some kind of sickness which must be cured. 'Dear, tell me what the trouble is and I will cure you of this kind of disease of anger which you have caught somewhere like a cold and then we will be all well and we will have nothing but kindly feelings toward each other and the class.'

"Obviously, this is a lot of baloney. It's dangerous, too. One way or another we seem to be illegitimatizing anger and conflict. We don't like anger and conflict. We don't know what to do with these perfectly legitimate feelings."

That's fine when you're one teacher dealing with one angry student. But what about the school where the large majority of children — because of poverty or race conflict or social dislocation — come to school terribly aggressive, terribly hostile, terribly upset? Do you dare let them express these feelings freely?

"George Dennison's new book, *The Lives of Children* [Random House] deals with that question. The book tells of a little school in New York, a private school for poor kids — black and Puerto Rican kids, disadvantaged kids, emotionally disturbed kids.

"It's a school full of problems where a lot of very different kids live and work in a loosely structured situation. The children are free to have conflicts with other children...and with the concerned adults who are there to help them. The children use moments of conflict to find out, deal with and work out the things within themselves in a way no conventional school would really permit.

"The teachers are always there, but they don't get in the

way of conflict. The children quarrel and sock and generally work hell out of one another. There are limits: When somebody says, 'Okay, I quit,' that's it. No pounding of the head into the floor. No knives. But beyond this the limits are very wide."

Is this education? Or therapy?

"There's no distinction. Absolutely no distinction. A kid drinks orange juice in the morning. Is that therapy? Is it nutrition? Health? Dennison points out again and again that education is about the growth of children — spiritual, emotional, moral growth."

What about the acquisition of knowledge?

"Knowledge doesn't just float around in the air. Neil Postman and Charles Weingartner make this point very eloquently in their book, *Teaching as a Subversive Activity* [Delacorte]. They say people don't make meaning the way you might make a suit of clothes. We make meaning by interacting with the world, by experiencing — whether firsthand or vicariously as in a book."

What's to guarantee that the child will ever get beyond firsthand experiencing — which is limited, largely, to interpersonal things? Can we be sure he will move on to the wider-ranging, vicarious experiences found in books?

"There's no guarantee. No assurance. The fact is, though, that if a kid is hung up on interpersonal relationships, he won't get much out of books anyway. Many teachers will say, 'Well, that kid has a learning problem.' But it's not a learning problem at all. His faculties are just hung up on something which, to him, are much more serious than books."

Surely teachers are being paid to help kids go beyond this!

"Well, they're drawing their salaries under false pretenses. Oh, I know. It's part of the mythology — teachers are being paid to get children to *learn. Things. Facts.* This is one of the neuroses of education. I think we simply have to fight it. Teachers are always asking how we can know whether children are learning or not and whether they're learning the right things. And I have to say, 'We don't know. These are only hints.'

"We see the difference between children who are bored and children who are interested, children who are withdrawn and children who are involved, children who are curious and children who aren't. We see the differences. But we can't add them up in little columns of figures and make any overall meaning of them. And if we're asked to, we must say no."

*But teachers are constantly being asked to assess learning
in some meaningful way. Their administrators ask them
to do this. Parents often demand it. How should a teacher
answer an angry parent who insists on knowing why her child
can't read, spell, or write?*

"There are many answers. Perhaps you have to say that
the kid isn't reading and all the rest of it because he has
become convinced that he can't, that he's too dumb, that it'll
never penetrate. Or perhaps you have to point out that the
kid isn't reading because his parents or other teachers have
made it a battleground. They've said, 'By God, you're going
to read whether you like it or not!' And the child has said,
'Well, we'll see about that.' And he's winning.

"I think we owe it to parents, as well as ourselves, to clarify
what teaching is all about. There's a sort of assumption that
teaching equals learning. But teaching as it is ordinarily
understood in school and by parents—the external direction
of learning—is the *enemy* of learning about 99 percent of the
time. Much of what a lot of teachers do, and of what a lot
of administrators and parents pressure them to do, is not
aimed at getting kids to read better or remember better, or
use what they know better. A lot of what teachers do is
merely self-protective. If something goes wrong—that is, if
a child doesn't do well by one standard or another—the
teacher wants to be able to say, 'Well, it's not my fault.'
So does just about everybody else connected with the child
for that matter.

"Now I know there are realities and teachers have to live
with them. But we can take tentative steps toward a better
reality. This is what Herb Kohl writes about; he says try
something different just ten minutes a day. It's what one of
my next books will be about—giving children a little more
room for choice, for decision, for judgment. It's letting the
children pick partners and decide for themselves how they're
going to use a textbook. Or having them write their own tests.
There's really no situation so confined that a teacher can't
do something along these lines.

"And I would say if that's the direction you want to go in,
go ahead. There's lots of evidence that you're not taking
your life in your hands by trying something different. It's less
of a gamble than it appears. There's as good a chance that
the kids will do better as there is that they'll do worse.
So be of good heart. Take a step."

The Moral Imperative in Contemporary American Education

by Philip H. Phenix

Reprinted from *Perspectives on Education*, Winter 1969, Teachers College, Columbia University. Used with permission.

Within the past three or four years there has occurred one of those sea changes in the American scene that radically alters the entire climate of common presuppositions and expectations. While in previous periods the central issues might be characterized as ideological, technical, political, and the like, I think the most apt term for what is new in the present atmosphere is moral concern.

By moral I do not mean moralistic. Few contemporary Americans are moved by the kind of self-assured reforming zeal that, for example, made possible the Eighteenth Amendment. When I say the dominant atmosphere is one of moral concern, I mean that questions of conscience have now moved into the foreground of the American cultural scene. The immediate stimulus is, of course, Vietnam, but Vietnam only symbolizes the conflicts of conscience in a wide range of social and personal issues, including those of race, poverty, sex, drugs, and politics, both national and international.

Americans are becoming increasingly aware that material and technical approaches to these issues do not suffice, that without a moral basis and the morale that flows from it, typical American practicalism and activism prove impractical and stultifying.

American schools and colleges are, naturally enough, deeply involved in these recent transformations in the cultural climate. It is in the young that the probings of conscience are most evident. Their lives and their futures are most at stake in the various social, political, economic, racial, and personal struggles of our time. Hence it is not surprising that the universities, inhabited by large numbers of young people with abundant resources of intelligence, imagination, and energy, should now be in the midst of a period of ferment unparalleled in the history of American education. The present student discontent is in large measure animated by a powerful undercurrent of profoundly moral concern.

What the morally concerned students are asking is nothing less than a thorough moral reconstruction of education itself. Most of them would not couch their protest and their aspiration in those terms; they would rather use a term like "relevant," meaning an education that will enable them to transform a world that their consciences bid them reject in its present form.

What are the prospects for such a transformation? What can teachers, students, and administrators do together to contribute constructively to the moral imperatives that are grasping the present generation? I am convinced that the present unrest offers signal opportunities for the educative enterprise and that we would do well to think carefully and to act resolutely to avail ourselves of the creative moment presented to us.

I wish to sketch in broad strokes a theory of moral education that aims to speak to the contemporary cultural and educational situation. One might argue that not theory but resolute practical action is what the current crisis and opportunity call for. To this I respond that just now nothing is more urgently needed than a moral theory — a vision that justifies and animates the educator's and the student's active moral endeavor. In this context, as in so many others, it turns out that nothing is so practical as theory.

If one presumes to engage in moral instruction, the basic question that arises concerns the value standards or norms that are to be used and the sources and justification for those norms. In this regard there are four possible orientations that one can take, each defining a practice-controlling theoretical outlook.

First, one can assume an essentially nihilistic position *vis a vis* values. Such a position of normlessness can be called *anomic*. It is a denial that there are really any standards of right or wrong, of better or worse, because the whole human endeavor appears to be meaningless and without purpose.

The anomic outlook is common in a time of widespread cultural change. When traditional values disintegrate because of altered social and material conditions, many persons become deeply anxious and disoriented. In the modern world the disintegration of norms caused by social and technical change is greatly accentuated by the meeting and mixing of many different cultural traditions. Travel and communication have brought about a situation of world-wide cultural pluralism which presents each individual with such a bewildering array of possible value-orientations that he is tempted to deny the meaning of any of them.

The practical consequence of the anomic position is an attitude of frustration and cynicism which leads one to drift aimlessly with the current and to react passively to internal impulses and external compulsions. In extreme cases it results in suicide, the culminating expression of the sense of meaninglessness. Many who adopt one or another of the forms of social deviance do so as an expression of their inability to find any meaning in the established orders of human life.

Obviously, the anomic outlook cannot provide a basis for moral education, if, indeed, for any kind of education. If life is essentially meaningless, there is no point in trying to promote it or to improve it. An anomic theory of values is fatal to education, as it is to any sustained cultural pursuit. Unfortunately, it is a theory all too widely held, either explicitly or tacitly, and it should be recognized as an enemy of human morale and of educational effectiveness.

A more constructive position, and one that its adherents are generally more willing to acknowledge and disseminate, may be termed the *autonomic*. The autonomist believes that there are norms or values and that their source and justification are in the persons who make them. Every individual invests existence with meaning, and its significance is nothing more nor less than the meaning he gives it.

The autonomic theory of values, like the anomic, constitutes a response to the dissolution of traditional value systems and

the confrontation of divergent cultural norms. Powerful
impetus for it comes from the scientific studies of cultures
that indicate the boundless varieties of institutions and
customs that human ingenuity has devised. A common result
of such investigations is the theoretical conviction that
values are nothing but human artifacts and that all standards
are relative to the persons and societies that make them.

The value theory of most contemporary philosophies,
including existentialism, is essentially autonomic. The
dominant empirical and naturalistic systems of thought,
denying transcendent realms of being, admit of no normative
reality beyond the observable natural and social orders.
Human beings are creative agents who make their own world
and who can depend on no objective moral order to guide
their choices. The only moral truth for man is in the
passionate subjectivity of his own creative value-projections.

The educational consequences of the autonomic theory of
value are far-reaching. If norms are simply what people posit
them to be—if human beings make values—then it is
inadmissible to teach people how they *ought* to behave. All
one can teach is how this person or that group of persons
have decided they will behave. The key educational problem
is to impart skill in adjusting the varieties of values that
people have so as to create a reasonably congruent social
scheme. Moral decision is thus defined by (or perhaps better,
replaced by) political strategy. It is not a question of learning
what is right or wrong, but what is socially expedient.

The prevalence of the autonomic theory of values is plainly
seen in the fact that the most crucial present-day value issues
are being dealt with mainly in political, not moral, terms. The
most dramatic case in point is the rapid transfer of the racial
question from the moral to the political arena. What was only
a few years ago argued in terms of right is now often treated
primarily as a matter of power, with scant reference to the
moral ends to be served. From the autonomic standpoint, why
should the black man want to become integrated into the
value structures of the white man, from whom he has suffered
such humiliation and deprivation? If people make their own
values, is it not high time black people claim their freedom to
create their own culture and to set their own norms, which
are neither better nor worse, but simply different from those
of white people? The result of such an argument is strong

educational emphasis on the integrity and distinctive cultural identity of black people and insistence on full treatment of the norms of the black community in education as valuable in their own terms, simply by virtue of their being the standards by which blacks have defined the meaning of their existence.

The same autonomic value theory is operative in the movement to politicize the institutions of education. The question increasingly being asked by those who hold school and college buildings under seige, and by strikers and pressure groups, whether of students, of teachers, or of parents, is not what is good and right, but who has the power—whose will is to prevail. I believe that one fundamental reason for this politicization is that the various parties to the conflict over policy do not believe there are any norms of judgment beyond the interests and prescriptions of the people and groups involved. Educational institutions, recognized as important agencies for the sorting and grading of persons for positions within the power structure of society, thus become key factors in the political struggle. The curriculum is judged in terms of "relevance" (a basic idea in current reform movements) which in political terms means effectiveness in promoting autonomous interests and demands.

In contrast to both of the foregoing value-orientations, a third theory, the *heteronomic*, asserts that there are objective standards of value that are known, that can be taught, and that provide clear and unambiguous norms of judgment for human conduct. According to this theory, people do not make values, they discover them. Right and wrong are just as real as the laws of physical nature, only they take the form of moral obligation not of physical necessity. These moral laws are sometimes regarded as divine commands, promulgated by an all-wise sovereign deity, and sometimes as rationally intuitable demands apprehended by the moral sensibility.

The heteronomic standpoint is operative in those who look with alarm and disapproval on the disintegration of traditional values, who decry the anomic and autonomic responses so widespread today, and who urge the adoption of strong programs of explicit religious and ethical instruction in order to restore the lost values to the coming generation. The heteronomists also stress law and order and the taking of all necessary enforcement measures to prevent deviance from established standards of belief and conduct.

Of many different persuasions, the heteronomists may be staunch conservatives, orthodox communists, or doctrinaire liberals of the middle way. What makes them heteronomic is their ideological certainty and their consequent pedagogical commitment to transmit and inculcate values they are convinced are right.

All three of the foregoing value theories fail to do justice to the realities of moral conscience and fail to provide a basis for moral education. It seems to me that heteronomy is unsatisfactory because of the perennial conflict of value systems. Each ideology is regarded by its adherents as the ultimate standard of value, by which all others must be criticized. It does not take a great deal of historical or anthropological perspective to see how untenable such ethnocentrism is. In the face of the staggering multiplicity of norms by which people have actually lived and do live, it is hard to justify an exclusivist ideological position. That is why so many adopt an anomic or an autonomic view. But these latter positions are unsatisfactory for a different reason, namely, that they cut the nerve of moral inquiry and effectively negate moral conscience. The anomist is not morally concerned because he regards the whole human enterprise as meaningless, while the autonomist substitutes political strategy for morality. If values are human creations, then there is no objective basis for judging their worth, analogous, for example, to the objective observational norms used in judging the truth of statements in natural science.

What serious moral education in the modern age requires is a theoretical persuasion that moral inquiry has some objective referent. Thus I propose that a fourth theory which I shall call *teleonomic* is required. By teleonomic I refer to the theory that the moral demand is grounded in a comprehensive purpose or "telos" that is objective and normative, but that forever transcends concrete institutional embodiment or ideological formulation.

Teleonomy, in short, is an interpretation of the persistent commitment of persons of conscience to the progressive *discovery* of what they ought to do. Just as the commitment to truth is a common presupposition of all scientific inquiry, expressing acknowledgement of an objective order of perceptual relationships in a world of great variety and complexity, so the commitment to right is a common presupposition of all moral inquiry, expressing dedication to an objective order of values in the domain of human choices, equally various and complex. Teleonomy interprets the moral enterprise as a venture of faith, not in the sense of blind adherence to a set of precepts that cannot be rationally justified, but in the sense of willingness to believe in and to pursue the right through the partial and imperfect embodiments of it in the concrete historical institutions of society, confident that these are always subject to criticism from the standpoint of an ideal order forever beyond specification and finite embodiment.

The practical operational consequence of the teleonomic outlook is to foster dialogue and to make moral inquiry a life-long practice. The person who believes that moral conscience is an essential concommitant of being human above all wants to do right. He is not satisfied with getting his own way and promoting his own demands. Furthermore, he readily sees that what is right is a very complicated matter and that the judgments he makes on the basis of his own limited experience are extremely partial and unreliable. Therefore he needs to associate with other persons who can complement and correct his understandings through bringing to bear other perspectives on the issues requiring decision. Furthermore, he has the grace to perceive that every value-determination is subject to further scrutiny and to continuing revision in the light of new understandings.

If we are convinced by the evidence of conscience in ourselves and by the deep and pervasive moral concern on the part of many Americans as they grapple with our critical social issues, then we will agree that there is a moral imperative in education that needs to be responded to by educational means both consonant with genuinely moral ends and not governed either by political or doctrinaire ideological considerations. The contemporary educational responses to the moral issues of our time tend to polarize into two opposing forces: the absolutists, who seek to inculcate some orthodoxy of law and order, whether of right, left, or middle; and the relativists, who aim to transform educational institutions into essentially political instrumentalities. What the moral imperative in education requires is the practice of teaching and learning in response to an absolute commitment to the good, by means of the relativities of concrete historical institutions to which humans as finite and fallible creatures are inescapably limited.

What, then, are the appropriate terms of the educative response to this imperative? I have already suggested that they should be dialogic. But who should participate in the dialogue, and according to what procedures? That is to say, what is the indicated methodology of moral instruction?

The distinctive office of the school, as I see it, in the domain of moral education, is to develop skills in moral deliberation through bringing to bear on concrete personal and social problems the relevant perspectives drawn from a variety of specialized disciplines. The premise on which moral instruction depends is that choices can be improved by widening and deepening one's understanding, both cognitive and affective, in particular decision-situations. Unwise choices result from partiality and narrowness of view, both of which can be overcome by exhibiting, through dialogue, the bearings of various specialized studies.

A dialogue whose participants are merely other concerned persons, without specialized competences directed toward the issue at hand, can provide alternative insights that may enlarge the chooser's perspective. But any improvement thus achieved is uncontrolled, accidental, and likely to be superficial. The use in the dialogue of relevant specialists allows for a far more profound transformation of understanding. Even a single specialized inquiry may afford a radically fresh outlook on a given problem. However, each such unitary modification of view by itself distorts the moral outlook, and therefore must be complemented and corrected by perspectives from other specialized studies.

I shall illustrate these general methodological recommendations by referring to the specific case of sex education. Let us assume that we do not adopt the heteronomic stand that we already know the absolute right about sexual conduct. Let us assume further that we do not regard sexual behavior as a matter of moral indifference, subject to no judgment beyond one's autonomous preferences. Let us assume, then, that we regard sex as a subject for conscientious moral decision.

Clearly, common sense and hearsay about sex are quite inadequate. Specialized knowledge must be brought to bear in sex education. Obviously relevant are the biologist's and the physician's knowledge of human physiology, of the reproductive process, of the means available for preventing conception, of abortion, and of the various pathologies associated with sex and their treatment. Yet important as such specialized knowledge is, by itself it does not constitute a basis for guiding responsible sexual conduct. It is necessary but not sufficient. I would hazard the judgment that the transformation of perspective effected by such studies offered in isolation from complementary disciplines may do more harm than good to the student. A genuinely moral decision depends on an outlook that is both deeply informed and comprehensively integrated.

Hence the physiology of sex needs to be complemented by psychological insights, including understanding of the role of affect in human personality, of the various motivations for sexual relations, and of how sexuality is sublimated or expressed in other human pursuits. To these insights should be added the important findings of social scientists concerning the family, the diverse patterns of sexual behavior actually practiced in various cultures, and the ways in which such patterns fit into the total complex of practices constituting these alternative ways of life.

Still the picture of what sexuality means is far from complete if based only on the inquiries of specialists in the natural and social sciences and psychology. These must be supplemented by humanistic perspectives. For example, literature contains profound expressions of the subjective meanings of sex. Sex is a central theme in much poetry, in the novel, and in drama. In these sources are articulated a great variety of attitudes of persons confronted with specific moral choices in the realm of sex, and one can imaginatively observe the outworkings of the various decisions made. Likewise, it is important to view sexuality in historical perspective in order to be freed from the provinciality of present preoccupations.

These scientific, aesthetic, and historical perspectives finally must be considered in the light of a comprehensive coordinating vision stemming from philosophical and theological inquiry. Such questions as the creation, nature, and destiny of the human person, the meaning of human relatedness, the uniqueness and sanctity of the person, and the significance of loyalty and promise-making are obviously fundamental to the question of sexual relations.

The insights provided by the various specialized studies do not, of course, yield any clear and conclusive answer to the moral inquirer. They do not simplify the problem of moral decision, they make it more complicated. In the end, each person must respond in conscience to the persuasion of the right that best commends itself to him. From an educational standpoint what matters is that the persuasion emerge from a mind deeply and widely informed and not from a congeries of chance impressions, haphazard impulses, and accidents of personal history.

In short, the moral imperative in education requires the nurture of intelligence in concrete decision-making. "Intelligent" choice, as I have indicated, includes not only scientific, but also affective, aesthetic, religious, and metaphysical elements.

The process of moral inquiry sketched above is designed to suggest justifiable principles of conduct in an area such as sex. Beyond such general principles of moral orientation, of course, lie matters of individual decision in particular contexts. Circumstances determine just how the general principles apply in a given case. Instruction might thus profitably include both multi-disciplinary critical elaboration of general rules and the use of case studies to illustrate the particular deployment of these rules.

I see the moral imperative requiring a substantial restructuring of the curriculum so as to institutionalize the requisite moral inquiry. This would not be done by creating separate courses in ethics taught by specialists. Instead, major, continuing study would be required in the basic personal and social issues, with instruction organized on a multi-disciplinary basis. At the same time, faculty and students should continue to pursue specialized disciplinary studies, which are the prime sources of significant and useful knowledge. This duality of specialized studies and multi-disciplinary moral investigations would be carefully guarded. Disciplinary studies alone tend toward academic fragmentation and a sense of academic irrelevance. Education organized exclusively on a problem basis, on the other hand, tends to degenerate into an insipid exchange of prejudices among the mutually uninformed.

The contemporary American scene provides a fertile field for

the deployment of moral imagination. There are abundant
signs that conscience is very much alive in many Americans,
especially of the younger generation. The problems that
confront us as a nation and world are enormous but so also
are our personal and material resources. It is a time of
magnificent prospects for an education reconstituted in
response to the moral imperative that is presented in these
stirrings of conscience. To counteract both static moralistic
traditionalism and moral nihilism and subjectivism, I believe
that we require a renewed conviction of the objective, though
ultimately transcendent, reality of the moral realm, together
with institutionalized procedures for moral instruction,
procedures based on the dialogic interpenetration of the
various academic specializations within dedicated
communities of inquiry.

The Child as a
Moral Philosopher

by Lawrence Kohlberg

Reprinted with permission from *Psychology Today* Magazine, September 1968. Copyright © Communications/Research/Machines, Inc.

How can one study morality? Current trends in the fields of ethics, linguistics, anthropology, and cognitive psychology have suggested a new approach which seems to avoid the morass of semantical confusions, value-bias, and cultural relativity in which the psychoanalytic and semantic approaches to morality have foundered. New scholarship in all these fields is now focusing upon structures, forms, and relationships that seem to be common to all societies and all languages rather than upon the features that make particular languages or cultures different.

For twelve years, my colleagues and I studied the same group of seventy-five American boys, following their development at three-year intervals from early adolescence through young manhood. At the start of the study, the boys were aged ten to sixteen. We have now followed them through to ages twenty-two to twenty-eight. In addition, I have explored moral development in other cultures – Great Britain, Canada, Taiwan, Mexico, and Turkey.

Inspired by Jean Piaget's pioneering effort to apply a structural approach to moral development, I have gradually elaborated over the years of my study a typological scheme describing general structures and forms of moral thought which can be defined independently of the specific content of particular moral decisions or actions.

The typology contains three distinct levels of moral thinking, and within each of these levels distinguishes two related stages. These levels and stages may be considered separate moral philosophies, distinct views of the socio-moral world.

We can speak of the child as having his own morality or series of moralities. Adults seldom listen to children's moralizing. If a child throws back a few adult clichés and behaves himself, most parents—and many anthropologists and psychologists as well—think that the child has adopted or internalized the appropriate parental standards.

Actually, as soon as we talk with children about morality, we find that they have many ways of making judgments which are not "internalized" from the outside and which do not come in any direct and obvious way from parents, teachers, or even peers.

Moral Levels

The *preconventional* level is the first of three levels of moral thinking; the second level is *conventional,* and the third *postconventional* or autonomous. While the preconventional child is often "well-behaved" and is responsive to cultural labels of good and bad, he interprets these labels in terms of their physical consequences (punishment, reward, exchange of favors) or in terms of the physical power of those who enunciate the rules and labels of good and bad.

This level is usually occupied by children aged four to ten, a fact long known to sensitive observers of children. The capacity of "properly behaved" children of this age to engage in cruel behavior when there are holes in the power structure is sometimes noted as tragic (*Lord of the Flies, High Wind in Jamaica*), sometimes as comic (Lucy in *Peanuts*).

The second or *conventional* level also can be described as conformist, but that is perhaps too smug a term. Maintaining the expectations and rules of the individual's family, group, or nation is perceived as valuable in its own right. There is a concern not only with *conforming* to the individual's social order but in *maintaining,* supporting, and justifying this order.

The *postconventional* level is characterized by a major

thrust toward autonomous moral principles which have
validity and application apart from authority of the groups or
persons who hold them and apart from the individual's
identification with those persons or groups.

Moral Stages

Within each of these three levels there are two discernable
stages. At the preconventional level we have:

Stage 1: Orientation toward punishment and unquestioning
deference to superior power. The physical consequences of
action (regardless of their human meaning or value) determine
its goodness or badness.

Stage 2: Right action consists of that which instrumentally
satisfies one's own needs and occasionally the needs of others.
Human relations are viewed in terms like those of the
marketplace. Elements of fairness, of reciprocity, and of
equal sharing are present, but they are always interpreted in
a physical, pragmatic way. Reciprocity is a matter of "you
scratch my back and I'll scratch yours" not of loyalty,
gratitude, or justice.

And at the conventional level we have:

Stage 3: Good-boy — good-girl orientation. Good behavior is
that which pleases or helps others and is approved by them.
There is much conformity to stereotypical images of what is
majority or "natural" behavior. Behavior is often judged by
intention — "he means well" becomes important for the first
time, and is overused, as by Charlie Brown in *Peanuts*. One
seeks approval by being "nice."

Stage 4: Orientation toward authority, fixed rules, and the
maintenance of the social order. Right behavior consists of
doing one's duty, showing respect for authority, and
maintaining the given social order for its own sake. One
earns respect by performing dutifully.

At the postconventional level, we have:

Stage 5: A social-contract orientation, generally with
legalistic and utilitarian overtones. Right action tends to be
defined in terms of general rights and in terms of standards
which have been critically examined and agreed upon by the
whole society. There is a clear awareness of the relativism of
personal values and opinions and a corresponding emphasis
upon procedural rules for reaching consensus. Aside from
what is constitutionally and democratically agreed upon,

right or wrong is a matter of personal "values" and "opinion."
The result is an emphasis upon the "legal point of view," but
with an emphasis upon the possibility of *changing* law in
terms of rational considerations of social utility, rather
than freezing it in the terms of Stage 4 "law and order."
Outside the legal realm, free agreement and contract are the
binding elements of obligation. This is the "official" morality
of American government and finds its ground in the thought
of the writers of the Constitution.

Stage 6: Orientation toward the decisions of conscience and
toward self-chosen *ethical principles* appealing to logical
comprehensiveness, universality, and consistency. These
principles are abstract and ethical (the golden rule, the
categorical imperative); they are not concrete moral rules like
the Ten Commandments. Instead they are universal principles
of *justice*, of the *reciprocity* and *equality* of human rights, and
of respect for the dignity of human beings as *individual persons.*

Up to Now
In the past, when psychologists tried to answer the question
asked of Socrates by Meno "Is virtue something that can be
taught (by rational discussion), or does it come by practice,
or is it a natural inborn attitude?" their answers usually
have been dictated, not by research findings on children's
moral character, but by their general theoretical convictions.

Behavior theorists have said that virtue is behavior
acquired according to their favorite general principles of
learning. Freudians have claimed that virtue is superego-
identification with parents generated by a proper balance of
love and authority in family relations.

American psychologists who have actually studied
children's morality have tried to start with a set of labels—the
"virtues" and "vices," the "traits" of good and bad character
found in ordinary language. The earliest major psychological
study of moral character, that of Hugh Hartshorne and
Mark May in 1928-1930, focused on a bag of virtues including
honesty, service (altruism or generosity), and self-control.
To their dismay, they found that there were *no* character
traits, psychological dispositions, or entities which
corresponded to words like honesty, service, or self-control.

Regarding honesty, for instance, they found that almost

everyone cheats some of the time, and that if a person cheats in one situation, it doesn't mean that he *will* or *won't* in another. In other words, it is not an identifiable character trait, *dis*honesty, that makes a child cheat in a given situation. These early researchers also found that people who cheat express as much or even more moral disapproval of cheating as those who do not cheat.

What Hartshorne and May found out about their bag of virtues is equally upsetting to the somewhat more psychological-sounding names introduced by psychoanalytic psychology: "superego-strength," "resistance to temptation," "strength of conscience," and the like. When recent researchers attempt to measure such traits in individuals, they are forced to use Hartshorne and May's old tests of honesty and self-control, and they get exactly the same results—"superego-strength" in one situation predicts little to "superego-strength" in another. That is, virtue-words like honesty (or superego-strength) point to certain behaviors with approval, but give us no guide to understanding them.

So far as one can extract some generalized personality factor from children's performance on tests of honesty or resistance to temptation, it is a factor of ego-strength or ego-control, which always involves nonmoral capacities like the capacity to maintain attention, intelligent-task performance, and the ability to delay response. "Ego-strength" (called "will" in earlier days) has something to do with moral action, but it does not take us to the core of morality or to the definition of virtue. Obviously enough, many of the greatest evildoers in history have been men of strong wills, men strongly pursuing immoral goals.

Moral Reasons

In our research, we have found definite and universal levels of development in moral thought. In our study of seventy-five American boys from early adolescence on, these youths were presented with hypothetical moral dilemmas, all deliberately philosophical, some of them found in medieval works of casuistry.

On the basis of their reasoning about these dilemmas at a given age, each boy's stage of thought could be determined for each of twenty-five basic moral concepts or aspects.

One such aspect, for instance, is "Motive Given for Rule Obedience or Moral Action." In this instance, the six stages look like this:

1. Obey rules to avoid punishment.
2. Conform to obtain rewards, have favors returned, and so on.
3. Conform to avoid disapproval, dislike by others.
4. Conform to avoid censure by legitimate authorities and resultant guilt.
5. Conform to maintain the respect of the impartial spectator judging in terms of community welfare.
6. Conform to avoid self-condemnation.

In another of these twenty-five moral aspects, "The Value of Human Life," the six stages can be defined thus:

1. The value of a human life is confused with the value of physical objects and is based on the social status or physical attributes of its possessor.
2. The value of a human life is seen as instrumental to the satisfaction of the needs of its possessor or of other persons.
3. The value of a human life is based on the empathy and affection of family members and others toward its possessor.
4. Life is conceived as sacred in terms of its place in a categorical moral or religious order of rights and duties.
5. Life is valued both in terms of its relation to community welfare and in terms of life being a universal human right.
6. Belief in the sacredness of human life as representing a universal human value of respect for the individual.

I have called this scheme a typology. This is because about 50 percent of most people's thinking will be at a single stage, regardless of the moral dilemma involved. We call our types *stages* because they seem to represent an *invariant developmental sequence.* "True" stages come one at a time and always in the same order.

All movement is forward in sequence and does not skip steps. Children may move through these stages at varying speeds, of course, and may be found half in and half out of a particular stage. An individual may stop at any given stage and at any age, but if he continues to move, he must move in accord with these steps. Moral reasoning of the conventional (Stages 3 and 4) kind never occurs before the preconventional (Stages 1 and 2) thought has taken place. No adult in Stage 4 has gone through Stage 6, but all Stage-6 adults have gone at least through Stage 4.

While the evidence is not complete, my study strongly suggests that moral change fits the stage pattern just described. (The major uncertainty is whether all Stage 6s go through Stage 5 or whether these are two alternate mature orientations.)

How Values Change

As a single example of our findings of stage-sequence, take the progress of two boys on the aspect "The Value of Human Life." The first boy, Tommy, is asked "Is it better to save the life of one important person or a lot of unimportant people?" At age ten, he answers "all the people that aren't important because one man just has one house, maybe a lot of furniture, but a whole bunch of people have an awful lot of furniture and some of these poor people might have a lot of money and it doesn't look it."

Clearly Tommy is Stage 1: He confuses the value of a human being with the value of the property he possesses. Three years later (age thirteen) Tommy's conceptions of life's value are most clearly elicited by the question, "Should the doctor 'mercy kill' a fatally ill woman who is requesting death because of her pain?" He answers, "Maybe it would be good to put her out of her pain; she'd be better off that way. But the husband wouldn't want it; it's not like an animal. If a pet dies you can get along without it—it isn't something you really need. Well, you can get a new wife, but it's not really the same."

Here his answer is Stage 2: The value of the woman's life is partly contingent on its hedonistic value to the wife herself but even more contingent on its instrumental value to her husband, who can't replace her as easily as he can a pet.

Three years later still (age sixteen) Tommy's conception of life's value is elicited by the same question, to which he replies: "It might be best for her, but her husband—it's a human life—not like an animal; it just doesn't have the same relationship that a human being does to a family. You can become attached to a dog, but nothing like a human you know."

Now Tommy has moved from a Stage-2 instrumental view of

the woman's value to a Stage-3 view based on the husband's distinctively human empathy and love for someone in his family. Equally clearly, it lacks any basis for a universal human value of the woman's life, which would hold if she had no husband or if her husband didn't love her. Tommy, then, has moved step by step through three stages during the age ten through sixteen. Tommy, though bright (I.Q. 120), is a slow developer in moral judgment. Let us take another boy, Richard, to show us sequential movement through the remaining three steps.

At age thirteen, Richard said about the mercy-killing: "If she requests it, it's really up to her. She is in such terrible pain, just the same as people are always putting animals out of their pain." His answer, in general, showed a mixture of Stage-2 and Stage-3 responses concerning the value of life. At sixteen, he said, "I don't know. In one way, it's murder, it's not a right or privilege of man to decide who shall live and who should die. God put life into everybody on earth, and you're taking away something from that person that came directly from God, and you're destroying something that is very sacred; it's in a way part of God and it's almost destroying a part of God when you kill a person. There's something of God in everyone."

Here Richard clearly displays a Stage-4 concept of life as sacred in terms of its place in a categorical moral or religious order. The value of human life is universal; it is true for all humans. It is still, however, dependent on something else, upon respect for God and God's authority; it is not an autonomous human value. Presumably if God told Richard to murder, as God commanded Abraham to murder Isaac, he would do so.

At age twenty, Richard said to the same question: "There are more and more people in the medical profession who think it is a hardship on everyone, the person, the family, when you know they are going to die. When a person is kept alive by an artificial lung or kidney it's more like being a vegetable than being a human. If it's her own choice, I think there are certain rights and privileges that go along with being a human being. I am a human being and have certain desires for life and I think everybody else does too. You have a world of which you are the center, and everybody else does too and in that sense we're all equal."

Richard's response is clearly Stage 5, in that the value of life is defined in terms of equal and universal human rights in a context of relativity ("You have a world of which you are the center and in that sense we're all equal.") and of concern for utility or welfare consequences.

The Final Step

At twenty-four, Richard says: "A human life takes precedence over any other moral or legal value, whoever it is. A human life has inherent value whether or not it is valued by a particular individual. The worth of the individual human being is central where the principles of justice and love are normative for all human relationships."

This young man is at Stage 6 in seeing the value of human life as absolute in representing a universal and equal respect for the human as an individual. He has moved step-by-step through a sequence culminating in a definition of human life as centrally valuable rather than derived from or dependent on social or divine authority.

In a genuine and culturally universal sense, these steps lead toward an increased *morality* of value judgment, where morality is considered as a form of judging, as it has been in a philosophic tradition, running from the analyses of Kant to those of the modern analytic or "ordinary language" philosophers. The person at Stage 6 has disentangled his judgments of — or language about — human life from status and property values (Stage 1), from its uses to others (Stage 2), from interpersonal affection (Stage 3), and so on; he has a means of moral judgment that is universal and impersonal. The Stage-6 person's answers use moral words like "duty" or "morally right," and he uses them in a way implying universality, ideals, impersonality: He thinks and speaks in phrases like "regardless of who it was," or "...I would do it in spite of punishment."

Across Cultures

When I first decided to explore moral development in other cultures, I was told by anthropologist friends that I would have to throw away my culture-bound moral concepts and stories and start from scratch, learning a whole new set of values for each new culture. My first try consisted of a brace of villages, one Atayal (Malaysian aboriginal) and the other Taiwanese.

My guide was a young Chinese ethnographer who had
written an account of the moral and religious patterns of the
Atayal and Taiwanese villages. Taiwanese boys in the ten
through thirteen age group were asked about a story
involving theft of food. A man's wife is starving to death
but the store owner won't give the man any food unless he
can pay, which he can't. Should he break in and steal some
food? Why? Many of the boys said, "He should steal the food
for his wife because if she dies he'll have to pay for her
funeral and that costs a lot."

My guide was amused by these responses, but I was
relieved: They were of course "classic" Stage-2 responses.
In the Atayal village, funerals weren't such a big thing, so
the Stage-2 boys would say, "He should steal the food
because he needs his wife to cook for him."

This means that we need to consult our anthropologists
to know what content a Stage-2 child will include in his
instrumental exchange calculations, or what a Stage-4 adult
will identify as the proper social order. But one certainly
doesn't have to start from scratch. What made my guide
laugh was the difference in form between the children's
Stage-2 thought and his own, a difference definable
independently of particular cultures.

At age ten in the United States, Taiwan, and
Mexico, the order of use of each stage is the same
as the order of its difficulty or maturity.

In the United States, by age sixteen the order is the
reverse, from the highest to the lowest, except that Stage 6
is still little-used. At age thirteen, the good-boy, middle
stage (Stage 3), is not used.

The results in Mexico and Taiwan are the same, except
that development is a little slower. The most conspicuous
feature is that at the age of sixteen, Stage-5 thinking is much
more salient in the United States than in Mexico or Taiwan.
Nevertheless, it *is* present in the other countries, so we
know that this is not purely an American democratic
construct.

There are strikingly similar results from two
isolated villages, one in Yucatan, one in Turkey.
Although conventional moral thought increases steadily
from ages ten to sixteen, it still has not achieved a clear
ascendency over preconventional thought.

Trends for lower-class urban groups are intermediate in the rate of development between those for the middle-class and for the village boys. In the three divergent cultures that I studied, middle-class children were found to be more advanced in moral judgment than matched lower-class children. This was not due to the fact that the middle-class children heavily favored some one type of thought which could be seen as corresponding to the prevailing middle-class pattern. Instead, middle-class and lower-class children move through the same sequences, but the middle-class children move faster and farther.

This sequence is not dependent upon a particular religion, or any religion at all in the usual sense. I found no important differences in the development of moral thinking among Catholics, Protestants, Jews, Buddhists, Moslems, and atheists. Religious values seem to go through the same stages as all other values.

Trading Up

In summary, the nature of our sequence is not significantly affected by widely varying social, cultural, or religious conditions. The only thing that is affected is the *rate* at which individuals progress through this sequence.

Why should there be such a universal invariant sequence of development? In answering this question, we need first to analyze these developing social concepts in terms of their internal logical structure. At each stage the same basic moral concept or aspect is defined, but at each higher stage this definition is more differentiated, more integrated, and more general or universal. When one's concept of human life moves from Stage 1 to Stage 2, the value of life becomes more differentiated from the value of property, more integrated (the value of life enters an organizational hierarchy where it is "higher" than property so that one steals property in order to save life), and more universalized (the life of any sentient being is valuable regardless of status or property). The same advance is true at each stage in the hierarchy. Each step of development, then, is a better cognitive organization than the one before it, one which takes account of everything present in the previous stage, but makes new distinctions and organizes them into a more comprehensive or more equilibrated structure. The fact that this is the case has been demonstrated by a series of studies indicating that children and adolescents comprehend all stages up to their own, but not more than one stage beyond their own. And importantly, *they prefer this next stage.*

We have conducted experimental moral discussion classes which show that the child at an earlier stage of development tends to move forward when confronted by the views of a child one stage further along. In an argument between a Stage-3 and Stage-4 child, the child in Stage 3 tends to move toward or into Stage 4, while the Stage-4 child understands but does not accept the arguments of the Stage-3 child.

Moral thought, then, seems to behave like all other kinds of thought. Progress through the moral levels and stages is characterized by increasing differentiation and increasing integration, and hence is the same kind of progress that scientific theory represents. Like acceptable scientific theory — or like *any* theory or structure of knowledge — moral thought may be considered partially to generate its own data as it goes along, or at least to expand so as to contain in a balanced, self-consistent way a wider and wider experiential field. The raw data in the case of our ethical philosophies may be considered as conflicts between roles, or values, or as the social order in which men live.

The Role of Society

The social worlds of all men seem to contain the same basic structures. All the societies we have studied have the same basic institutions — family, economy, law, government. In addition, however, all societies are alike because they *are* societies — systems of defined complementary roles. In order to *play* a social role in the family, school, or society, the child must implicitly take the role of others toward himself and toward others in the group. These role-taking tendencies form the basis of all social institutions. They represent various patternings of shared or complementary expectations.

In the preconventional and conventional levels (Stages 1-4), moral content or value is largely accidental or culture-bound. Anything from "honesty" to "courage in battle" can be the central value. But in the higher postconventional levels, Socrates, Lincoln, Thoreau, and Martin Luther King tend to speak without confusion of tongues, as it were. This is because the ideal principles of any social structure are basically alike, if only because there simply aren't that many principles which are articulate, comprehensive, and integrated enough to be satisfying to the human intellect. And most of these principles have gone by the name of justice.

Behavioristic psychology and psychoanalysis have always upheld the Philistine view that fine moral words are one thing and moral deeds another. Morally mature reasoning is quite a different matter and does not really depend upon "fine words." The man who understands justice is more likely to practice it.

In our studies, we have found that youths who understand justice act more justly, and the man who understands justice helps create a moral climate which goes far beyond his immediate and personal acts. The universal society is the beneficiary.

An Exchange of Opinion Between Kohlberg and Simon

Reprinted by special permission from *Learning*, a magazine for creative teaching, December 1972. © Copyright 1972 by Education Today Company, Inc., 530 University Avenue, Palo Alto, California 94301.

Kohlberg and Simon talked with *Learning* about each other's work and how it relates to his own. Their exchange of opinions should help the teacher who wants to choose between the constructs or create his own synthesis of the two.

"I think Kohlberg has developed a very sound research instrument in a developmental framework that one can respect fully," Simon said. "I admire the cross-cultural research that he's done. I think he's into something very, very important. I also think he needs some specific things for teachers to do with the insights of his theory. But he'll get to that in a few years. I think we already have things that teachers can do—that's our particular gift. Our work is based on a sound theory *that's manageable* for the classroom teacher. Kohlberg will continue to be attractive to researchers. And classroom teachers will barely know his name."

We asked Simon if he believes that his strategies will help stimulate growth through the stages of moral thinking that Kohlberg has defined.

"Yes," he answered, "they're almost instinctively within Kohlberg's framework. Because his framework is right. But when he says a teacher should strive to help children progress, the teacher looks and says, 'By doing what?' And I don't think he has enough answers to that now. I think he has a staff developing that. In the next five or six years, he will probably accomplish that."

Kohlberg agrees that "there are tremendous difficulties in putting this sort of thing into practice. We're just beginning to know how to do it."

He feels that his is the only construct in moral education that is sound philosophically, morally, constitutionally, and psychologically. So how does he view the values work of Raths, Simon, and their colleagues?

"I think they have some useful techniques. Values clarification is a very useful component of moral education, and we try to do some of that ourselves. But they really have not defined their objectives. So no one can tell yet whether it works. No one has ever assessed what good their work has done because they have no criteria of what developmental improvement would be. I think they deal with a much broader field than moral values or moral development. Values cover everything under the sun. A lot of what they call values clarification is what other people would call psychological education. They talk about feelings, needs, and desires as equivalent to values. When you do that, you get into interesting aspects of psychological education that we don't deal with."

Simon wonders why Kohlberg thinks that "I convey such overwhelming relativism." He added, "But because he believes it so strongly, I'd like not to just write it off."

Kohlberg's criticism is that the Raths construct, unlike his, does not define either more advanced or less advanced processes of thinking about moral issues. Research on the procedures used by Simon indicates that they help students to overcome such limiting patterns of behavior as apathy, flightiness, overconformity, nagging dissension, and chronic posturing and become more purposeful, enthusiastic, positive, and clear about what is worth striving for. But only Kohlberg has done extensive research on the levels of moral reasoning and their development.

Kohlberg's painstaking research to document the universality of the sequence of processes he describes has been motivated partly by his keen awareness that any widespread application of educational processes having to do with morals and values is likely to meet public opposition and possibly court tests. "I think his analysis is probably accurate," Simon commented, "although I wouldn't see it as grimly as he has stated it."

Both Simon and Kohlberg referred to a flap that took place in Great Neck, New York. The school district's proposed budget included a small amount of money for Simon to train some of their teachers in values clarification. "An orthodox Jewish, right-wing group got hold of it and just raised hell!" Simon said. Kohlberg said the protestors insisted that "values shouldn't be dealt with in the school, but should be left for the church and home." (Although Kohlberg testified in favor of the Simon training, it was cut from the budget.)

To sum up: Kohlberg's work concerns itself with the cognitive processes of making moral decisions, while values clarification is involved with both the emotions and thinking. Simon thinks Kohlberg has an important construct but lacks strategies of implementation. Kohlberg thinks the strategies Simon uses are good but the theory is inadequate in supplying objectives. Both think the Raths-Simon strategies help to stimulate the progression in levels of moral thinking that Kohlberg has defined.

For the teacher who is aware of both developmental processes and works to facilitate both in his classroom, there are great and exciting potentials.

Persuasion That Persists

by Milton Rokeach

From *Psychology Today*, September 1971. Used with permission of the author.

Suppose you could take a group of people, give them a twenty-minute pencil-and-paper task, talk to them for ten to twenty minutes afterward, and thereby produce long-range changes in core values and personal behavior in a significant portion of this group. For openers, it would of course have major implications for education, government, propaganda, and therapy. Suppose, further, that you could ascertain quickly and that you could predict accurately the nature and direction of these changes.

Scientists have urged us all to consider the consequences of research in this area, warning that we are on the brink of breakthroughs that will demand new levels of social responsibility. According to these predictions, we will soon face several major ethical questions that have to be answered.

My colleagues and I have in the last five years achieved the kinds of results suggested in the first paragraph of this article. As a result we must now face up to the ethical implications that follow from the fact that it now seems to be within man's power to alter experimentally another person's basic values, and to control the direction of the change.

Dissonance. Contemporary social psychologists generally agree that before changes in attitudes or in value-related behavior can occur, there must first exist what John Dewey had called a "felt difficulty" and what social psychologists nowadays call a state of psychological imbalance or dissonance.

There are two major experimental methods for creating dissonance: 1) You can force a person to act in a way that is incompatible with his professed or real attitudes and values, or 2) You can expose him to conflicting attitudes or values held by persons who are in some way important to him.

We used a third method. We exposed a person to information designed to make him consciously aware of inconstancies within his own value-attitude system, inconsistencies of which he is normally unaware.

We have also differed in our definition and measurement of dissonance itself. Dissonance requires at least two elements — let us call them X and Y — that stand in some dissonant or unharmonious relationship with each other. Leon Festinger's theory and other similar theories usually identify X and Y as two "ideas" (beliefs, attitudes, values, or rationalizations) about some particular situations or actions that will occasionally differ from or be incompatible with one another.

In contrast, we identified X and Y in such a way that they are not two ideas that vary from one situation to another, but rather are elements that remain invariant across all situations. In our hypothesis, X was equivalent to self. We defined Y as a person's interpretation of his own performance or behavior in any given situation.

Gauge. Dissonance occurs whenever a person's behavior in any given situation, Y, leads him to become dissatisfied with himself, X. Conversely, if a person is pleased with himself in any given situation, we consider that X and Y are nondissonant, or harmonious. We can measure such states of dissonance and self-satisfaction in any experiment simply by asking the subject how he feels about what he may have said or done in a given situation.

It might be objected that such a question really tests the subject's general self-esteem; self-confident persons would probably report satisfaction with their behavior, while a person with low self-esteem would probably report chronic dissatisfaction with his achievement, no matter how acceptable that achievement might be in some objective sense. Although a number of psychiatric theories seem to predict such an outcome, it is nevertheless also true that self-confident persons are not always satisfied with what they do and say in certain situations, and, conversely, that persons of low self-confidence are not always dissatisfied with what they do or say.

We also made a firm operational distinction between attitudes and values, and, unlike many researchers in the field of social psychology, we focused on the latter. We also defined values as more fundamental to human personality than attitudes, for values serve as determinants of attitudes as well as of behavior.

Hotpants. For the purposes of our research we identified an attitude as a more or less enduring organization of interrelated thoughts and feelings called into being by a specific object or situation. Thus an attitude always has a historical context as well as a personal one—toward the Pill, for instance, or civil-rights demonstrations, hotpants, or J. Edgar Hoover. Assuming that values are less embedded in particular temporal or socioeconomic contexts, we used the word *value* to describe either a desirable end-state of existence (a terminal value) or a desirable mode of behavior (an instrumental value). In a sense, values are the source and foundation of attitudes and behavior toward specific events, people, or situations. A person can have thousands of attitudes but only a few values that transcend and dynamically determine these thousands of attitudes.

My colleagues and I performed a number of experiments in which we induced in our subjects feelings of self-dissatisfaction about specific values and behavioral situations, and we measured the long-range effects that such self-dissatisfaction produced.

We took two groups of college students—usually twenty to twenty-five in a group—and asked them to rank eighteen terminal values in an order of perceived importance. The eighteen values were: a comfortable life, an exciting life, a sense of accomplishment, a world at peace, a world of beauty, equality, family security, freedom, happiness, inner harmony, mature love, national security, pleasure, salvation, social recognition, self-respect, true friendship, and wisdom.

Grade. We asked each subject to rank each value from

one to eighteen in order of its personal importance. We then asked members of both groups to state in writing their attitudes toward civil-rights demonstrations. After this was done, we dismissed one group, which became our control group.

Members of the remaining or experimental group then viewed a chart that showed the average rankings of the eighteen terminal values obtained from students in a previous experiment conducted at their school. We drew their attention especially to the data concerning two of the eighteen values shown in the chart—equality and freedom— pointing out that students in previous tests had ranked freedom first and equality eleventh. We interpreted these findings to mean that "students are, in general, much more interested in their own freedom than other people's." We then invited students to compare their own value rankings with those of their peers.

To raise levels of self-dissatisfaction further, we asked students to indicate the extent of their sympathy with the aims of civil-rights demonstrators by agreeing to one of the following phrases: "Yes, I am sympathetic, and I have personally participated in a civil-rights demonstration"; "Yes, I am sympathetic, and I have not participated in a civil-rights demonstration"; or "No, I am not sympathetic."

After this, students viewed a second table from previous tests that showed correlations between rankings of freedom and equality and positions on civil-rights issues. The main finding brought out in this table is that those who are unsympathetic with civil rights rank freedom high and equality low, while those who are sympathetic rank both freedom and equality high. We explained that the findings of this table can be interpreted to mean that persons who are against civil rights are really saying that they are indifferent to other people's freedom, while they care a great deal about their own. Those who are *for* civil rights want freedom not only for themselves, but for other people too. We then invited students to compare their own rankings of equality and freedom and their own positions on the civil-rights issue with those on the table.

Dismay. In this procedure, many of the experimental subjects—about 40 percent—became aware of certain inconsistencies within their own value and attitude systems.

Some students discovered to their dismay that they had placed a high value on freedom but a low value on equality. Others discovered that they cared about civil rights but had ranked equality low in their scaling values. Many thus discovered that they had been doing their liberal thing because it was fashionable rather than because of principle.

At the end of the experiment, we asked students to rate – on a scale ranging from one to eleven – how satisfied or dissatisfied they were in general with what they had found out about their values and attitudes. More importantly, we asked them to indicate whether they were satisfied or dissatisfied with their ranking of each of the eighteen values considered separately. This latter, more specific rating proved to be a significant predictor of subsequent changes in the value hierarchy.

Members of the control group, you will recall, had no opportunity to think about their values or possible conflicts among them; they did not see the tables that the experimental subjects saw. Sessions for the control group lasted only about twenty minutes, and the experimental session ran from thirty to forty minutes.

Change. Follow-ups on the experimental and control groups indicated that the experimental groups experienced highly significant changes in values and attitudes, increases in the value placed on equality and freedom, and increases in favorable attitudes toward civil rights that were evident three to five months after the ten-to-twenty minute experimental "treatment." Further, the self-ratings on satisfaction-dissatisfaction obtained at the end of the experimental sessions predicted the value changes that were to be observed three weeks and three to five months afterward.

We were extremely reluctant to accept these experimental findings as evidence of genuine, long-range changes in values and attitudes. It seemed unlikely that any single, brief experimental session could produce such effects. We therefore did more experiments – II and III – to monitor the long-term effects more closely and in more detail.

Subtlety. Experiments II and III were basically identical in procedure to the initial series. However, this time we used more subtle measures of behavioral effects in addition to paper-and-pencil tests of change in value and attitude. We extended post-testing to include more intervals, among them three-week, three-to-five month and fifteen-to-seventeen month intervals.

The subjects of Experiments II and III were newly entering freshmen of two small new residential colleges at Michigan State University, James Madison College, and Lyman Briggs College. Both experiments were identical in all respects; only the students were different. In both cases, we aroused feelings of self-dissatisfaction by making the subjects aware that certain of their values or attitudes were possibly incompatible with one another. As in previous experiments, the only difference between the experimental and the control groups was that we exposed the experimental students to tables, along with a brief commentary on the tables, and did not do so with the control students.

Join. Pretesting showed no significant differences between the two groups. On the average, both groups ranked equality and freedom approximately the same, and took the same range of civil-rights positions toward black Americans. Post-testing techniques included unobtrusive measurements of behavior along with questionnaires. For example, three to five months and fifteen to seventeen months after the experiment, each subject received a direct solicitation through the mails from the National Association for the Advancement of Colored People (on N.A.A.C.P. stationery). The letter invited the student to join the N.A.A.C.P. To do this, the student had to fill out an application blank, enclose a dollar, and mail back a prestamped return envelope.

We found significant increases in ranking for both equality and freedom in the experimental students on all the post-tests. After fifteen to seventeen months, for example, the experimental group had increased its ranking of equality an average of 2.68 units (on the eighteen-point scale) while the control group had increased its ranking only .32 units. Freedom also rose in value. Within the same period, the experimental ranking of freedom increased an average of 1.59 units, while the control ranking increased only .22 units. This suggests that significant changes in bedrock standards or broad normative beliefs about social ends and means took place as a result of a relatively short experimental session.

Backlash. The findings in relation to attitude-change (how do you think/feel about civil rights for blacks?) also

were significant. Three weeks after the session, we noticed
what might be called a sleeper effect among the experimental
students. There was no positive change in attitude toward
civil rights. In fact, there was a slight backlash. However, we
did find significant increases in pro-civil-rights attitudes
among these same experimental subjects three to five months
later, and fifteen to seventeen months later. These results
point to long-range attitude change, and the time-lag suggests
that a change in the ordering of values preceded the change of
attitude.

In contrast to the findings for the experimental group,
there were no significant changes in value hierarchy or
attitude among the control students at any of the post-test
intervals. After fifteen to seventeen months' exposure to the
college environment, the students in the control groups
had essentially the same value and attitude profiles they
started with.

Range. I come now to the long-range behavioral effects of the
experimental session. In the first N.A.A.C.P. solicitation of all
experimental and control subjects, undertaken three to five
months after the experimental session, forty students
responded by joining N.A.A.C.P., and thirteen more responded
by writing sympathetic letters asking for more information.
In all, fifty-three of 366 students responded; of these, thirty-
nine were experiment subjects and fourteen were control
subjects.

A full year after the first solicitation—and fifteen to
seventeen months after the experimental sessions—each
experimental and control subject received another invitation
to join N.A.A.C.P. or to renew his membership by paying
another dollar. The second letter resulted in six new
memberships—five experimental and one control. In
addition there were eleven favorable letters, seven from
experiment subjects, four from controls, one of whom had
also written after the first solicitation. There were six
renewals, half of them by experimental students and half
by control students. There were two indignant letters—both
from experimental students complaining about the
N.A.A.C.P.'s year-long silence. In all, seventeen experimental
subjects responded as against eight controls. When the
results of both N.A.A.C.P. solicitations are combined, we
find that a total of sixty-nine persons out of 366—about 20

percent—responded to the letters. Of these sixty-nine persons, fifty-one were from the experimental group and only eighteen were from the control group. This represents a statistically significant response rate of about one out of ten for the control group and one out of four for those students who had been in the briefing.

The data produced by the satisfaction-dissatisfaction ratings throw some light on the basic psychological processes that underlie the long-range changes seen in the experimental groups. Experimental subjects substantially revised their rankings of equality and freedom over the long haul, whether they reported themselves initially satisfied or dissatisfied. But it is apparent that those students who reported themselves dissatisfied with parts of their original value heirarchy changed more significantly than those who reported themselves satisfied. Reports of specific satisfaction or dissatisfaction predicted changes in value rankings that could be observed three weeks after the experiment, three to five months afterward, and fifteen to seventeen months afterward. Any value that caused dissatisfaction typically changed place in latter rankings. On the other hand, reports of general dissatisfaction did not predict as reliably, although they had some predictive value.

Ethics. In the very process of conducting our experiment we caused an unsolicited reordering of people's value systems and behavioral choices. It might be argued that no scientist should be permitted or required to cause such changes without some broad social or consensual ethical framework to refer his work and its effects to. We should remember that institutions—such as public schools—are based upon the assumption that such changes are not only desirable but do in fact occur.

Every teacher I have ever met who takes professional pride in his work would like to think that his teaching somehow changes the values, attitudes, and behavior of his students in some significant way. So long as he cannot prove that what he does in the classroom actually results in such change, no one will bother him or raise questions about the ethics of changing other people's values. But when the day comes that he can demonstrate that certain changes in values, attitudes, and behavior have in fact occurred, the teacher exposes himself to the danger of being accused, by the

community in which he lives and by his colleagues, of
unethically manipulating his students' values, attitudes,
and behavior without their informed consent.

I believe that educational institutions have always been in
the business on the one hand of transmitting knowledge and
on the other of shaping the values of students in certain
directions. Psychologists like Jerome Bruner and
B. F. Skinner have spent a good deal of their professional
lives trying to figure out better ways of transmitting
knowledge from one generation to succeeding generations,
and we all applaud such efforts. But if we agree that
educational institutions are also in the business of shaping
values, then we should encourage scientific research on better
ways of shaping values.

But which values, and in which directions?

Market. If it is possible to alter the process of valuation
so that freedom and equality go up in the value market, it is
also possible to short sell them. We obviously need safeguards
to ensure that the values we choose to change in our students
and the direction we choose in changing them are consistent
with the values of our educational and scientific institutions,
and are consistent with the values of political democracy and,
above all, with interests of all humanity.

What exactly are the values of education, science,
democracy, and humanity?

Importance of Values as Ranked in Previous Tests

1. freedom
2. happiness
3. wisdom
4. self-respect
5. mature love
6. a sense of accomplishment
7. true friendship
8. inner harmony
9. family security
10. a world at peace
11. equality
12. an exciting life
13. a comfortable life
14. salvation
15. social recognition
16. national security
17. a world of beauty
18. pleasure

Average Rankings of Freedom and Equality For and Against Civil Rights in Previous Tests

	Yes, sympathetic and have participated in a demonstration.	Yes, sympathetic but have not participated in a demonstration.	No, not sympathetic to civil rights.
freedom	6	1	2
equality	5	11	17
difference	+1	−10	−15

Toward a Modern Approach to Values: The Valuing Process in the Mature Person

by Carl R. Rogers

Reprinted from the *Journal of Abnormal and Social Psychology*, vol. 68, no. 2, 1964, pp. 160-167. Copyright 1964. Reproduced by permission of the American Psychological Association and the author.

There is a great deal of concern today with the problem of values. Youth, in almost every country, is deeply uncertain of its value orientation; the values associated with various religions have lost much of their influence; sophisticated individuals in every culture seem unsure and troubled as to the goals they hold in esteem. The reasons are not far to seek. The world culture, in all its aspects, seems increasingly scientific and relativistic, and the rigid, absolute views on values which come to us from the past appear anachronistic. Even more important, perhaps, is the fact that the modern individual is assailed from every angle by divergent and contradictory value claims. It is no longer possible, as it was in the not too distant historical past, to settle comfortably into the value system of one's forebears or one's community and live out one's life without ever examining the nature and the assumptions of that system.

In this situation it is not surprising that value orientations from the past appear to be in a state of disintegration or collapse. Men question whether there are, or can be, any universal values. It is often felt that we may have lost, in our modern world, all possibility of any general or cross-cultural basis for values. One natural result of this uncertainty and confusion is that there is an increasing concern about, interest in, and a searching for, a sound or meaningful value approach which can hold its own in today's world. I share this general concern. I have also experienced the more specific value issues which arise in my own field, psychotherapy. The client's feelings and convictions about values frequently change during therapy. How can he or we know whether they have changed in a sound direction? Or does he simply, as some claim, take over the value system of his therapist? Is psychotherapy simply a device whereby the unacknowledged and unexamined values of the therapist are unknowingly transmitted to an unsuspecting client? Or should this transmission of values be the therapist's openly held purpose? Should he become the modern priest, upholding and imparting a value system suitable for today? And what would such a value system be? There has been much discussion of such issues, ranging from thoughtful and empirically based presentations such as that of D. D. Glad to more polemic statements. As is so often true, the general problem faced by the culture is painfully and specifically evident in the cultural microcosm which is called the therapeutic relationship.

I should like to attempt a modest approach to this whole problem. I have observed changes in the approach to values as the individual grows from infancy to adulthood. I observe further changes when, if he is fortunate, he continues to grow toward true psychological maturity. Many of these observations grow out of my experience as a therapist, where I have had the rich opportunity of seeing the ways in which individuals move toward a richer life. From these observations I believe I see some directional threads emerging which might offer a new concept of the valuing process, more tenable in the modern world. I have made a beginning by presenting some of these ideas partially in previous writings; I would like now to voice them more clearly and more fully.

I would stress that my vantage point for making these observations is not that of the scholar or philosopher: I am speaking from my experience of the functioning human being, as I have lived with him in the intimate experience of therapy and in other situations of growth, change, and development.

Some Definitions

Before I present some of these observations, perhaps I should try to clarify what I mean by values. There are many definitions which have been used, but I have found helpful some distinctions made by Charles Morris. He points out that *value* is a term we employ in different ways. We use it to refer to the tendency of any living beings to show preference, in their actions, for one kind of object or objective rather than another. This preferential behavior he calls "operative values." It need not involve any cognitive or conceptual thinking. It is simply the value choice which is indicated behaviorally when the organism selects one object, rejects another. When the earthworm, placed in a simple Y maze, chooses the smooth arm of the Y, instead of the path which is paved with sandpaper, he is indicating an operative value.

A second use of the term might be called "conceived values." This is the preference of the individual for a symbolized object. Usually in such a preference there is anticipation or foresight of the outcome of behavior directed toward such a symbolized object. A choice such as "honesty is the best policy" is such a conceived value.

A final use of the term might be called "objective value." People use the word in this way when they wish to speak of what is objectively preferable, whether or not it is in fact sensed or conceived of as desirable. What I have to say involves this last definition scarcely at all. I will be concerned with operative values and conceptualized values.

The Infant's Way of Valuing

Let me first speak about the infant. The living human being has, at the outset, a clear approach to values. He prefers some things and experiences and rejects others. We can infer from studying his behavior that he prefers those experiences which maintain, enhance, or actualize his organism and rejects those which do not serve this end. Watch him for a bit:

Hunger is negatively valued. His expression of this often comes through loud and clear.

Food is positively valued. But when he is satisfied, food is negatively valued, and the same milk he responded to so eagerly is now spit out, or the breast which seemed so satisfying is now rejected as he turns his head away from the

nipple with an amusing facial expression of disgust and
revulsion.

He values security and the holding and caressing which
seem to communicate security.

He values new experience for its own sake, and we observe
this in his obvious pleasure in discovering his toes, in his
searching movements, in his endless curiosity.

He shows a clear negative valuing of pain, bitter tastes,
sudden loud sounds.

All of this is commonplace, but let us look at these facts in
terms of what they tell us about the infant's approach to
values. It is first of all a flexible, changing, valuing *process*,
not a fixed system. He likes food and dislikes the same food.
He values security and rest and rejects it for new experience.
What is going on seems best described as an organismic
valuing process in which each element, each moment of what
he is experiencing, is somehow weighed and selected or
rejected, depending on whether, at this moment, it tends
to actualize the organism or not. This complicated weighing
of experience is clearly an organismic, not a conscious or
symbolic function. These are operative, not conceived values.
But this process can nonetheless deal with complex value
problems. I would remind you of the experiment in which
young infants had spread in front of them a score or more of
dishes of natural (that is, unflavored) foods. Over a period of
time they clearly tended to value the foods which enhanced
their own survival, growth, and development. If for a time
a child gorged himself on starches, this would soon be
balanced by a protein "binge." If at times he chose a diet
deficient in some vitamin, he would later seek out foods rich
in this very vitamin. He was utilizing the wisdom of the body
in his value choices, or perhaps more accurately, the
physiological wisdom of his body guided his behavioral
movements, resulting in what we might think of as objectively
sound value choices.

Another aspect of the infant's approach to values is that
the source or locus of the evaluating process is clearly within
himself. Unlike many of us, he *knows* what he likes and
dislikes, and the origin of these value choices lies strictly
within himself. He is the center of the valuing process, the
evidence for his choices being supplied by his own senses.
He is not at this point influenced by what his parents think

he should prefer, or by what the church says, or by the opinion
of the latest "expert" in the field, or by the persuasive talents
of an advertising firm. It is from within his own experiencing
that his organism is saying in nonverbal terms, "this is good
for me," "that is bad for me," "I like this," or "I strongly
dislike that." He would laugh at our concern over values, if he
could understand it. How could anyone fail to know what he
liked and disliked, what was good for him and what was not?

The Change in the Valuing Process

What happens to this highly efficient, soundly based valuing
process? By what sequence of events do we exchange it for
the more rigid, uncertain, inefficient approach to values which
characterizes most of us as adults? Let me try to state
briefly one of the major ways in which I think this happens.

The infant needs love, wants it, tends to behave in ways
which will bring a repetition of this wanted experience. But
this brings complications. He pulls baby sister's hair and
finds it satisfying to hear her wails and protests. He then
hears that he is "a naughty, bad boy," and this may be
reinforced by a slap on the hand. He is cut off from affection.
As this experience is repeated, and many, many others like it,
he gradually learns that what "feels good" is often "bad"
in the eyes of others. Then the next step occurs, in which
he comes to take the same attitude himself which these
others have taken. Now, as he pulls his sister's hair, he
solemnly intones, "Bad, bad boy." He is introjecting the value
judgment of another, taking it as his own. He has deserted
the wisdom of his organism, giving up the locus of evaluation,
and is trying to behave in terms of values set by another,
in order to hold love.

Or take another example at an older level. A boy senses,
though perhaps not consciously, that he is more loved and
prized by his parents when he thinks of being a doctor than
when he thinks of being an artist. Gradually he introjects the
values attached to being a doctor. He comes to want, above
all, to be a doctor. Then in college he is baffled by the fact that
he repeatedly fails in chemistry, which is absolutely necessary
to becoming a physician, in spite of the fact that the guidance
counselor assures him he has the ability to pass the course.
Only in counseling interviews does he begin to realize how
completely he has lost touch with his organismic reactions,

how out of touch he is with his own valuing process.

Let me give another instance from a class of mine, a group of prospective teachers. I asked them at the beginning of the course, "Please list for me the two or three values which you would most wish to pass on to the children with whom you will work." They turned in many value goals, but I was surprised by some of the items. Several listed such things as "to speak correctly," "to use good English, not to use words like ain't." Others mentioned neatness—"to do things according to instructions"; one explained her hope that "When I tell them to write their names in the upper right-hand corner with the date under it, I want them to do it *that way*, not in some other form."

I confess I was somewhat appalled that for some of these girls the most important values to be passed on to pupils were to avoid bad grammar, or meticulously to follow teacher's instructions. I felt baffled. Certainly these behaviors had not been *experienced* as the most satisfying and meaningful elements in their own lives. The listing of such values could only be accounted for by the fact that these behaviors had gained approval—and thus had been introjected as deeply important.

Perhaps these several illustrations will indicate that in an attempt to gain or hold love, approval, esteem, the individual relinquishes the locus of evaluation which was his in infancy and places it in others. He learns to have a basic *dis*trust for his own experiencing as a guide to his behavior. He learns from others a large number of conceived values, and adopts them as his own, even though they may be widely discrepant from what he is experiencing. Because these concepts are not based on his own valuing, they tend to be fixed and rigid, rather than fluid and changing.

Some Introjected Patterns

It is in this fashion, I believe, that most of us accumulate the introjected value patterns by which we live. In this fantastically complex culture of today, the patterns we introject as desirable or undesirable come from a variety of sources and are often highly contradictory in their meanings. Let me list a few of the introjections which are commonly held.

Sexual desires and behaviors are mostly bad. The sources of this construct are many—parents, churches, teachers.

Disobedience is bad. Here parents and teachers combine with the military to emphasize this concept. To obey is good. To obey without question is even better.

Making money is the highest good. The sources of this conceived value are too numerous to mention.

Learning an accumulation of scholarly facts is highly desirable.

Browsing and aimless exploratory reading for fun is undesirable. The source of these last two concepts is apt to be in school, the educational system.

Abstract art or "pop" art, or "op" art is good. Here the people we regard as sophisticated are the originators of the value.

Communism is utterly bad. Here the government is a major source.

To love thy neighbor is the highest good. This concept comes from the church, perhaps from the parents.

Cooperation and teamwork are preferable to acting alone. Here companions are an important source.

Cheating is clever and desirable. The peer group again is the origin.

Coca-Colas, chewing gum, electric refrigerators, and automobiles are all utterly desirable. This conception comes not only from advertisements, but is reinforced by people all over the world. From Jamaica to Japan, from Copenhagen to Kowloon, the "Coca-Cola culture" has come to be regarded as the acme of desirability.

This is a small and diversified sample of the myriads of conceived values which individuals often introject, and hold as their own, without ever having considered their inner organismic reactions to these patterns and objects.

Common Characteristics of Adult Valuing

I believe it will be clear from the foregoing that the usual adult — I feel I am speaking for most of us — has an approach to values which has these characteristics:

The majority of his values are introjected from other individuals or groups insignificant to him, but are regarded by him as his own.

The source or locus of evaluation on most matters lies outside of himself.

The criterion by which his values are set is the degree

to which they will cause him to be loved or accepted.

These conceived preferences are either not related at all, or not clearly related, to his own process of experiencing.

Often there is a wide and unrecognized discrepancy between the evidence supplied by his own experience, and these conceived values.

Because these conceptions are not open to testing in experience, he must hold them in a rigid and unchanging fashion. The alternative would be a collapse of his values. Hence his values are "right" – like the law of the Medes and the Persians, which changeth not.

Because they are untestable, there is no ready way of solving contradictions. If he has taken in from the community the conception that money is the *summum bonum* and from the church the conception that love of one's neighbor is the highest value, he has no way of discovering which has more value for *him*. Hence a common aspect of modern life is living with absolutely contradictory values. We calmly discuss the possibility of dropping a hydrogen bomb on Russia, but then find tears in our eyes when we see headlines about the suffering of one small child.

Because he has relinquished the locus of evaluation to others and has lost touch with his own valuing process, he feels profoundly insecure and easily threatened in his values. If some of these conceptions were destroyed, what would take their place? This threatening possibility makes him hold his value conceptions more rigidly, or more confusedly, or both.

The Fundamental Discrepancy

I believe that this picture of the individual, with values mostly introjected, held as fixed concepts, rarely examined or tested, is the picture of most of us. By taking over the conceptions of others as our own, we lose contact with the potential wisdom of our own functioning, and lose confidence in ourselves. Since these value constructs are often sharply at variance with what is going on in our own experiencing, we have in a very basic way divorced ourselves from ourselves, and this accounts for much of modern strain and insecurity. This fundamental discrepancy between the individual's concepts and what he is actually experiencing, between the intellectual structure of his values and the valuing process

going on unrecognized within him—this is a part of the
fundamental estrangement of modern man from himself.
This is a major problem for the therapist.

Restoring Contact with Experience

Some individuals are fortunate in going beyond the picture
I have just given, developing further in the direction of
psychological maturity. We see this happen in psychotherapy
where we endeavor to provide a climate favorable to the
growth of the person. We also see it happen in life, whenever
life provides a therapeutic climate for the individual. Let me
concentrate on this further maturing of a value approach
as I have seen it in therapy.

In the first place let me say somewhat parenthetically that
the therapeutic relationship is *not* devoid of values. Quite the
contrary. When it is most effective, it seems to me, it is
marked by one primary value: namely, that this person, this
client, has worth. He as a person is valued in his separateness
and uniqueness. It is when he senses and realizes that he is
prized as a person that he can slowly begin to value the
different aspects of himself. Most importantly, he can begin,
with much difficulty at first, to sense and to feel what is going
on within him, what he is feeling, what he is experiencing,
how he is reacting. He uses his experiencing as a direct
referent to which he can turn in forming accurate
conceptualizations and as a guide to his behavior. E. T.
Gendlin has elaborated the way in which this occurs. As his
experiencing becomes more and more open to him, as he is
able to live more freely in the process of his feelings, then
significant changes begin to occur in his approach to values.
It begins to assume many of the characteristics it had
in infancy.

Introjected Values in Relation to Experiencing

Perhaps I can indicate this by reviewing a few of the brief
examples of introjected values which I have given and
suggesting what happens to them as the individual comes
closer to what is going on within him.

The individual in therapy looks back and realizes, "But
I *enjoyed* pulling my sister's hair—and that doesn't make me
a bad person."

The student failing chemistry realizes, as he gets close to

his own experiencing—"I don't value being a doctor, even though my parents do; I don't like chemistry; I don't like taking steps toward being a doctor; and I am not a failure for having these feelings."

The adult recognizes that sexual desires and behavior may be richly satisfying and permanently enriching in their consequences, or they can be shallow and temporary and less than satisfying. He goes by his own experiencing, which does not always coincide with the social norms.

He considers art from a new value approach. He says, "This picture moves me deeply, means a great deal to me. It also happens to be an abstraction, but that is not the basis for my valuing it."

He recognizes freely that this communist book or person has attitudes and goals which he shares as well as ideas and values which he does not share.

He realizes that at times he experiences cooperation as meaningful and valuable to him, and that at other times he wishes to be alone and act alone.

Valuing in the Mature Person

The valuing process which seems to develop in this more mature person is in some ways very much like that in the infant, and in some ways quite different. It is fluid, flexible, based on this particular moment and the degree to which this moment is experienced as enhancing and actualizing. Values are not held rigidly, but are continually changing. The painting which last year seemed meaningful now appears uninteresting, the way of working with individuals which was formerly experienced as good now seems inadequate, the belief which then seemed true is now experienced as only partly true, or perhaps false.

Another characteristic of the way this person values experience is that it is highly differentiated, or as the semanticists would say, extensional. As the members of my class of prospective teachers learned, general principles are not as useful as sensitively discriminating reactions. One says, "With this little boy, I just felt I should be very firm, and he seemed to welcome that, and I felt good that I had been. But I'm not that way at all with the other children most of the time." She was relying on her experiencing of the relationship with each child to guide her behavior. I have

already indicated, in going through the examples, how much
more differentiated are the individual's reactions to what
were previously rather solid monolithic introjected values.

In another way the mature individual's approach is like
that of the infant. The locus of evaluation is again established
firmly within the person. It is his own experience which
provides the value information or feedback. This does not
mean that he is not open to all the evidence he can obtain
from other sources. But it means that this is taken for what
it is—outside evidence—and is not as significant as his own
reactions. Thus he may be told by a friend that a new book
is very disappointing. He reads two unfavorable reviews of
the book. His tentative hypothesis is that he will not value
the book. Yet, if he reads the book, his valuing will be based
upon the reactions it stirs in him, not on what he has been
told by others.

There is also involved in this valuing process a letting
oneself down into the immediacy of what one is experiencing,
endeavoring to sense and to clarify all its complex meanings.
I think of a client who, toward the close of therapy, when
puzzled about an issue, would put his head in his hands and
say, "Now what *is* it that I'm feeling? I want to get next to it.
I want to learn what it is." Then he would wait, quietly and
patiently, trying to listen to himself, until he could discern
the exact flavor of the feelings he was experiencing. He, like
others, was trying to get close to himself.

In getting close to what is going on within himself, the
process is much more complex than it is in the infant. In the
mature person, it has much more scope and sweep, for there
is involved in the present moment of experiencing the
memory traces of all the relevant learnings from the past.
This moment has not only its immediate sensory impact,
but it has meaning growing out of similar experiences in the
past. It has both the new and the old in it. So when I
experience a painting or a person, my experiencing contains
within it the learnings I have accumulated from past
meetings with paintings or persons, as well as the new
impact of this particular encounter. Likewise the moment of
experience contains, for the mature adult, hypotheses about
consequences. "I feel now that I would enjoy a third drink,
but past learnings indicate that I may regret it in the
morning." "It is not pleasant to express forthrightly my

negative feelings to this person, but past experience indicates that in a continuing relationship it will be helpful in the long run." Past and future are both in this moment and enter into the valuing.

I find that in the person I am speaking of (and here again we see a similarity to the infant) the criterion of the valuing process is the degree to which the object of the experience actualizes the individual himself. Does it make him a richer, more complete, more fully developed person? This may sound as though it were a selfish or unsocial criterion, but it does not prove to be so, since deep and helpful relationships with others are experienced as actualizing.

Like the infant, too, the psychologically mature adult trusts and uses the wisdom of his organism, with the difference that he is able to do so knowingly. He realizes that if he can trust all of himself, his feelings and his intuitions may be wiser than his mind, that as a total person he can be more sensitive and accurate than his thoughts alone. Hence he is not afraid to say — "I feel that this experience (or this thing, or this direction) is good. Later I will probably know *why* I feel it is good." He trusts the totality of himself.

It should be evident from what I have been saying that this valuing process in the mature individual is not an easy or simple thing. The process is complex, the choices often very perplexing and difficult, and there is no guarantee that the choice which is made will in fact prove to be self-actualizing. But because whatever evidence exists is available to the individual, and because he is open to his experiencing, errors are correctable. If a chosen course of action is not self-enhancing, this will be sensed, and he can make an adjustment or revision. He thrives on a maximum feedback interchange, and thus, like the gyroscopic compass on a ship, can continually correct his course toward becoming more of himself.

Some Propositions Regarding the Valuing Process

Let me sharpen the meaning of what I have been saying by stating three propositions which contain the essential elements of this viewpoint. While it may not be possible to devise empirical tests of each proposition in its entirety, each is to some degree capable of being tested through the methods of science. I would also state that though the following propositions are stated firmly in order to give them clarity, I am actually advancing them as decidedly tentative hypotheses.

1. There is an organismic base for an organized valuing process within the human individual.

It is hypothesized that this base is something the human being shares with the rest of the animate world. It is part of the functioning life process of any healthy organism. It is the capacity for receiving feedback information which enables the organism continually to adjust its behavior and reactions so as to achieve the maximum possible self-enhancement.

2. This valuing process in the human being is effective in achieving self-enhancement to the degree that the individual is open to the experiencing which is going on within himself.

I have tried to give two examples of individuals who are close to their own experiencing: the tiny infant who has not yet learned to deny in his awareness the processes going on within; and the psychologically mature person who has relearned the advantages of this open state.

3. One way of assisting the individual to move toward openness to experience is through a relationship in which he is prized as a separate person, in which the experiencing going on within him is empathically understood and valued, and in which he is given the freedom to experience his own feelings and those of others without being threatened in doing so.

This proposition obviously grows out of therapeutic experience. It is a brief statement of the essential qualities in the therapeutic relationship. There are already some empirical studies, of which the one by Barrett-Lennard is a good example, which give support to such a statement.

Propositions Regarding the Outcomes of the Valuing Process

I come now to the nub of any theory of values or valuing. What are its consequences? I should like to move into this new ground by stating bluntly two propositions as to the qualities of behavior which emerge from this valuing process. I shall then give some of the evidence from my own experience as a therapist in support of these propositions.

4. In persons who are moving toward greater openness to their experiencing, there is an organismic commonality of value directions.

5. These common value directions are of such kinds as to

enhance the development of the individual himself and of others in his community and to make for the survival and evolution of his species.

It has been a striking fact of my experience that in therapy, where individuals are valued, where there is greater freedom to feel and to be, certain value directions seem to emerge. These are not chaotic directions but instead have a surprising commonality. This commonality is not dependent on the personality of the therapist, for I have seen these trends emerge in the clients of therapists sharply different in personality. This commonality does not seem to be due to the influences of any one culture, for I have found evidence of these directions in cultures as divergent as those of the United States, Holland, France, and Japan. I like to think that this commonality of value directions is due to the fact that we all belong to the same species—that just as a human infant tends, individually, to select a diet similar to that selected by other human infants, so a client in therapy tends, individually, to choose value directions similar to those chosen by other clients. As a species there may be certain elements of experience which tend to make for inner development and which would be chosen by all individuals if they were genuinely free to choose.

Let me indicate a few of these value directions as I see them in my clients as they move in the direction of personal growth and maturity.

They tend to move away from facades. Pretense, defensiveness, putting up a front, tend to be negatively valued.

They tend to move away from "oughts." The compelling feeling of "I ought to do or be thus and so" is negatively valued. The client moves away from being what he "ought to be," no matter who has set that imperative.

They tend to move away from meeting the expectations of others. Pleasing others, as a goal in itself, is negatively valued.

Being real is positively valued. The client tends to move toward being himself, being his real feelings, being what he is. This seems to be a very deep preference.

Self-direction is positively valued. The client discovers an increasing pride and confidence in making his own choices, guiding his own life.

One's self, one's own feelings, come to be positively valued. From a point where he looks upon himself with contempt and despair, the client comes to value himself and his reactions as being of worth.

Being a process is positively valued. From desiring some fixed goal, clients come to prefer the excitement of being a process of potentialities being born.

Perhaps more than all else, the client comes to value an openness to all of his inner and outer experience. To be open to and sensitive to his own *inner* reactions and feelings, the reactions and feelings of others, and the realities of the objective world—this is a direction which he clearly prefers. This openness becomes the client's most valued resource.

Sensitivity to others and acceptance of others is positively valued. The client comes to appreciate others for what they are, just as he has come to appreciate himself for what he is.

Finally, deep relationships are positively valued. To achieve a close, intimate, real, fully communicative relationship with another person seems to meet a deep need in every individual and is very highly valued.

These then are some of the preferred directions which I have observed in individuals moving toward personality maturity. Though I am sure that the list I have given is inadequate and perhaps to some degree inaccurate, it holds for me exciting possibilities. Let me try to explain why.

I find it significant that when individuals are prized as persons, the values they select do not run the full gamut of possibilities. I do not find, in such a climate of freedom, that one person comes to value fraud and murder and thievery, while another values a life of self-sacrifice, and another values only money. Instead there seems to be a deep and underlying thread of commonality. I dare to believe that when the human being is inwardly free to choose whatever he deeply values, he tends to value those objects, experiences, and goals which make for his own survival, growth, and development and for the survival and development of others. I hypothesize that it is characteristic of the human organism to prefer such actualizing and socialized goals when he is exposed to a growth-promoting climate.

A corollary of what I have been saying is that in *any* culture, given a climate of respect and freedom in which he is valued as a person, the mature individual would tend to choose and prefer these same value directions. This is a highly significant hypothesis which could be tested. It means that though the individual of whom I am speaking would not have a consistent or even a stable system of conceived values, the valuing process within him would lead to emerging value directions which would be constant across cultures and across time.

Another implication I see is that individuals who exhibit the fluid valuing process I have tried to describe, whose value directions are generally those I have listed, would be highly effective in the ongoing process of human evolution. If the human species is to survive at all on this globe, the human being must become more readily adaptive to new problems and situations, must be able to select that which is valuable for development and survival out of new and complex situations, must be accurate in his appreciation of reality if he is to make such selections. The psychologically mature person as I have described him has, I believe, the qualities which would cause him to value those experiences which would make for the survival and enhancement of the human race. He would be a worthy participant and guide in the process of human evolution.

Finally, it appears that we have returned to the issue of universality of values, but by a different route. Instead of universal values "out there," or a universal value system imposed by some group—philosophers, rulers, or priests—we have the possibility of universal human value directions emerging from the experiencing of the human organism. Evidence from therapy indicates that both personal and social values emerge as natural, and experienced, when the individual is close to his own organismic valuing process. The suggestion is that though modern man no longer trusts religion or science or philosophy nor any system of beliefs to *give* him his values, he may find an organismic valuing base within himself which, if he can learn again to be in touch with it, will prove to be an organized, adaptive, and social approach to the perplexing value issues which face all of us.

Summary

I have tried to present some observations, growing out of experience in psychotherapy, which are relevant to man's search for some satisfying basis for his approach to values.

I have described the human infant as he enters directly into an evaluating transaction with his world, appreciating or rejecting his experiences as they have meaning for his own actualization, utilizing all the wisdom of his tiny but complex organism.

I have said that we seem to lose this capacity for direct evaluation, and come to behave in those ways and to act in terms of those values which will bring us social approval, affection, esteem. To buy love we relinquish the valuing process. Because the center of our lives now lies in others, we are fearful and insecure and must cling rigidly to the values we have introjected.

But if life or therapy gives us favorable conditions for continuing our psychological growth, we move on in something of a spiral, developing an approach to values which partakes of the infant's directness and fluidity but goes far beyond him in its richness. In our transactions with experience we are again the locus or source of valuing, we prefer those experiences which in the long run are enhancing, we utilize all the richness of our cognitive learning and functioning, but at the same time we trust the wisdom of our organism.

I have pointed out that these observations lead to certain basic statements. Man has within him an organismic basis for valuing. To the extent that he can be freely in touch with this valuing process in himself, he will behave in ways which are self-enhancing. We even know some of the conditions which enable him to be in touch with his own experiencing process.

In therapy, such openness to experience leads to emerging value directions which appear to be common across individuals and perhaps even across cultures. Stated in older terms, individuals who are thus in touch with their experiencing come to value such directions as sincerity, independence, self-direction, self-knowledge, social responsivity, social responsibility, and loving interpersonal relationships.

I have concluded that a new kind of emergent universality of value directions becomes possible when individuals move in the direction of psychological maturity, or more accurately, move in the direction of becoming open to their experiencing. Such a value base appears to make for the enhancement of self and others and to promote a positive evolutionary process.

Beyond Values Clarification

by Howard Kirschenbaum

Reprinted by permission of the author and the Adirondack Mountain Humanistic Education Center, Upper Jay, New York 12987.

PART ONE

Since the publication of *Values and Teaching*,[1] in 1966, proponents of the values-clarification approach in education have continued to develop scores of new *techniques* and *applications* for their work.[2,3] There has, however, been little or no change in the *theoretical foundation* upon which the approach is built. This has been especially true of Louis Raths' seven criteria for a value—the Gibraltar upon which values clarification has rested for many years.

Like many other approaches in the humanistic education field, values clarification has grown up as a separate "movement" with its own terminology, concepts, and methods. Although I believe the approach, by itself, has a great deal to offer, over the last several years I have felt increasingly hamstrung by some of its theories and concepts. Many of my colleagues and students in this field have expressed similar misgivings. The problem seems to be that many of us have experienced several different branches of humanistic education and are not convinced that any one approach has all the answers or even the best answers. What many people

are seeking is a wider view of our goals as humanistic
educators—one that encompasses values clarification, but
also integrates it with the other valuable approaches which
exist. In this essay, I would like to describe my own evolution
on this issue and my attempts, both theoretical and practical,
to move beyond values clarification as a separate approach.

My first introduction to values-clarification theory was back
in 1964 when one of Sid Simon's students told me about
Louis Raths' seven criteria for a value. I learned that if a
belief or behavior were to qualify as a value, according to
Raths, it must be: 1) chosen from alternatives; 2) chosen after
thoughtful consideration of consequences; 3) chosen freely;
4) prized and cherished; 5) publicly affirmed; 6) acted upon;
and 7) acted upon with some pattern and repetition.

I was very impressed. My friends and I had grown up in an
educational system which did little but moralize and
indoctrinate. Rarely were we given a chance to get in touch
with what we thought was important, what we prized and
cherished. Nor did we have much of a chance to explore
alternatives or make free choices as a part of our education.
And schooling certainly didn't involve action for us; it had
little to do with our lives in the real world. Moreover, I had
just been very involved with the civil-rights movement in
Mississippi. I saw in values clarification—in the methods and
approaches that fostered Raths' seven criteria—the
educational implementation of my political and social views.
If young people could only be encouraged to see more
alternatives, to question their values, to act on their ideals,
I felt certain they could play an integral role in changing
and improving our society and world.

So when I began teaching in 1966, values clarification was
one important part of my repertoire. I believed then (and
do now) that few educational goals are more important than
helping young people determine who they are, what they
stand for, and where they want to go. I was also very
impressed with the by-products of the approach when used in
a group setting—the greater tolerance of others' points of
view, the realization that we are not so unique and that
others share our problems and concerns, the sense of trust
and community the activities foster, and so on.

But I soon became aware that values clarification wasn't
all that was important in education. In 1968 I took a group

dynamics course at Temple University and a Human
Relations Workshop at the National Training Laboratories
in Bethel, Maine. In these powerful educational experiences,
I realized how the goals of more effective *communication* and
the ability to deal with one's *feelings* were as important as the
choosing, prizing, and acting goals of values clarification.
Simultaneously, Sid Simon and Merrill Harmin also were
experiencing the power of verbal and nonverbal
communication exercises in their work.

In the summers of 1968 and 1969, we began to introduce
these communication and awareness exercises into our
week-long values workshops. We made two big charts, headed
"Values-Clarification Strategies" and "Feeling Strategies"
(or "Emotional-Awareness Exercises"), and after the group
had participated in or observed a particular strategy, we
would write the name of the technique on the appropriate
chart. The implication was that "values" was the primarily
cognitive area and "feelings" was, of course, the affective
area. We even set aside the first hour of every morning for
nonverbal activities, which were usually very powerful,
emotion-laden experiences for those who participated. At the
end of the workshop, we would offer a theory I had developed,
based on an essay by Carl Rogers,[4] for how the feeling area
and the values area fit together.

Not everyone, however, appreciated the affective
component in these workshops. It often produced some threat
and resistance for many of the participants who had come
for values clarification and were not interested in these
"touchy-feely" exercises. We wanted to respect their rights,
too. It was something of a dilemma. In the long run, we
decided we had little enough time in a weekend or a week to
do all we wanted with values clarification, let alone introduce
these deeper communication and feeling-awareness exercises.
So we abandoned most of these in our values workshops and
saved them for separate human relations and personal growth
workshops which we began to conduct at about that time.

Perhaps we had been close to something important – an
integration of values clarification with other areas of
humanistic education. At any rate, we backed off from that
and went back to thinking of values clarification as including
only those exercises that could be seen to stem directly from
Raths' seven criteria. Over the years, we continued to

introduce, from time to time, different types of activities into
our workshops—listening exercises, reevaluation counseling
methods, Gestalt approaches. But we did this mostly in an
intuitive way, making little attempt to consciously or
explicitly integrate them with values clarification.

In effect, we were still teaching values clarification
augmented when appropriate by various strategies from
other approaches. Our workshops continued to be very
satisfying, challenging, and transferable experiences for the
participants. But I always felt bad that we had not found
a way to expand our concepts and designs so as to include
other goals, methods, and approaches in a systematic way.

Meanwhile, I was becoming increasingly dissatisfied with
Raths' seven criteria—for two reasons. First, I didn't like the
notion of "criteria." Secondly, I had a lot of problems with
several of the seven criteria.

In *Values and Teaching*, the authors had written:

> We therefore cannot be certain what values, what style of
> life, would be most suitable for any person. We do, however,
> have some ideas about what *processes* might be most effective
> for obtaining values. These ideas grow from the assumption
> that whatever values one obtains should work as effectively
> as possible to relate one to his world in a satisfying and
> intelligent way.
>
> From this assumption comes what we call the *process of
> valuing*. A look at this process may make clear how we define
> a value. Unless something satisfies *all* seven of the criteria
> noted below, we do not call it a value. In other words, for a
> value to result, all of the following seven requirements must
> apply. Collectively, they describe the process of valuing.[5]

I have never heard anyone dispute that Raths did identify
seven ways that our beliefs or behaviors take on added value
for us—seven processes of valuing. But when the authors
extended these processes to also serve as "criteria," they
created a problem.

For the word "criterion" to have some meaning, other than
theoretical, it must be usable. By definition, a criterion is
a standard. It is used to determine whether whatever is being
evaluated measures up to the standard. Whether the criterion
is an objective one (New York City policemen must be at least
5′8″ tall) or a subjective one (my house site must be secluded
and quiet) the principle is the same: if we know all the criteria

and we know all the facts of the situation, we should be able to tell whether the criteria are met or not.

In the case of Raths' seven criteria for a value, this principle does not apply.

How proud must someone be of his belief or behavior in order to meet the prizing criteria? Very proud? Just a little proud? What about pleased? When does pleased turn into proud?

How many times must someone publicly affirm something in order to satisfy the fifth criteria? Is once enough? If I publicly affirmed my views on pollution six years ago, have I satisfied that criteria?

How many alternatives does one have to choose from before whoever is doing the judging tells me I have met the third criteria?

How many consequences must I thoughtfully consider? If I spend one minute thoughtfully considering one consequence, have I satisfied the criteria? How much consideration is involved in being thoughtful?

And how free does my choice have to be? And how many times must I act before I've "actualized" my value? And how many inconsistencies am I allowed before I flunk the test of its being a pattern in my life?

The argument becomes almost absurd. Of course, no one can answer these questions. Ultimately each individual must decide for himself how many alternatives to consider, how many times to act, or how proud he must feel about something before wanting to do it or repeat it. By using the word and the concept "criteria," we suggest that it is possible for someone (perhaps I, the workshop leader) to judge whether or not a particular belief or behavior of someone else is a value. Time and again, I have seen this implicit suggestion produce resistance among workshop participants. Understandably, they resent having someone else define for them what their values are or aren't. As a consequence, they often deny the importance of some of the valuing processes, rather than accept that certain values they thought they held are not values after all (they're only "value indicators," we say). Ironically, we become another type of moralizer, making people feel guilty because they haven't met this or that criterion on a given issue.

Therefore, I prefer to talk only of the *processes* of valuing,

to emphasize that here are seven ways we develop and enrich
the values in our lives—by getting in touch with what we
prize and cherish, by considering alternatives, by acting on
our beliefs and goals, by examining our patterns, and so on.
My goal is not for people to be able to say, "Look here, I've
got five values which meet all seven criteria," but to help
people, including myself, learn to use skillfully the seven
processes in our lives. Then, as a matter of course, we will
continue to examine what we prize and cherish, make
thoughtful choices from alternatives, act on our beliefs and
goals—*but only when we feel the need to do so and not just to
meet someone else's criteria*. It seems to me that one of the
overall goals of values clarification is to return the locus of
evaluation to the person, so that he is the controller of his own
valuing process. The seven criteria imply an external frame
of reference which seems inimical to values clarification.
I want to use the seven valuing processes in my life because
they help my inner needs find expression and fulfillment.
I do not want to use them because they are criteria.

This differentiation between "processes" and "criteria"
may seem like only a semantic distinction, important only
in its possibility for producing less resistance when
explaining the seven processes at values-clarification
workshops. On the contrary, I think that once one firmly
shifts his focus to the valuing *process* the very nature of the
seven processes begins to change.

Consider the fourth process or criteria—that of prizing
and cherishing. To hold beliefs and engage in behaviors that
one prizes and cherishes is clearly one of the goals of values
clarification. In this sense, the prized beliefs or behaviors
are a *product* of values clarification; the "criterion" of prizing
and cherishing has been met. But, in reality, we know two
things: first, that one does not quickly or easily arrive at
fully developed beliefs and behaviors that are prized and
cherished; second, what one prizes and cherishes continually
changes, from moment to moment or from year to year.
Again, we see that prizing and cherishing is not so much
an attained state as it is an ongoing process.

What, then, is this ongoing process by which one
continually discovers what he prizes and cherishes? Here we
return to the problem we experienced several years ago
when we abandoned the use of the emotional-awareness

exercises in the values-clarification workshops. Whether we know how to integrate it in workshops or not, it seems clear that the affective realm, the feeling area, is one of the crucial ingredients in values clarification, and that the process by which one discovers what he prizes and cherishes is, in part, a deepening awareness of one's own feelings. In Carl Rogers' terminology, it would be an "openness to our inner experience." And this includes not only the positive experience; it involves the full gamut of human emotion.

One needs only to recall the most recent, extremely important decision in his life — perhaps involving a love relationship, a choice or change of job, a move to another locality, or the like. It was probably necessary to process numerous emotions — fear, hope, anxiety, excitement, dependence, love, hate, loneliness, competence, incompetence — before coming to a better understanding of which choices one would prize or cherish the most.

What all this implies is that if we are describing the valuing process, instead of the criterion, we shall have to adopt new terminology. For the fourth process, we might move from "prizing and cherishing," which is the by-product, to talk about *discovering* what one prizes and cherishes. Yet even this is perhaps a misnomer for the task, placing too much emphasis on the results. I prefer "being open to one's inner experience," as this connotes an ongoing process of identifying and sorting through one's feelings in order to keep arriving at choices which one can prize and cherish. But the terminology is far less important than the process described and the implications of such a shift in emphasis. What is implied is that values clarification, which has been treated as primarily a cognitive process even by the leaders in the approach, must be much more fully recognized as also an in-depth affective process. If this is so, then we can no longer exclude the learnings and techniques from psychotherapy, human relations training, Gestalt therapy, bioenergetics, and many other areas from our concepts or from our practices in values clarification. These latter methods may focus more on discovering all of one's feelings in the present moment (the "here and now"), and values-clarification strategies may focus more on discovering our prizing and cherishing feelings as evident in our beliefs and behavior patterns; but both are needed and complementary.

All the methods by which people become aware of all their feelings and learn to deal with and understand them are crucial for developing one's own values and making difficult values decisions. The "criteria" of beliefs and behaviors which are prized and cherished are reached only through an ongoing awareness of one's inner, feeling world.

I believe a similar extension of the meaning of values clarification takes place when we view what has been, traditionally, the fifth criterion for a value, that of "public affirmation."

I can't remember all the times I've seen participants at workshops raise objections when we told them that, if they didn't publicly affirm something, it wasn't a value. Some participants have admitted later that they were uncomfortable because of certain beliefs they held which they felt guilty about not standing up to be counted for. To deny the importance of public affirmation was to escape from some of their guilt feelings. But many participants raised valid objections to the public affirmation criterion, or process, which were more than personal defenses. What about the person who gives to charity but also holds a value of *not* publicly identifying himself as the donor? What about the many times in history when to publicly affirm one's beliefs on religion or politics would mean death or imprisonment or dismissal for the affirmer? What about the times when public affirmation would be hurtful to some individual or group that is also valued? In short, what happens when the value and benefits of public affirmation conflict with other values that need to be considered? Are there not times when it is inappropriate to publicly affirm one's values?

To answer these objections, we would have to backtrack. We were forced to admit that, yes, there are some times when other values are stronger than that of public affirmation. And, yes, there are some times when the risk of public affirmation overshadows its advantages. Ultimately, we conceded, each person must decide for himself when *not* to publicly affirm is the better part of valor and when it is a cowardly cop-out. In practice, the criterion became: public affirmation, *when appropriate*. We even developed the Privacy Circles strategy to help people discover their own standard of appropriateness in affirming their values. The strategy demonstrates that we reveal different things about ourselves to intimates, to friends, to colleagues, to acquaintances, and to strangers, and that each of us must decide the patterns we want to develop for what we will reveal on different issues to each group.

Similarly, the word "share" began to replace the word "affirm" in our instructions for discussion topics during workshops and classes. Affirmation seems most appropriate in public settings or when we feel extremely strongly about an issue. The picture of publicly affirming something to one's intimate friend is slightly ludicrous. *Affirm* often takes on connotations of rigidity and imposition. *Share* conveys much more of the flavor for what we hope most discussions of values might become. It suggests more of an offering—we offer our value alternatives to others for their consideration. They are free to reject the offering, without our rejecting them. For these reasons, I have gradually begun to describe the fifth process of valuing as that of "appropriate sharing" instead of public affirmation. In some ways, I regret that we maintained that latter use in *Values Clarification: A Handbook of Practical Strategies* and in *Clarifying Values through Subject Matter.*

But, as with the prizing and cherishing process, once we move away from the original criteria-oriented description, a whole new dimension of the process is suggested. One might ask: Why *is* appropriate sharing a valuing process? Why is it even a valuable process?

When we were only speaking of public affirmation, we could describe how standing up for one's opinions and beliefs is a necessary condition for democracy to be successful. Whether it is a family, a small group, a class, an organization, or a society, only as the group takes into consideration the feelings and views of all its members, can it reach its most effective decisions—decisions which are not undermined later by the minority whose views were not expressed. It was also clear that public affirmation helped other people clarify their values by giving them new alternatives to consider. But little emphasis was ever placed on how public affirmation is a valuing process or a clarifying process for the individual doing the affirming. Again, we might ask: Why is appropriate sharing a valuable valuing process?

Sidney Jourard[5] has answered this in the context of

"self-disclosure." Only as we are willing to reveal our inner selves to others, he says, can we fully understand and accept ourselves. Why is this so? These are my impressions: First, because we are social beings whose self-concept is developed through interaction with others. Only by sharing our inner selves with others and by receiving their acceptance or successfully coping with their rejection can we fully accept ourselves or deal with the parts of ourselves which we, to some extent, reject. And if we do not accept ourselves, then neither can we be open to our inner experiences nor can we have the confidence to make our own choices. Secondly, self-disclosure has a clarifying effect. As we reveal ourselves, we hear ourselves speak, we get others' reactions, we think "that's not exactly what I meant to say" or "I haven't conveyed what I'm really feeling" or "next time I'd like to put it differently." Thus, by taking the risk of self-disclosure, we become more closely attuned to the inner selves that even we are not fully aware of. The self-disclosure process puts us more closely in touch with our inner experience.

Again, the implications for our work are profound. If self-disclosure is an essential part of values clarification, then our concept of values clarification must be expanded to include all those processes by which effective self-disclosure takes place — in a word: communication. Once more we return to the dilemma of several years ago. In the long run, the human relations-encounter-communications area cannot be excluded from the values-clarification process. Verbal and nonverbal communication, the giving and receiving of feedback, sending clear messages, empathic listening — all these processes and others foster self-disclosure and exposure to alternatives and, therefore, are part and parcel of the values-clarification process.

PART TWO

The door is open. Once we change the emphasis from *criteria* for a value to the *processes* of valuing, we are forced to ask: What are all the processes by which individuals achieve an identity, develop values, and decide what they stand for and what they wish to live for? The older "choosing, prizing, and acting" areas of values clarification are no longer enough to encompass the answer.

In my own thinking, I would expand the three major areas
of valuing into these five major processes:

1. Feeling
2. Thinking
3. Communicating
4. Choosing
5. Acting

It seems to me that each of these areas is an essential part
of the valuing process. Individually, each area is comprised
of several subprocesses of valuing which I will discuss
briefly below. Collectively, these five valuing processes
describe an effective human being, utilizing most of his
or her faculties for living fully and satisfyingly in our
society. Moreover, these five areas seem necessary for living
fully and satisfyingly in any society. True, different societies
have different norms; for example, one society might have
standards for self-disclosure that would be entirely
inappropriate in another society. But to live effectively in
either society, one has to learn the *skills* for knowing when
and how to reveal himself. Therefore, each of the areas
is not only a major valuing process; each is also a set of *life
skills* that can be learned, practiced, and improved in time.

Feeling

This is the area that schools have studiously avoided
throughout history, believing that wisdom resided in the
mind and the solution to most of life's problems lay in the
rational processes. Today, there is a significant movement to
bring *affective* education into the schools.

The primary process in the feeling area of valuing, as
discussed at length above, is to be "open to one's inner
experience." Others have described this process, or parts
of it, in various terms: "Know thyself." "Be in touch with your
feelings." "Know what you prize and cherish." All these
things are part of the bigger process. To be open implies an
acceptance of one's feelings. The person who distrusts himself,
who is guilty about certain feelings, who is fearful of certain
of his emotions, cannot be open to all portions of his
inner experience. To the extent that he denies these feelings
(or thoughts) or distorts them in his awareness, he will
deprive himself of important data in making values
decisions. His thinking, communicating, choosing, and acting
processes will all suffer as a result. Therefore, all the

approaches which have been or are being developed to help
people learn the skills for becoming aware of and sorting
through or "processing" their feelings are extremely
important for the values-clarification process to operate
effectively.

Thinking

Most of us would assume that thinking skills are necessary
to develop clear values; but this has rarely been made
explicit by humanistic educators. Probably the reason for this
is that it is widely assumed that schools are being effective in
the cognitive realm (a questionable assumption). Therefore,
humanistic educators have spent most of their time focusing
on the affective realm. But, both in theory and in practice, the
thinking area should not be slighted.

People have thought of thinking skills in a variety of ways,
and it seems to me that all are important. Benjamin Bloom
and Norris Sanders have emphasized the levels of thinking—
memory, translation, interpretation, application, analysis,
synthesis, and evaluation, for example, and have encouraged
teachers to help students learn the higher levels of thinking,
not only memory.[6,7] Others have taught "critical thinking,"
distinguishing fact from opinion, analyzing propaganda, etc.
Logic is another thinking skill that is taught in many
schools, often through the math department.[8,9] Creative
thinking is yet another.[10]

Clearly, the choosing and communicating processes of
valuing, especially, are dependent on the thinking process. In
my own high school teaching experience, I have been guilty at
times of emphasizing the other four major valuing processes
to the detriment of the cognitive, without which no person
can be an effective human being. We sometimes assume that
people learn to think by themselves. Piaget and Kohlberg,
however, have demonstrated, both in the areas of pure
cognition and in moral reasoning, that by manipulating the
environment, we can help people advance to higher, more
flexible levels of thinking. The dichotomy between
"traditional" and "humanistic" education is often misleading
in this respect. Thinking always has been—and should
continue to be—a major concern for the humanist.

Communicating

As discussed earlier, the process of communicating can be

both verbal and nonverbal. In either case, some of the major subprocesses or separate skills are: sending clear messages, empathic listening, and giving and receiving feedback. Drawing another person out and asking clarifying questions could also be listed. Conflict resolution might be mentioned as another valuing process, for whenever conflicts arise, this skill is necessary to resolve the conflict in a way that best realizes the values of all the parties involved. Many other approaches in humanistic education have emphasized the importance of the communication area.[11-15]

Choosing

The discussion of this area will also be short, because I would list the three standbys in Raths' seven processes as subprocesses in the choosing area—choosing from alternatives, choosing after thoughtful consideration of consequences, and choosing freely. Perhaps different types of planning and problem-solving processes could also be included here; for example, the type of achievement-planning strategy advocated and taught by Alfred Alschuler and his colleagues.[16] Clearly, choosing is a process that is dependent on both feeling and thinking skills and enhanced by good communication skills.

Acting

Here again, Raths' subprocesses would apply. One way we value is to act upon something with repetition. The more we act on it, the more our behavior shows that we value it. Quantity is the issue. Second, the *quality* of our actions also shows what we value. As I build patterns into my life, as I eliminate the inconsistencies, my actions take on a harmonious and cumulative momentum which has that much more chance of actualizing what I prize and cherish. This emphasis is consistent with those existentialists who say that we define ourselves through our actions.*

Thus, the school program that wishes to encourage the action aspect of valuing provides opportunities for students

---

*It is interesting that, while some existentialists and others say that our actions reveal our values, there are others who equate our beliefs and opinions with our values. Still others see values as synonymous with attitudes and preferences. Values clarification is unique in that it sees the valuing process as involving feelings, thoughts, and actions, not one to the exclusion of the others.

to examine the patterns of action and inaction in their lives
and, moveover, provides them with the opportunity to act
on the choices they make. This may mean that they actually
control some aspects of their education (choice of classes,
choice of reading, choice of how they spend their time during
the day, etc.), or it may mean that they get out into the
world and involve themselves in action projects where they
can put some of their beliefs and ideals into real practice.

The school which is interested in building skills in this
action area not only allows students to act on their choices,
it helps them learn to act more effectively. This may be done
in two ways. One is to help the student learn the other four
major valuing processes. Simply by being more skillful as a
feeler, thinker, communicator, and chooser, it follows that
a person's chosen actions will work out that much more
successfully. Whether the student chooses to write, work
with automobiles, or engage in social change, the school
can provide the settings or resources whereby he can learn to
do those chosen actions more effectively. Not only schools,
but parents, group leaders, peers, or anyone else can help
foster this and the other valuing processes.

The discussion of each of the five major processes of valuing
is intentionally short and suggestive. The more I think
about the valuing process, the more it seems to encompass.
The present enlarged view of the valuing process could be
outlined in the following form. Each major process (for
example, thinking) and each subprocess (for example,
critical thinking) is considered a valuing process, because
if an individual can and does utilize the process effectively,
he is more likely to guide his life in a satisfying and
continually growing direction.

THE VALUING PROCESS

I. Feeling
1. Being open to one's inner experience.
    a. awareness of one's inner experience
    b. acceptance of one's inner experience
II. Thinking
1. Thinking on all seven levels.
    a. memory
    b. translation

       c. application
       d. interpretation
       e. analysis
       f. synthesis
       g. evaluation
2. Critical thinking.
       a. distinguishing fact from opinion
       b. distinguishing supported from unsupported arguments
       c. analyzing propaganda, stereotypes, etc.
3. Logical thinking (logic).
4. Creative thinking.
5. Fundamental cognitive skills.
       a. language use
       b. mathematical skills
       c. research skills

III. Communicating – Verbally and Nonverbally

1. Sending clear messages.
2. Empathic listening.
3. Drawing out.
4. Asking clarifying questions.
5. Giving and receiving feedback.
6. Conflict resolution.

IV. Choosing

1. Generating and considering alternatives.
2. Thoughtfully considering consequences, pros and cons.
3. Choosing strategically.
       a. goal setting
       b. data gathering
       c. problem solving
       d. planning
4. Choosing freely.

V. Acting

1. Acting with repetition.
2. Acting with a pattern and consistency.
3. Acting skillfully, competently.

This expanded conception of the valuing process, or the life skills, leaves many questions unanswered. In closing this essay, I would like to elaborate on the tentative character of this formulation and some of its limitations.

First, the five particular major valuing processes I have

chosen are not necessarily the most useful categories. For
example, one might ask whether choosing is an act that is
really separate from feeling and thinking. If it is not, then
perhaps the choosing area should be dropped, and we should
speak only of teaching the feeling and thinking skills.
(Personally, I think this would be a mistake. It seems to me
that choosing is such an important act of valuing—one that
integrates the feeling and thinking processes in order to
perform a particularly important human function—that it
deserves special consideration, both theoretically and
practically.) I mention this example merely to indicate that
the five categories are only one organizational model. If a
better organization can be created to subsume all the
separate skills and processes that are important for values
clarification and humanistic education, then that newer
organization should be employed.

Second, the various subprocesses and skills which I have
listed under each major process are incomplete—in two ways.
First, there are probably many other valuing subprocesses
or skills which should be added to the list. I hope others will
do so. Second, each subprocess could be divided into many
other "sub-subprocesses." In the communication area, for
example, empathic listening is a process that really involves
many separate subskills—the appropriate amount of eye
contact and head-nodding, focused attention, adopting the
other's frame of reference, and so on. So, while the listing
seems to be a more detailed look at the values-clarification
process than any which has been published before, it can still
be broken down into many finer categories; and it probably
should, if we are to find the most effective way of teaching
all the various valuing skills.

A third limitation of this formulation is that values
clarification is only one approach to humanistic education.
And although the valuing processes have been described
as also being "life skills," there are other life skills which are
not necessarily valuing processes. For example, under the
feeling process, I have discussed "being open to one's inner
experience" as an important valuing process. Yet, many
educators who are concerned with helping people develop
to their fullest human potential would emphasize also the
processes and skills of being open to one's *outer* experience.
This could include the *sensory awareness* movement that

teaches us to more fully apprehend the world through our five senses, or it could include the *mystical awareness* movement that teaches us to be more open to the intangible phenomena — enlightenment, religious experience, extrasensory perception, psychic phenomena, and the like. Through nonverbal exercises, sense relaxation, meditation, prayer, special types of concentration, the skills for being open to the outer environment are cultivated. There are probably many other life skills worthy of our serious attention.

In other words, this schema is only the first step in what could be a very exciting project. Perhaps the next few years will see some individual or group compile a listing of all the different skills and processes which the various approaches to humanizing education attempt to teach. The listing could then be organized into some framework, as I have attempted above. Hopefully, this would result in: 1) a clearer conception of the goals of humanistic education; 2) a greater understanding of how values clarification (or any other approach) fits in with the other approaches in the field; and 3) a stimulus to further curriculum projects and research.

Finally, if these five major areas do give a fuller picture of what the values-clarification process is like, what implications does this have for the way values clarification is used in schools or groups or taught in workshops for educators? This seems to me to be one of the most difficult problems and brings us back to the dilemma which faced us several years ago. Do we try to focus on all five major valuing processes and, perhaps, cover none of them adequately? Or do we limit our goals and hope that the emphasis we delete will be dealt with at some other time? Or do we only give longer workshops, hoping there will be time for everything, but knowing that many fewer people will be able to attend?

There are questions in another aspect of the problem. Even in a short presentation on values clarification, should we try to explain the much fuller conception of the valuing process and risk overloading the listeners with too much detail? Or do we stick with the shorter, safer version of the seven processes which have worked well for many years? What are some other alternatives? If, in a workshop, we have decided to emphasize only some of the major valuing processes, how do we set our priorities? Is feeling more

important than acting? Which is more likely to result in
consistent actions that are in harmony with what people say
they prize and cherish—the values-clarification choosing
strategies, the Hilda Taba critical thinking strategies, the
Gestalt feeling exercises, or the Kohlberg-derived moral
reasoning activities?

We don't really know the answers to these and many other
questions. And, although they offer rich possibilities for
research, it will probably be some time before answers begin
to emerge. Meanwhile, undoubtedly, we will continue to insert
all kinds of feeling-oriented and communication-oriented
exercises into our workshops and our writings. Intuitively, we'll
know we have to go beyond the original confines of values-
clarification theory. I ask that those of us who are interested
in this work admit that we are going beyond values
clarification, that we expand our conception of what values
clarification is, that we encourage dialogues with other
branches of humanistic education, and that, together, we
build new theoretical models and practical designs which
mutually enhance what we all are seeking—the more effective,
more fulfilled, more self-actualizing human being.

—April 1973

NOTES

1. Louis E. Raths, Merrill Harmin, and Sidney B. Simon, *Values and Teaching*
(Columbus, Ohio: Charles E. Merrill Publishing Co., 1966).
2. Sidney B. Simon, Leland W. Howe, and Howard Kirschenbaum, *Values
Clarification: A Handbook of Practical Strategies for Teachers and Students*
(New York: Hart Publishing Company, Inc., 1972).
3. Merrill Harmin, Howard Kirschenbaum, and Sidney B. Simon, *Clarifying
Values Through Subject Matter: Applications for the Classroom* (Minneapolis:
Winston Press, Inc., 1973).
4. Carl R. Rogers, "A Modern Approach to the Valuing Process," *Freedom to
Learn* (Columbus, Ohio: Charles E. Merrill Publishing Co., 1969).
5. Sidney Jourard, *The Transparent Self* (New York: Van Nostrand Reinhold
Company, 1964).
6. Benjamin S. Bloom et al., *Taxonomy of Educational Objectives* (New York:
David McKay Company, 1956).
7. Norris M. Sanders, *Classroom Questions: What Kinds?* (New York: Harper
& Row, Publishers, 1966).
8. Louis E. Raths et al., *Thinking and Teaching* (Columbus, Ohio: Charles E.
Merrill Publishing Co., 1966).
9. Hilda Taba et al., *Elementary Curriculum in Intergroup Relations*
(Washington, D.C.: American Council of Education, 1950).

10. William J. Gordon, *Synectics: The Development of Creative Capacity* (New York: Collier Books, 1961).

11. Richard Schmuck and Patricia Schmuck, *Group Processes in the Classroom* (Dubuque, Ia.: William C. Brown & Company, 1971).

12. Carl R. Rogers, *On Encounter Groups* (New York: Harper & Row, Publishers, 1971).

13. Seville Sax and Sandra Hollander, *Reality Games* (New York: The Macmillan Company, 1971).

14. Gene Stanford and Barbara Stanford, *Learning Discussion Skills through Games* (New York: Citation Press, 1969).

15. Thomas Gordon, *Parent Effectiveness Training* (New York: Peter H. Wyden, 1970).

16. Alfred Alschuler, Diane Tabor, and James McIntyre, *Teaching Achievement Motivation* (Middleton, Conn.: Education Ventures, 1971).

Values Clarification and School Subjects

INTRODUCTION

The articles in this section need little introduction. They all attempt to apply the values-clarification approach to the various academic subjects usually taught in schools. Generally, these articles follow either or both of two patterns. The first is to use the three-level conception of subject matter (facts, concepts, and values) as the basis for the application to a particular subject. The second approach is to use the values-clarification strategies to help teach the subject with a focus on values. The Osman article on health education is interesting in that it also describes a research effort using the values-clarification strategies.

Since the articles in this section were written before the publication of a new book on the subject, perhaps it would be appropriate here to mention that book. It integrates many of the ideas and examples which follow: Merrill Harmin, Howard Kirschenbaum, and Sidney B. Simon, *Clarifying Values through Subject Matter: Applications for the Classroom* (Minneapolis: Winston Press, Inc., 1973).

The job af applying values clarification to the different subject areas goes on continually. This is an area which is in desperate need of additional articles, programs, and books. Many classroom teachers, without knowing it, have made applications of values clarification to their subject areas that are definitely deserving of publication. We would encourage readers to submit their ideas to the education journals. Such articles would benefit many teachers.

Subject Matter with a Focus on Values

by Sidney B. Simon and Merrill Harmin

From *Educational Leadership*, October 1968. Reprinted with permission of the Association for Supervision and Curriculum Development and the authors. Copyright © 1968 by the Association for Supervision and Curriculum Development.

How increasingly irrelevant the schools seem! Social conflicts range all around us, and the schools (the universities, too) go trotting down their "bland" alleys and continue to devote teaching time to grammar drills, the founding of Jamestown, and the urgent problem of how tall the flagpole is if its shadow is fifty feet at high noon.

If only we could see that the confrontation of high noon is here now, and if any drills are in order, perhaps they ought to be riot drills. If we must measure shadows, let them be the shadows of de facto segregation which cloud our land.

Of course this is not easy. Almost all of us feel tremendous ambivalence as we wrestle with that question of just how much of the standard subject matter of the school is to be set aside to make room for dealing with the current concerns of our society. We can all too quickly cite the fact that these problems are not the schools' fault, and that they are too big, too all-encompassing to be tackled in school anyhow. Or we say we have other obligations, like teaching our students the inheritance of man's intellectual past.

What a school budgets time and money for, however, tells what it prizes. What and who it rewards tell what it cherishes.

What the school asks on its true and false questions says
more than almost anything else what it cares about, and
just now, with the heavy emphasis upon college entrance, the
schools care most deeply about putting in more subject matter.

We are not going into that weary either/or argument about
subject matter *or* play-play-play. We have nothing against
subject matter, per se. We do have an urgent need, however,
to make subject matter more relevant, and to us, relevancy
means that the subject matter *must* illumine a student's
values. Louis Raths puts it this way: "The function of
information is to inform. To inform what? To inform
our values."

THREE LEVELS

Information which stays merely at the level of filling in the
holes of a crossword puzzle, or name-dropping at a suburban
cocktail party, is information which we really do not need.
So much of schooling is at this facts-for-facts level. There is a
second level, a higher level, engagingly presented by Bruner,
and this is called the concepts level. We believe that there
is still a higher level, a level which makes use of facts and
concepts, but which goes well beyond them in the direction of
penetrating a student's life. This we call the *values level*.

Let us look at an example to make this point. Take the
favorite social studies topic, "The United States Constitution."
We can teach this at the facts level, the concepts level, or
the values level.

> Facts Level:
> 1. Information about where and when the Constitution
> was drawn up.
> 2. Who was involved and which colonies wanted what in it.
> 3. Information about how it differed from the Articles
> of Confederation.
> 4. Data on what was in the preamble and perhaps asking
> the class to memorize it.
> 5. A list of the first ten amendments and why they were
> called the Bill of Rights.
> 6. The order in which the colonies ratified the document.

The above items should be fairly familiar facts to most
of us, although we have probably forgotten the specifics. At

one time this topic was presented to us in an organized
manner, each fact building upon fact. Unfortunately, it was
difficult to remember then and it still is hard to retain. It was
of interest to only a few students and of little use even to
them in any relevant search for values which might enlighten
living in today's world.

Thus, many teachers, encouraged by Bruner and his
followers, tried to teach the Constitution at the concepts level.

Concepts Level:

1. Our Constitution as a landmark in the evolving concept of
democratic forms of government.

2. The concept of "compromise" and how it operated in
reconciling the economic forces of the period.

3. The motives of the signers and the constituencies all
representatives are obligated to serve.

4. The social injustices which the Bill of Rights attempted
to correct.

5. The concept of amendment and how it has operated in state
legislatures and in Congress.

6. The Constitution today as seen in the actions of the
Supreme Court and the Americal Civil Liberties
Union, etc.

The above "subject matter" will be seen as the basis for
good teaching. It attempts to build relationships between
random facts and to pull together generalizations supported
by data. Many educators would be proud to have this kind
of teaching going on in their schools, but we would argue that
this approach is simply not good enough for these complex
times. Let us look now at the values level, that third level
to which subject matter needs to be lifted.

Values Level:

1. What rights and guarantees do you have in your family?
Who serves as the Supreme Court in disputes?

2. Have you ever written a letter to the editor of a newspaper
or magazine?

3. Many student governments are really token governments
controlled by the "mother country," i.e., the administration.
Is this true in your school? What can you do about it?
If not you, who should do it?

4. Should the editorial board of your school newspaper have
the final say about what is printed in it? How do you

reconcile the fact that the community will judge the school, a tax supported institution, by what is printed in the school paper?

5. When was the last time you signed a petition? Have you ever been the person to draw one up? What did the last sign you carried on a picket line say?

6. Where do you stand on wire tapping, financial aid to parochial schools, censorship of pornographic magazines, or the right of a barber to decide if he wants to cut a Negro's hair?

This kind of teaching is not for the fainthearted. It often hits at the guts, but if we are to see the school as more than a place from which we issue the press release each spring which tells which colleges our students made, then we must do more teaching at this third level, this values level.

Let us be clear that teachers are not to throw out facts and concepts. Obviously, these are essential if we are to have anything to base our values upon. On the other hand, let us say forcefully that the facts and concepts levels, no matter how brilliantly taught, do not clarify students' values. That third level has to be consciously and consistently pushed.

TO INFORM OUR VALUES

Here is another example to argue for our third level point of view. Take Shakespeare's *Hamlet*. It is a good example for three reasons. It is taught universally, it is universally taught badly, and it is a play particularly ripe with values-teaching possibilities.

Facts Level:

1. Information on the year the play was written and the sequence it occupies in Shakespeare's works.

2. What country did Rosencrantz and Guildenstern come from?

3. How did Hamlet's father die? How do we know that?

4. What is the relationship between Hamlet and Queen Gertrude? Between Hamlet and Polonius? Hamlet and Ophelia?

5. Identify these quotations and explain why Shakespeare put them in the play.

6. What is Hamlet's tragic flaw?

7. Who are all the people dead at the end of the play?

The above list is not meant to be all-inclusive by any means. Many other facts and details would be stressed by different teachers. Most teachers, however, feel at ease with such material. Students have been trained to feel comfortable with it, too. They know how to give the teacher what he wants on the kinds of questions which will be asked on tests. (True or False: Ophelia died from an overdose of rosemary.)

Teachers who are more aware will more often be teaching at the second level, the concepts level.

> Concepts Level:
>
> 1. The concept of tragedy as opposed to comedy and how Shakespeare departed from the Aristotelian concepts of drama.
> 2. To understand the various thematic threads of: incest, indecision, revenge, etc.
> 3. To know the dramaturgy behind the "play within a play" concept.
> 4. The concept of "ghost" as it was understood by an Elizabethan audience.
> 5. Psychological concepts which motivate Hamlet, Gertrude, Laertes, etc.
> 6. The various ways *Hamlet* has been played by the great Shakespearean actors.

Again, our lists are merely suggestive. It should, however, be quite apparent that this kind of teaching is much more lively and meaningful as compared with the survey of routine facts or going over the play line for line. Nevertheless, it is a serious error *not* to take your teaching to that third level, the values level. *Hamlet* is so very well-suited to help students develop the skills of clarifying their values and evaluating their lives. We believe that questions like the ones below should help students to do this.

> Values Level:
>
> 1. King Claudius supposedly killed to get ahead. How far will you go to get what you want?
> 2. Laertes hears his father's advice, and it comes out a string of clichés. What kind of advice do you get which falls on *your* deaf ears?
> 3. Part of *Hamlet* is about the obligation of a son to seek revenge for his father. Where do you stand on that kind of act?

4. Hamlet is cruel to Ophelia. In what ways have you ever been cruel to members of the opposite sex? When have you been the recipient of cruelty? Is cruelty an essential part of love to you?

5. What are some things about which you are having trouble making up your mind? Where will you go for help? Whom do you trust? How will you know that you have made a wise decision?

6. What kind of son or daughter do you want to be?

7. Death is a regular happening in *Hamlet*. How close have you ever come to death? What part of you responds to a news story of death on the highway? Death in Vietnam?

It might be well to take a look at the third level, the values level, questions posed here. For one thing, the questions have a heavy component of "you" in them. Among these "you-centered" questions there are some which invite a student to examine alternatives and to follow out the consequences. Some search for elements of pride in his choices. All of them, hopefully, cause him to look more closely at his present life, to see it as related to the subject matter he is studying. Some of the alternatives show that the subject matter could be pertinent to his personal existence. This is essential, this linking of the facts and concepts to the choices and decisions in the student's real life, at least if we are serious about teaching for the clarification of values.

Among these "you-centered" questions there are several which get the student to look at what he is actually *doing* in his life. The questions about the United States Constitution at the third level illustrate this clearly. This action emphasis is very important in the search for values. Many of the social conflicts of our time rage on because so many of us have a giant gap between what we say and what we do. For many of us this gap is a chasm.

These are troubled and confused times in which to grow up. To live life with integrity becomes more and more difficult for more and more people. The threads of alienation which are increasingly woven into our youth must give us all deep concern.

We must demand of the subject matter we teach that it makes us more than politely erudite. We must insist that it relate to students' lives. It must pertain to the realities of life in this complex and confusing time. Subject matter which is lifted to that third level, the values level, will give us a fighting chance. We must not be guilty of ignoring Dag Hammarskjöld's warning: "In modern times we are in danger of taking facts for knowledge, and knowledge for wisdom."

Teaching English with a Focus on Values

by Howard Kirschenbaum and Sidney B. Simon

From the *English Journal*, October 1969. Reprinted with permission of the National Council of Teachers of English.

There must be some reason that we assign all of those compositions, read all of that Shakespeare, and work our way through such a vast quantity of novels, short stories, essays, plays, poetry, and other gems of the English teacher's repertoire.

One possible explanation for what we do is simply that we ourselves love the literature and relish the excitement we have known through reading and writing. We know that writing is an authentic way of achieving better self-understanding. We have tasted the adventure of trying to communicate our ideas and feelings. We have seen literature open up whole new worlds of experience and deepen our insight into ourselves, our fellowman, and our society. We agree with Camus that literature "illuminates the problems of the human conscience in our time." For many of us, leading young people to the edge of these discoveries is what teaching English is all about, and why we are in it.

Yet, sometimes we forget, and in the pressure of our day-to-day teaching, we often allow a giant gap to develop—a gap between what we say and what we do. It is in this gap that the realm of values lies. John Holt asked a college

student who had received straight "A's" in high school
English if he could see some of her high school compositions.
She answered, "What would I save any of those for? I never
wrote anything which really mattered to me for *English*."
She probably echoes the thoughts of more students than we
may care to acknowledge, for until we make the search for
values a consistent and persistent objective (and a behavioral
one at that), we will witness all too many students going
through the motions without writing or reading much of
anything which really "matters" to them in English classes.

There are many things an English teacher can do about
values. We, however, want to discuss one particular strategy
for clarifying values which we have found especially
productive. It is called the Value Sheet.

A Value Sheet is simply a ditto upon which is written a
provocative, perhaps even threatening, but always
value-laden statement. For example, with one of your own
classes, try this rather eloquent example taken from
Russell Baker's "Observer" column in the *New York Times*.
Value Sheet: "Under the Sway of the Great Apes"

    Edwin P. Young, an uncelebrated philosopher, once observed
of football, "After all, it's only a game that kids can play."
This is no longer strictly true. If it were, the networks would
not have bought it up as a vehicle to sell cigarettes, cars,
and beer.

    The evidence suggests that it satisfies some inner need of
the spectator so completely that it can rivet him to his chair
through a holiday in disregard of family life or bring him to
his feet howling for (Allie) Sherman's head when the
outcome fails to gratify.

    If sports have ceased to be only games that kids can play
and become psychotherapy for the mob, it is too bad,
especially for kids who will grow up hating them or busting
gussets to achieve professional excellence.

    What is worse, though, is the distortion of values that
radiates throughout the society. For thirty minutes of farce,
Liston and Clay can earn more than the entire faculty of a
public school can make in a decade.

                     —January 5, 1965

That first part of the Value Sheet is the stimulator. It can
come from essays, quotations, definitions, poetry, cartoons.
Anything the teacher is imaginative enough to find or create

can involve the students in serious consideration of some area of values — politics, religion, money, love, work, friends, family, death, leisure.

The second half of the Value Sheet asks a series of directed questions which help the student to clarify his thinking about the values problems raised by the stimulator. The emphasis here is upon "you-centered" questions. What we are after is what the student himself thinks, not what he believes is the answer the teacher is looking for. Our questions must never be moralizing ones, and we must do everything possible to see that there are no implied right or best answers. For example, we would never ask the question: "Don't you think man should help his fellowman?"

Here are some "you-centered" questions which could be used with the "Under the Sway of the Great Apes" Value Sheet: 1) Did you watch football on New Year's Day? 2) Is it a pattern of yours? Are you proud of it? 3) How would you answer Mr. Baker? 4) Do you think the publishers of *Harper's* or *Atlantic* could benefit from taking ads during the televising of a football game? Comment. 5) Does this sheet make you want to do anything different in your life?

Using this general form, an English teacher can make use of Value Sheets to lift his subject matter beyond the factual and conceptual levels and raise it to a third level which we call the values level. The Value Sheet is particularly useful in making poetry lessons more relevant to the search for values. Here are examples of the Value Sheet being used in two poetry lessons.

The essence of the first lesson is a comparison between the points of view expressed in Tennyson's "Charge of the Light Brigade" and e. e. cummings' "next to god america." The first poem illustrates one kind of patriotism ("Ours is not to reason why...Ours is but to do or die"), while the second satirizes it ("what could be more beautiful than these heroic happy dead...they did not stop to think they died instead..."). Which attitude is the better? What are the alternatives? We believe that this is for the student to decide for himself. The following Value Sheet immediately *involves* the student in the poetry and in this important area of values.
Value Sheet: Patriotism[1]

(The following statements, except for the last, are from the *NEA Journal*, January 1967.)

"To me, patriotism is one's love or devotion to one's country. Having its roots in religion, it includes respect for our leaders, honor for our heroes, belief in our ideals, and a stout defense of the integrity of America."   —J. Edgar Hoover

"Many men have assumed that blind support of their country 'right or wrong' is the very essence of patriotism. But I agree with the view that 'he loves his country best who strives to make it best.' Our schools will produce true patriots capable of saving this nation and all that makes it dear only if they turn out youngsters alert and alive to our society's shortcomings and weaknesses; only if they instill in our children a social conscience, a fervor for righting old wrongs, defying old fears, surmounting old prejudices, and banishing old social taboos."   —Carl T. Rowan

"We love our country, in the final analysis, because it is *ours*, because it is an extension of ourselves, and because we love ourselves... But the highest ethical command is to love others as we love ourselves. The best patriotism, then, does not exclude and despise the foreigner, but gives him the love and respect to which all men are entitled."   —Steve Allen

"To me, strong 'national patriotism' is undesirable. What we need is devotion to self and all mankind. Rather than more persons blindly loyal to a particular group, we need more persons who see that in this shrinking world all humans must share responsibility for each other's trouble and joy."   —Tamaji Harmin

1. Which of these four statements sounds like things you were taught about patriotism? Put an "O" (for old) or an "N" (for new) next to the statements which seem old or new to you.

2. If the world's people chose one of these statements rather than the others as its position on patriotism, which one or two statements, in your opinion, would lead to the best kind of world? Discuss fully.

3. If all the world's people chose one of these statements rather than the others as its position on patriotism, which statement(s) would lead to a world that was most undesirable? Discuss fully.

4. According to the definition of patriotism which appeals to you the most, are *you* a patriotic American? Discuss. (Here you might want to write down *your own* definition of patriotism if you think it more meaningful than any of the four above.)

This Value Sheet may be used by the teacher in a number of different ways: 1) If used as a prelude to the reading of the poems, the Value Sheet is an excellent motivational device, which also focuses students' attention on the major ideas in the poems. 2) The questions can be assigned for homework before or after reading the poems. 3) The second question on the Value Sheet is guaranteed to start an exciting classroom controversy which could lead directly to the reading of the poems and the values question: Which poet's point of view do you prefer? 4) A composition assignment: Now that we have discussed patriotism in reference to the Value Sheet and have seen what two poets with different ideas have had to say on the subject, write a composition on what patriotism means to you. 5) A follow-up activity: Which statement about patriotism on the Value Sheet would Tennyson most likely subscribe to? Support your answer with specific references to the statement and poem. Which statement would e. e. cummings most likely subscribe to? Support your answer.

The Value Sheet is no gimmick. It is a meaningful way of encouraging careful reading and critical thinking and of helping the poetry to come alive for the students.

Here is another poetry lesson following the same pattern. John Donne's "No Man Is an Island" is an excellent contrast to the popular folk-rock singers Simon and Garfunkel's song-poem "I Am a Rock (I Am an Island)." The students read the Donne poem, and as they hear the recording, read the words to the Simon and Garfunkel song. The following Value Sheet can be used with these poems in similar ways to those outlined.

Value Sheet: Mind Your Own Business vs. Help Those in Need

"Some people say that man is basically selfish, that one must watch out for himself, and that it's best to serve your own purposes, avoid hurting others, and mind your own business."

"Other people say that men must stick together and help one another or they will fall separately, that no man is an island, that each man's fate is intertwined with other men's fates, and that one should help those in need."

1. What label might be appropriate for each position?
2. Is this a case of "either-or" (*either* you support one position *or* the other)? Can you think of other possible

positions one could take concerning this issue? If possible, identify some of these positions.

3. Professor Laurence Topp of Rutgers University suggests that persons who have experienced social injustice and who have experienced feelings of being unfairly treated are likely to take the second position. Would you agree? Have you any evidence for your ideas about this?

4. Read each of the situations below and try to identify *what you would do* in each case. Although not all the information is complete for any of the situations, make the best estimate of *what you would do if you were faced with situations like these in the future.* Try to be as realistic as possible in your choice of actions. When you are finished, try to summarize *your* position regarding the issue: Mind Your Own Business vs. Help Those in Need.

Situation A: You are walking down a busy shopping street in the middle of the afternoon. You hear screams across the street and see a man choking a woman in a doorway. Several persons on both sides of the street notice, but nobody moves as the woman continues to scream and the man tries to drag her indoors by the throat.

Situation B: You are in a group of persons with whom you would like to be friends. Two members of the group begin to tease a nearby girl who has some awkward physical characteristics. Others in the group join in, although a few are silent.

Situation C: The young married couple that lives next to you has a little boy, three years old. During a friendly visit with them, you observe that they are energetically teaching that boy to hate a minority group.

The top of a Value Sheet can serve both as the motivation for and the subject of a composition assignment. If we want our students to write a composition on patriotism, we could easily say, "Write a composition on what patriotism means to you." But how much more effective it is to distribute that Value Sheet on patriotism, provoke a heated discussion, and use *that* as the starting point for the composition. The students, then, have thought about the topic and can use the composition to put down the ideas they wanted to get across in the discussion, when they hadn't as yet formulated their thoughts or where they didn't get a chance to speak.

This principle works for any topic. If the composition were

to be on *courage*, a Value Sheet on courage could be used.
The questions, if possible, could come from the class's readings.
Value Sheet: Courage

"Courage is to fight when someone insults you, no matter
who he is." —a gang leader

"True courage is to do without witness everything that
one is capable of doing before all the world." —La
Rochefoucauld

"Ultimate bravery is courage of the mind."   —H. G. Wells

"Courage is...when you know you're licked before you begin
but you begin anyway and you see it through no matter
what."   —Harper Lee

(Add more. Include your favorites. Make them up yourself,
appropriate to your needs. Have the students give *their*
definitions.)

> 1. Consider the different acts of courage which are part
> of the above definitions. Which kind of action, in your opinion,
> takes the *most* courage? Why?
> 2. Do you think everyone possesses courage? How? If not,
> why not?
> 3. Describe a time you acted courageously. Why did you?
> 4. Describe a time you acted without courage. What would
> you do if the situation arose again?

From this, the teacher can devise a variety of composition
assignments. We have used a similar approach with a
composition assignment, for high school students, on the
draft. For the top part of the sheet, we presented many
different views on the Selective Service System—it should
be abolished, no college deferments should be granted, it is
fine as it is, women should be drafted for noncombatant
service. In this case, we did not ask any questions but went
right into the composition assignment: Choose *one* position
and support it.

A poem might serve as the top half of the Value Sheet. The
questions, then, would refer to values areas raised in the
poem. For example, if the top half were "The Road Not
Taken" by Robert Frost, the questions might go something
like this:

> 1. What was the *most important choice* in *your* life that
> you have had to make between two divergent roads?
> 2. Which one was the "grassy" one that "wanted wear"?

3. In what way(s) has the choice made a "difference" in your life?

4. Are you proud of your choice? If yes, why? If not, why not?

5. Was there any adult who could have given you good advice at the time? Any of your friends?

6. Are you at or are you coming to any new forks in the road? How do you think you'll choose? What are the pros and cons of either choice?

Such questions get the student to personalize the major issues in the poem, to focus on specific words or phrases, and to look more deeply into his own values.

Instead of a special top for a Value Sheet, you might simply write: *Silas Marner*, Chapter 6. Your questions will relate the subject matter with the student's own experience. 1) Briefly characterize the major people you meet at the Rainbow. 2) Do you know any people who are similar to those at the Rainbow? Discuss briefly. 3) Consider the topics of conversation at the Rainbow. Do those topics persist to this day with the people you know? How much of your discussions involve those topics? 4) How would *you* define gossip?

Another top for a Value Sheet could be some *moral dilemma* which is relevant to the literature your class has read. The dilemma might be about money or women or man's relation to the state or a question of ends and means or a dozen other problems. Questions: 1) How would Character A from Book X solve this dilemma? Support your answer based on.... 2) How would *you* solve this dilemma? Why? 3) In what ways are you and Character A similar? 4) In what ways are you and Character A different?

A variation on this idea would be to present a situation, not necessarily a moral dilemma, and ask the student to consider how he and the literary character would probably act in that situation.

Now take another type of approach toward teaching literature, that is, teaching literature in *thematic* units. Your Value Sheet, on the particular theme, could precede or follow the unit. If, for example, you are concluding a literary unit on "Man and God," and have read books with different points of view on the subject *(Oedipus, Job, The Rubaiyat of Omar Khayyam, Crime and Punishment, The*

Plague), you might devise a Value Sheet with some controversial statement and then ask questions which call for the student to compare and/or contrast his *own* views on the statement with those of the various authors. So it goes with other thematic units—"courage," "patriotism," "man's relation to his fellowman," and so on.

For whatever objectives—language arts, ideas, motivation, —you hold a class discussion, Value Sheets are an excellent way to begin. If students are required to answer the questions for homework first, you will find that you get much more participation, because the students will have had time to formulate their ideas. Below is an example of a Value Sheet used in just that way.

Value Sheet: Speak Up

"In Germany, first they came for the Communists, and I didn't speak up because I wasn't a Communist. Then they came for the Jews, and I didn't speak up because I wasn't a Jew. Then they came for the trade unionists, and I didn't speak up because I wasn't a trade unionist. Then they came for the Catholics, and I didn't speak up because I was a Protestant. Then they came for me—and by that time no one was left to speak up." —Pastor Martin Niemoller

> 1. Which category are *you* in? When would they have come for you?
> 2. Is there something in your school, some "injustice," about which you might well speak out?
> 3. Why stick *your* neck out? Why not?
> 4. If you decide to speak up, how do you go about it? What are the best ways?
> 5. Some people say: "We need to value what we do and to do something about what we value." Do you agree? If not, why? If so, what have you done lately?

Summary

It will come as no surprise that most of our students do not care as deeply about English as we would like them to care. On the other hand, if there is one subject they do feel passionately about, it is themselves and their attempts to develop clear, viable, and sound values in a confused and confusing world.

The Value Sheet is one excellent way of bringing these two concerns—the personal and the academic—together. Value

Sheets involve students personally in the reading and writing adventure, and help them, through increased self-awareness, to make better, wiser, and more thoughtful choices in life.

If we had to choose but one objective for our teaching, it would be to help students search for values. The English teacher with his unique, value-oriented subject matter can do more about values than almost any other teacher in the school. Values are the stars by which men steer their lives, and luckily enough, most of us who teach English are born stargazers.

NOTE

1. This Value Sheet is from the work of Dr. Merrill Harmin of Southern Illinois University.

The Free-Choice English Curriculum

by Howard Kirschenbaum

Presented at the annual convention of the National Council of Teachers of English, Washington, D.C., November 1969. Used by permission of the author and the Adirondack Mountain Humanistic Education Center, Upper Jay, New York 12987.

What course of study is relevant for the middle 75 percent of English students?

That's a big question. And, frankly, I'd feel very presumptuous if I had a direct answer for it.

How can one individual know what is relevant for the "middle 75 percent"—or the top and bottom 12.5 percent, for that matter? When I have free time for reading, I am hard-pressed to know what's relevant for myself. I scan my bookshelves, trying to find a book that relates to my thoughts, feelings, problems, and concerns of the moment. I see whole sections of unread books which I once bought because they were relevant to me at the time. But I never opened them because my concept of relevance changed over the years.

Last year, I recommended *Catch-22* to one of my closest friends, a man I've worked closely with for many years. I had no doubt that this great modern novel would mean as much to him as it did to me. He gave up on it after fifty pages. "What in the world made you think I'd like that?" he asked me. "I was bored to death with it."

And now I am asked to say what is relevant for the middle 75 percent.

The point I make is that we are on very dangerous ground when we propose to determine what is relevant for another human being—let alone 75 percent of a given group. Albert Camus once noted that we have had too many benevolent leaders whose only goal was the "happiness of the people." But the leaders failed to ask the people what it would take to make them happy and how they hoped to become so. Significantly, I note there are no students on the panel today. As long as we English teachers continue to take it solely upon ourselves to decide what is relevant for our students, I think our role is analogous to that of the benevolent despots to whom Camus referred.

Now, I don't mean to totally condemn benevolent despots. History shows us many examples of those who have done much to advance the progress of civilization. In fact, some of my best friends are benevolent despots—some in their classrooms, some in their businesses, and some in their homes.

It's just that benevolent despotism has many drawbacks, especially for curriculum builders. The drawback I want to mention here is that the benevolent despot may be wrong in his perceptions of his people's needs. In which case he is no longer called a benevolent despot, but a tyrant, a dictator, or a bad guy. A critical question for English teachers is whether our perceptions of what is relevant for our students have been right or wrong.

Speaking of English teachers collectively, I would say, up to now, we have failed abysmally in determining what is relevant for our students. How many of them read Shakespeare after completing their formal education? How many of them continue to write poetry? How many write essays and submit them to magazines? How many return to the classics? How many write anything more than postcards to their friends and relatives? And how many continue to present speeches in public or enter public debates or symposia?

On the other hand, how many become avid students of Reader's Digest or the Book-of-the-Month-Club? And how much time do adult Americans spend watching TV, compared to the time spent reading books?

Where have we failed? Why is it that only a small percentage of the millions of English students who have passed through our classrooms have developed the skills, attitudes, and behaviors we tried to teach them?

I would say that our failure lies, primarily, in our stance of benevolent despotism in creating curriculum. With the best of intentions, we have decided what our students *need* and what is *relevant* to them. But history has proved us wrong. We've incorrectly judged what is relevant for our students and have, thus, defeated our own purposes.

Which brings us to a point in history where we must decide to either ignore our own failure and proceed as usual or to acknowledge our failure and do something differently. Assuming we would do something differently, the question arises, *what?*

One alternative would be to hold a convention and call in "experts" to give a prescription for what is relevant for the middle 75 percent. Perhaps the experts' perceptions will be better than those of the average English teacher. They might tell us, for example, that Richard Wright's *Black Boy* is more relevant than *Silas Marner.* Or they might say the poetry of Bob Dylan or Paul Simon is more relevant than that of Chaucer or Spenser. And they might be right.

Perhaps more students enjoy Dylan than Chaucer. But what about the students, and there are many, who prefer the classical writers to the modern writers? What about the students who see *Silas Marner* as more relevant to them than *Black Boy?* And what about the students who know of other writers who are more relevant to them than either Richard Wright or George Eliot?

We come right back to the same problem. As long as one person or group of people, no matter what their expertise, determines what is relevant for another person or group of people, there is bound to be enormous inaccuracy and self-defeating results.

Clearly there is only one alternative that can help curriculum makers build a curriculm relevant to students. That alternative is to meaningfully involve the students in curriculum building and to structure the curriculum so that as many students as possible can pursue a course of study which is, in fact, relevant to their needs.

As I see it, this can be done in one or both of two ways. It can be done by an individual teacher and his students within a given classroom, or it can be done by a whole English department within a given school. While both of these are probably essential if a curriculum is really to be relevant to any group of students, I would like to suggest one model for how an English department, in an average size school, might build a curriculum which is not only relevant to the middle 75 percent, but the other 25 percent as well.

I will call this innovation the "free-choice English curriculum" and would like to note that many schools are already trying it on an experimental basis. Two such schools are Meadowbrook Junior High School in Newton, Massachusetts and Abington High School in Abington, Pennsylvania.

Picture Janie Smith, a tenth-grade student in this innovative school. It is April, and Janie, along with her classmates, must decide the courses she is going to take the following year. In some cases she has no choice, in other areas there is limited choice, in other areas considerable choice. One of the areas of considerable choice is English.

Janie must choose one English course. But she may choose from among the following alternatives, described in the English department's catalogue. Here is a sample of some of Janie's choices:

Modern Drama: This course will explore the beginnings and the evolution of modern drama. Beginning with Ibsen's *The Master Builder*, the course will include Shaw's *Caesar and Cleopatra* and *Man and Superman*, Wilde's *The Importance of Being Earnest*, Williams' *The Glass Menagerie*, Brecht's *Good Woman of Setsuan*, Sartre's *No Exit*, Miller's *Death of a Salesman*, and several productions of the 1960s. What can we expect in the theatre of the 70s? This, too, will be a subject of discussion. The course will include several trips to local performances of plays.

The Classics: What are the origins of Western literature? This course will explore some of the earliest and greatest literary works of the Western world and trace their influence through the centuries. Three major areas of literature will be stressed—the literature of the Bible and Greek and Roman literature. Some of the works considered will be: Genesis, Psalms, Matthew, Homer's *Odyssey*, Plato's *Apology* and several of his dialogues, Sophocles' *Antigone*, Edith Hamilton's *Mythology*, Virgil's *Aeniad*, and several other works.

Utopian Thought: What is the ideal society for man? Numerous works of literature and philosophy have attempted to answer this question. This course will explore different views of societies of the future—both those offered as ideals and those offered as warnings. These include: Plato's *Republic*, More's *Utopia*, Hilton's *Lost Horizon*, Skinner's *Walden Two*, Huxley's *Brave New World*, Orwell's *1984*, Neill's *Summerhill*, and modern writings by members of communes and the "counter-culture."

Great Men and Women in Literature: What is greatness? What is courage? Different people have lived lives that have illustrated greatness and courage in different ways. This course is designed especially for those students who would like to improve their reading and writing skills, and will explore these concepts of greatness and courage through the lives of famous men and women. Readings include: Helen Keller's *The Story of My Life*, the *Autobiography of Malcolm X*, Bob Feller's *Fear Strikes Out*, Audie Murphy's *To Hell and Back*, Sammy Davis, Jr.'s *Yes I Can*, and other biographies and autobiographies of famous politicians, military figures, scientists, sports heroes, and celebrities.

Man and God in Literature: Throughout the ages, man has attempted to define his relationship to God, to the universe, to the infinite, to the unknown. He has attempted to find the meaning in life, a reason for suffering. Out of this attempt have come organized religions, personal moral philosophies, atheism, agnosticism, and many other group and individual answers to metaphysical questions. This course will explore many of these answers and will use literature to illustrate alternative views. Readings are often long and difficult, so this course is recommended only for those students who are good readers and who like to read a lot. Readings include: Sophocles' *Oedipus Rex*, Job, Ecclesiastes, the Bhagavad Gita, Dostoevski's *Crime and Punishment*, *The Rubaiyat of Omar Khayyam*, Camus' *The Plague* and *The Myth Of Sysiphus*, and others.

These were only five of the courses from which Janie could choose. At Abington High School, the list of thirty-two

courses offered by the English department to ninth and tenth
graders this year includes:

> Creative Interpretations of Literature
> East Meets West
> Black Voices
> Basic Grammar
> Creative Writing
> How Man Expresses Himself about War
> Great Tales of the Supernatural
> Mirror of the Russian Mind
> Modern European Drama

Can you picture some of the books, films, activities you
would include in these courses? What is a course you would
really like to teach? Here are some others from the Abington
English Department's list:

> The Nature of Poetry
> Psychology and Literature
> The Roaring Twenties—Views of the Lost Generation
> Selected Plays of Shakespeare
> Twentieth Century Literature
> The Fall from Innocence
> The Impact of the City on People and Literature.

This list continues and is equally as exciting; but this is a
representative sample of the types of courses which might
be offered as part of the free-choice English curriculum. In
some schools, the course may run for the whole year; in
others, they may be semester long.

Now, what are the advantages of this kind of curriculum
structure, and what are the disadvantages?

First, *it allows the students to decide what is relevant to
them.* Because the student chooses from alternatives, he has
some commitment to his choice. (The more attractive his
alternatives are, the truer it is that his choice indicates a
commitment.) Because of this commitment, the student is
more motivated to work with interest in that course. And
because most of the class has made a similar commitment,
the class takes on a very special atmosphere—a group of
students committed to pursuing a common learning goal.

A second major advantage is that the free-choice English
curriculum maximizes staff effectiveness and morale.
Teachers have the opportunity to teach in the areas of

their special competency and interest. They relish their subject more, and this is conveyed to the students. They enjoy their work more, and this creates a happier, healthier feeling within the department. Over the years, as a given teacher's interests change, he can change his course offerings. The system allows the teacher to grow, learn, and change.

These two factors—increased student commitment and increased faculty interest and competence—lead to better performance by students and teachers, the goal of any curriculum innovation. However, all curriculum innovations have possible drawbacks, and this one is no exception.

If the course offerings are designed without meaningful participation by students, they stand to be just as irrelevant as most English curricula have been in the past. The English department has the responsibility of holding meetings with students, using questionnaires, getting feedback on student reaction to present course offerings, and involving the students in other ways before it comes out with its catalogue of courses for the new year or new semester.

Another danger is that the sum total of course offerings will be too narrow or restricted and that many student interests will not be covered. The department must make every effort to present as broad a selection of offerings as is possible, taking into account student interest and faculty interest and competence. This might have certain implications for hiring policies. The English department chairman, for example, might consciously seek new teachers who can offer new viewpoints and areas of interest and competence to the department.

Another pitfall is that student ability will not be considered as teachers propose courses which interest themselves. I'm not too worried about the students on top. There will be no problem finding teachers to offer "college-level courses" for them. And I'm not too worried about that middle 75 percent. They will have plenty of alternatives to choose from, and because they have chosen areas of their own interest, these so-called "average" students will do surprisingly well. But I am worried about those kids in what we call the "slow" classes or "low-ability" groups. It would be very easy for a department to forget these students, and after almost all the course offerings have been decided, to throw these students one or two courses as a sop. The department chairman has a special responsibility here to coordinate the course offerings so that *all* the students have real choices from attractive alternatives.

Still another possible drawback is that in smaller schools, the course offerings would necessarily be more limited in number. One way to compensate for this is to form interage classes. I taught that course in Utopian Literature, described above, to a group of eleventh and twelfth graders and found that the interaging actually increased the interaction. A colleague taught a psychology and literature class to tenth, eleventh, and twelfth graders. It, too, was a success.

Then there are the problems of scheduling, student and teacher rostering, course selection, who signs up for what, proper guidance for students, and so on. I'm afraid there are no easy answers here. But at Abington High School, where thirty-two English courses were offered to two thousand ninth and tenth graders, every single student in the school was given his first, second, or third choice, and every teacher was able to teach the courses he wanted. If the commitment is there, the solutions to the nitty-gritty problems will follow.

I've saved the biggest objection until last. It is often phrased like this: "Do you mean to tell me a student could go through four years of high school and never read Shakespeare or Milton?" In other words, are there not certain reading experiences a student needs if he is to be considered an educated person?

My answer to that is "No." Maybe it was true at one time. But with the vast proliferation of knowledge today, a person can be quite well-educated and well-rounded without studying Shakespeare or Milton. The problem is that as soon as we begin to prescribe what a student needs, we never know where to draw the line. I say Shakespeare, you say Milton, someone else says the Bible, and we're back where we started from — back to being benevolent despots with the same highly structured curriculum that we have had for years. One that is no longer working.

As far as specific content goes, I no longer feel comfortable prescribing certain "musts" for students. As far as skills go, that's another story. As English teachers, we still have the responsibility of teaching our students to effectively communicate with the English language. Students must have effective reading ability and the skill of literary analysis; clear and cogent writing skills; the ability to listen and hear another person's views and feelings; and the skill of verbally communicating their own thoughts and feelings. This has not changed, and these skills can all be taught in the context of any course within the free-choice English curriculum.

Certainly there are other drawbacks and other advantages of the curriculum design I have outlined. Nevertheless, to the limited extent that I have seen it used, this curriculum has offered exciting results and prospects for English teachers and students.

Teaching History with a Focus on Values

by Merrill Harmin, Howard Kirschenbaum, and
Sidney B. Simon

Reprinted with permission of the National Council for the Social Studies
and *Social Education*, May 1969.

Students today, with ever-increasing frequency and volume,
are demanding a curriculum pertinent to their own needs and
concerns. They want to understand what's going on and what
to do about it. How can the history teacher answer these
demands?

"We study history to better appreciate our cultural
heritage."

"We study history to better understand the present."

"We study history to avoid the mistakes of the past."

As important as these motivations may be, and as sincerely
as we may posit them, students are no longer getting the
message. With rare exceptions these noble goals offered in
September are forgotten by the first of October, and by
Columbus Day the students once again are convinced that
history is, at worst, a series of meaningless facts and, at best,
a series of probably important but definitely dull ideas.
This pattern is too true, too often.

FOCUS ON VALUES

We believe that students' need for relevance plus all the
traditional goals of the study of history can be met by

teaching history with a focus on values.

What do we mean by a focus on values?

First, we believe that every subject in the curriculum can be dealt with on three levels: *the facts level, the concepts level,* and *the values level.* To illustrate how these three levels differ, let us consider a typical subject-matter area in American history—the formation of the constitutional system and how it contributed to the workings of our American government.

On the *facts level,* we might find questions like these:

> 1. In what order did the states ratify the Constitution?
> 2. What were the major differences between the Constitution and the Articles of Confederation?
> 3. Name the founding fathers who were most instrumental in the formation of the Constitution, and tell the part that each played.
> 4. What resolutions did the Constitutional Convention pass on the issue of slavery?
> 5. Describe the ten amendments which make up the Bill of Rights.

Obviously, the factual level has its importance; but few would dispute the point that teachers must go beyond this level. It is widely recognized today that teachers must help students to understand concepts and to see how separate facts can be related through the process of generalization. Jerome Bruner's work has helped give this notion widespread attention.

On the *concepts level,* then, we might entertain questions such as these:

> 1. Why did the founding fathers believe it necessary to have a Bill of Rights? Relate their thinking to Washington's Farewell Address.
> 2. What were the causes of the American Revolution and how typical were they of revolutions in general?
> 3. How did the Constitution prevent "taxation without representation"?
> 4. If the Constitutional Convention had declared slavery illegal, how might the course of American history have been different?
> 5. What was the reasoning behind separating the powers into three branches of government?

Students do not really understand a subject until they can deal skillfully with it at the conceptual level—until they can see interrelationships, support generalizations, and understand causes and effects. It is skillful teaching at this level which makes us feel proud and excited to be history teachers. However, a student may be able to think and learn at the concept level and still find history irrelevant and boring.

This is where the values level comes in. On the values level the student is asked not only to understand history, but to become personally involved in it, perhaps to take a stand, to relate the concepts to his own times, and to consider alternatives of action for his own life.

Here are some questions that raise issues to the *values level:*

1. If *you* were at the Constitutional Convention, how would you have voted on the question of slavery? What are some things students your age have done about the race problem in America today? Have you done anything?

2. Compare the ways in which decisions are made in the United States government with the ways decisions are made in your family. Are there checks and balances? What part do *you* play in family decisions?

3. If you wanted to change something in our society or in this school, what are some ways you would go about it? Have *you ever tried any of them?*

4. The First Amendment affirms the right of freedom of speech. Have you made use of that freedom recently in **a** way of which you are proud? Name five things more important to *you* than freedom of speech.

5. Here are five civil liberties issues which have recently come up before the Supreme Court. Before I tell you the Court's decisions, I would like you to divide into committees and pretend that you are the Supreme Court. How would *you* decide on each? Give your reasons.

Notice how often the word "you" appears on the values level. The emphasis is on the student's values, beliefs, and behavior. By beginning with these questions of values, he can be led to see the relevance of history to the present and to his own life. By ending with these value questions, prior studied facts and concepts come alive in a context of reality.

UNIT IN HISTORY

Any unit in history can be seen on these three levels. For example, consider the topic of war.

Facts Level

1. Name the wars in which the United States has been directly involved since 1776.
2. Which wars took place at home and which on foreign soil?
3. Which wars contributed to the territorial expansion of the United States?
4. What were the major provisions of the 1954 Geneva Agreements on Vietnam?

Concepts Level

1. What are the major causes of war?
2. What factors have contributed to the United States generally being on the winning side of wars it has fought?
3. What are the main positive and negative results of war?
4. What are the likely outcomes of an American withdrawal from Vietnam?

Values Level

1. In *your* opinion, to what extent has the United States been justified in each of the wars it has fought? Which wars would you have considered just?
2. Should an individual be allowed to refuse to serve in the armed forces? For what reason(s)? Under what circumstances would *you* kill? What are some living things you have killed?
3. Have *you* ever done anything to promote world peace? What things might you do? Do you know some people already doing some of these things?
4. Have *you* ever been in a physical fight? What caused it? What were the results? Would you respond in the same way again?
5. How are disputes settled in *your* family? By force? By reason?
6. Where do *you* stand on the Vietnam War? Have you done anything to convince others of your point of view? Should you?

We cannot emphasize enough that the purpose of these questions is not to transmit the teacher's values to the students, but to stimulate the students to formulate their own values as a vital part of the process of learning a body of knowledge.

History is filled with values issues to stimulate the students' thinking and to bring the subject close to home, thus making it much more relevant and interesting. As examples, here are other topics lifted to the values level.

1. The increase of prosperity and the rise of the middle class raise values issues about money and material possessions in our own lives today.

2. The shortening of the work week raises values issues about the purposes of work and leisure time.

3. Advances in world communication (television, electronic media, etc.) raise values issues about the responsibility for truth.

4. Scientific advances (space travel, contraception, atomic energy, safe abortions) raise values issues about morality and religion.

5. An examination of family structure in pioneer times raises values issues about family and home life in suburbia today.

6. The ebb and flow of Negro history raises values issues about race relations today.

These examples may well make the conscientious teacher weary, since there is so much information to transmit on the factual and conceptual levels of history without getting to values. But as Louis Raths used to ask rhetorically of his students: "What is the purpose of information?"

"To inform," he would answer. "To inform our *values.*"

It is an important point. Information for its own sake becomes mere decoration, not wisdom. The facts and concepts of history can add to the substance of our students' values – values which will help them guide their lives wisely through a confusing and complex world. But this goal of the study of history will not be gained by paying lip service to it in September. It can be done only by consistently elevating the subject matter we teach to the third level – the level of values.

Teaching is not easy. The profession does not need dry, drab assignments, recitations, and tests. Instead, we need teachers who will sensitize themselves to the values issues present in their subject matter. Such teachers must be willing to risk some lively discussions and controversy. They must continually remind themselves not to moralize and not to foist values on students. And, of course, we need teachers who know their subject well enough to be able to recommend readings and areas to explore, to help students further their thinking and knowledge as they search for value clarity.

Teaching history with a focus on values is indeed a challenge. But once students have faced it, facts and concepts alone seem much too tame. Nothing is quite as gratifying for teachers and students as dealing with real and relevant questions and being deeply involved in the values quest.

Teaching Afro-American History with a Focus on Values

by Sidney Simon and Alice Carnes

From *Educational Leadership*, December 1969. Reprinted with permission of the Association for Supervision and Curriculum Development and the authors. Copyright © 1969 by the Association for Supervision and Curriculum Development.

A fair treatment of the black man's role in history is long overdue. More and more material is available to teachers to make the black experience really come alive. It cannot be taught without emotional reaction, however. Inevitably, the student's own racial values will get in the way of levelheaded consideration of innocent enough historical facts, but to teach it with utter blandness would be all wrong. Negro history is too viable to justify name-dropping Crispus Attucks and then rushing on to the next Negro in order to make sure we get through the Coolidge administration so we can mention Malcolm X in time for the final exam.

The study of Afro-American history is particularly ripe with values implications because the jump between *then* and *now* is too often not very startling. Many white students will not find it hard to think like a plantation owner, and a fair percentage of the black students may do everything but call the teacher Mistah Charlie. Working on black history will bring to the surface many of the conflicts which too often only break out on the playground.

It is these very values conflicts which need to be aired, faced, and clarified if we are to have hope for some racial peace in this country.

THE HOT PASSION OF VALUES

Teachers would be more willing to deal with the hot passion of values in the classroom if they knew some techniques for working with values in more systematic ways. Perhaps, too, they would avoid those typical pitfalls of moralizing, indoctrinating, or preaching. The sad truth is that there is probably no worse way to grapple with values than to insist that every student come out with the accepted set of values. What we advocate is the *search* for values, and our entire approach is focused upon the *process* which teaches how to build values, rather than memorize them.

Take the following, for example. We call it Rank Order.

Rank Order. Put questions like these to one student at a time. Write alternatives on the board and ask him to rank them 1-2-3.

    1. You are a slave who has been promised a brutal whipping. After thinking out the consequences, do you:

        a. run away?

        b. fight the master?

        c. take the whipping?

    2. You are a slave woman with children who has a chance to escape. Do you:

        a. escape alone?

        b. stay with the children?

        c. take them along?

    3. You are a plantation slave whose master has fled before the Union Army. Do you:

        a. try to carry on the work of the plantation?

        b. ransack the place?

        c. run away to the Union lines?

It should be apparent that these Rank Orders can involve students almost immediately. Although they are supposedly rank ordering what they would do as a slave who has been promised a whipping, their own lives and their own values are what they are really talking about.

Briefly, the aim of this approach to values is to direct the student toward the examination and clarification of his own values. A "value" is defined operationally as something freely chosen, after due reflection, from among alternatives; it is, moreover, something which is prized, publicly affirmed, and acted upon. Students are encouraged to apply these criteria to the beliefs they voice in class.

As students learn to apply these criteria consistently in their study of history, they become skillful in carrying these standards over to their understanding of current events and to those more personal things which surround their daily living. For example, take the technique we call the Values Continuum.

Values Continuum: the image of the slave. "Sambo" and Nat Turner are at opposite poles, and although polar thought is useful at times, in the case of slavery it is probably a distortion of reality. To help students imagine the shades of gray between two stereotypes, draw a line on the board to represent a continuum of values.

"Sambo" |———————————————————————| Nat Turner
(complete submission)   (open revolt)

Make a list of alternative positions (aiding fugitives, playing a role for the white man, attending secret church services, escaping via the Underground Railway, informing on other slaves, etc.). The students individually or as a group try to place these and other alternatives along the continuum. (It's not as easy as it looks!)

Some teachers would now be content to move on to the next topic of study. Others would, perhaps, try to raise the strategy another notch in the process of values clarification. Such teachers might ask:

> 1. In your way of dealing with teachers, where are *you* on the continuum?
> 2. Make a Rank Order of the various stances people take when black people move into a previously all-white neighborhood.
> 3. What do *you* really want to achieve in terms of race relations for America? What are you willing to do about it?

It is important to stress that if the teacher is really to help the search for values, he must not punish those students who give him the "wrong" values and reward those who feed him the party line. On the other hand, he is not to remain chameleon-like and agree with everything. He may have a position which he states strongly, but he offers it as only one alternative, for consideration, not for adoption.

In fact, just to keep the issue alive, and in a sense,

confused, he may play Devil's Advocate to great advantage.

Devil's Advocate. Put on your horns and challenge the class to disagree, as you play the devil's role broadly and sardonically. "What was wrong with slavery anyway? Why, the slave worked in the fields only fourteen hours a day, which was two hours less than his white counterpart in the factories. He had housing, sometimes even with windows and floors; he got half a pound of meat a week; and after he was old enough to work he'd get a new pair of jeans every year. The slave had no responsibilities. He didn't have to marry or stand trial in court. And his kindly ol' massa took care of him in his old age."

Open-Ended Questions. Give as an essay assignment: "If I were in charge of the Freedmen's Bureau, I would…."

Role-Playing. Establish a plantation system in the classroom. (The teacher should immediately volunteer to be a slave.) Set up situations: the slave too sick to work, the father who watches his son get whipped, the master's amorous overtures to a slave woman. Introduce alternatives by bringing in other characters. Have students switch roles within the same situation.

Value Sheet. Here is a sample Value Sheet taken from *Values and Teaching.*[1] It can be assigned in class or as homework. It is important to give students time to think. Later, the sheets may be used as the basis for discussion; or the teacher can simply leave them in the hands of the students.

> Merry-Go-Round
> Where is the Jim Crow section
> On this merry-go-round, Mister,
> Cause I want to ride?
> Down South where I come from
> White and colored
> Can't sit side by side.
> Down South on the train
> There's a Jim Crow car.
> On the bus we're put in back—
> But there ain't no back
> To a merry-go-round!
> Where's the horse
> For a kid that's black?
>   — Langston Hughes

1. When was the last time you were on a merry-go-round?

2. If you happened to be in line and overheard the incident that takes place in the poem, is there anything *you* might have said to that little boy?

3. Have you ever experienced anything similar to that boy's feeling?

4. What prejudice, subtle or otherwise, have you ever personally faced?

5. If you wanted to *do* something about the problem of "civil rights," what are some things you could do:

    a. in this school, through some school group?

    b. in your town, with some community organization?

    c. on the national level?

6. Perhaps you believe that nothing needs to be done about this problem. If so, state that position clearly and forcefully.

These are not techniques which "reach" every child; but they have a marked effect upon some. A child who expresses racist beliefs may come to see that his belief was accepted *per se* from his parents, friends, or other persons, without questioning or without considering the alternatives. Students who profess liberal or militant views may begin to weigh the extent to which they are willing to act upon them. If nothing else, these strategies encourage students to think.

The teaching of Afro-American history is a trend we can little ignore. Riots are a reality we had better heed, but more tokenism is not what we need. Black history must be taught as more than a reluctant submission to a fad. Giving it the highly charged focus of the search for values could make the difference.

NOTE

1. Louis E. Raths, Merrill Harmin, and Sidney B. Simon, *Values and Teaching* (Columbus, Ohio: Charles E. Merrill Publishing Co., 1966).

Teaching Science with a Focus on Values

by Merrill Harmin, Howard Kirschenbaum, and
Sidney B. Simon

From *The Science Teacher*, January 1970. Reprinted with permission.

Amid the screaming headlines and the general patriotic
fervor surrounding the moon shot this past summer, there
were many sober-faced people asking some values questions
about the entire event. Almost no one denied the smashing
success of the scientific and technological achievements
which put our men on the moon, but there were many citizens
who expressed cynicism about what the moon shot seems
to say about our society's values.

Particularly bitter were some black city dwellers who
raised important values questions against a backdrop of
decaying slums, rat-infested flats, malnutrition, disease,
polluted air, and cities which become increasingly unfit for
human habitation.

They were raising questions about national priorities, about
where science and technology should be putting their
energies. Once we get into "shoulds" and to the rank ordering
of where time, money, and talent are to go, we are walking
in the realm of values.

What are science teachers doing about values? To us, it
seems that too much of science teaching has assiduously
stayed away from dealing with values. Under the guise of
objectivity, too many of us have simply avoided dealing with

the hot and always controversial issues surrounding the
science we teach. Maybe we feel that issues like biochemical
warefare, the antiballistic missile system, the "unsafety"
of cars and highways, nonbiodegradable detergents, or the
fact that ghetto children get fewer vaccinations than do their
suburban age-mates will somehow be taken up in social
studies classes or in some bull session later in a college
dormitory. To take a kinder view: Perhaps we stay clear of
raising values issues because we do not wish to be guilty of
hustling our own point of view and thus rubbing our
students' noses in our own values.

Whatever the case, the writers want to argue strongly and
forcefully that values issues must become a part of the
teaching of science — so much a part of it that almost no topic
in any science class will be taught without some opportunity
to consider the values implication of that content. "Just the
facts, Ma'am," must be banished from anything to which we
give the name science teaching. The factual approach may
have sufficed in an earlier, less complex and confusing world,
but today, with nuclear holocaust just outside the window
and the polluted atmosphere already seeping in, we simply
cannot afford to train a generation of students who know the
how and *why* of scientific phenomena, but do not have a
process for inquiring into the values issues raised by the
topics they study. In today's world, a two-and-a-half-year-old
seems to be able to speak easily about the "we-entwy cwisis"
of our astronauts, but we also want an adolescent to
understand his own reentry crisis when he returns home
after spending all summer at camp. Or consider the reentry
crisis of the white commuters, making the round trip through
the ghetto on their way to and from work. Or the black
domestic workers, taking the trip the other way.

All right, then, how can it be done? How can we deal with
values in our science teaching while avoiding the problems
of indoctrinating students with our own values, or equally
bad, unquestioningly inculcating society's values, many of
which we believe are fraudulent? Can you deal with values
without teaching one set?

It has been helpful to see that almost any subject matter
taught in science (or in any other discipline, for that matter)
can be looked at on three different levels. The first level is

the facts level; the second, the concepts level; and the third,
the values level.

Take this simple example of a piece of subject matter
taught at least once in almost every science curriculum:

Newton's Laws of Motion

Facts Level:

1. What are Newton's laws? Learn the formulas derived
from the laws.

2. When were the laws formulated? What laws did they
make obsolete?

3. Which is called the first law, etc.?

Concepts Level:

1. Demonstrate, via certain laboratory experiments, that you
know these laws.

2. How are these principles used in recent inventions?

3. Attempt to invent something useful by applying one or
more of Newton's laws.

4. Describe the applications of these laws in certain simple
machines and devices used in the moon shot last summer.

Note: It is important to realize that just because questions
at the facts and concepts levels recognize an application
in today's world, they do not automatically become values
level material. There needs to be a real connection with the
students' lives, attitudes, and feelings for the questions to be
raised to the third level, the values level.

Values Level:

1. How, if at all, have these laws touched your own life?

2. Seat belts in cars stem from one of these laws. Do you
have them in the car you drive in most often? Do you use
them? Explain.

3. What's the fastest you have ever driven in a car? Were you
driving? If you weren't driving, at what speedometer
reading would you have insisted that the driver slow down?

4. Driving a car into a wall is like swinging a one-ton sledge
hammer at that wall. Would you rather be the wall or the
sledge hammer?

5. Where do you stand on the idea that scientists have an
obligation to see that their discoveries, like the automobile,
are not used to hurt man?

6. What do you believe automobile manufacturers should be

doing to save lives? Would you be willing to start a petition drive on that subject?

Here is another topic frequently covered in science classes across America. We shall examine it from the same three-level view.

The Earth's Crust

Facts Level:

1. What are the three major groups of rocks?
2. Name three ways water can change the earth's surface.
3. What precious gems are found among the minerals in the earth?
4. How are volcanoes formed?

Concepts Level:

1. Show how two recent dramatic changes of the earth's surface were similar to changes which took place a million or more years ago.
2. Compare and contrast two theories of how mountains were formed. Which do you accept? Give your reasons.
3. Discuss the similarities and differences between precious and semiprecious stones from a scientific point of view.
4. Where on the earth's surface are volcanoes most likely to occur today? Why?

Values Level:

1. Are you someone who is likely to become a rock hound some day?
2. Are the mountains a place where you really like to spend your vacations?
3. Where do you stand on oil companies' getting a depletion allowance?
4. In some states, strip miners find it cheaper to pay the fine than to do the reforestation the law requires. What is your reaction to this? What other information do you feel you need to know about this?
5. Which, if any, of these worry you at all or more than the others?
   a. Converting the Florida Everglades into housing for senior citizens.
   b. Bulldozing a mountain to build a four-lane road.
   c. Cities spreading out over the earth's surface, leaving less and less open space.

6. When you get married, do you think you will give an expensive ring to your wife, or if you are a girl, do you think you will want one? Can you think of any alternative ways a husband might show affection for his bride?

7. Grass is too hard to maintain in a city; cities should be all asphalt. Do you agree or disagree? Give your reasons.

8. How do you think you would have answered these questions last year? Describe how your answers have changed, if they have.

It should be obvious from the above that we are not against subject matter. All three levels are important; yet we like to think of a teacher's job as that of elevating subject matter to the third level, that is, making the information taught relevant to the students' lives. The values level usually requires the use of information available from the facts and concepts levels, but it often demands additional information and insight. The additional information can rarely be found in textbooks. It is more likely to come from keeping up with the daily newspaper, the weekly magazines, and the special-interest publications, such as conservation magazines for the example above or magazines having to do with automobiles for the Newton's laws example. The science classroom which has a rack of current magazines would be just that much more likely to get students to examine topics at the third level. Insights, too, come from many sources, such as a personal experience, observations of human behavior, and art and literature.

An important element of the values level approach is that it makes consistent use of what we call "you" questions. These are questions which attempt to involve the student in an issue by hitting him where he lives. They strive to make topics relevant in the best sense of the word because the student is asked to take a stand and to sometimes *do* something about the problem raised. It isn't just learning for the hundred true or false questions at the next midterm. It is teaching which aims at a student's values, at his life.

Here are some other examples of the direction a values level inquiry might take on three topics taught in typical science classes. Again notice that these issues all contain the "you" component and almost always demand current information over and above the facts and concepts of the science topics themselves. Often the information they require comes right out of the student's life.

Electricity

1. Have you ever really received an electrical shock? Why did it happen? Was something broken? What did you do to see that it didn't happen again?

2. Could you fix an electric motor that wouldn't run? Would this be something you'd like to learn how to fix? What if it were the starter on your own car?

3. Most power tools need to be grounded. What is done about grounding power tools around your house? Could you convince careless power-tool users to change their habits? How would you go about it?

4. Calculate how much it costs when the light in your room is on for one hour. For 365 hours. Do you ever leave the light on after you've left your room? Is it a habit you want to change?

Weather

1. How often, per year, do you phone the weatherman? Do you trust the weather reports as given on TV? Do you base any of your decisions on them?

2. Where do you stand on man's efforts to manipulate weather through cloud seeding? What about the issue of taking someone else's rain away from him? Or the conflicts between people who need the rain and others who may be hurt by it?

3. Weather-related accidents kill many private plane pilots. Would you be the kind of pilot who assumes the weather will get "better up ahead"?

4. If the points on your car got wet because of rain, would you know what to do about the situation?

5. Which is your favorite season of the year? Do you have any plans for that season when it comes up next?

6. Rank order these three things to do on a spring day. Which is your first choice, second choice, third choice?
   a. Walk in the woods in a light rain.
   b. Roam a deserted beach in the sun.
   c. Buy an Easter outfit in a busy shopping center.

The Frog

1. In dissecting a frog, we remove the pancreas and the messentery. What would happen to you if we removed yours? Would you give your eyes to science when you die?

2. Would you dissect a cat?

3. Would you eat a frog? Have you ever done it?

4. If you were lost in the woods and were starving, where would you draw the line about what you would or would not eat? Would you eat worms, mice, any mushrooms?

5. Should scientists use live things and kill them, if necessary, for their experiments?

6. Why not use live people in the same way?

All of these questions about electricity, weather, and frogs are merely suggestive of what might be asked. Different teachers are excited about different kinds of values issues. Raise whatever values questions you care to raise, but note these cautions. Do not insist that there be one right answer which all students must arrive at following the discussion. This would be antithetical to encouraging students to search for their own values, the only values that will ever mean anything to them. After students get the hang of confronting values issues, dealing with "you" questions, and pushing their subject matter beyond the facts and concepts levels, they will start raising values issues. One more caution: We believe it is essential for the teacher to declare where he stands on most of these values issues. However, he must do it with a quiet dignity which does not demand that every student line right up behind him. It means he must suspend his punishment-and-reward system during values discussions or too many students will feed the teacher the values statements he wants to hear. Sometimes the teacher postpones telling the class his position for a week or so. He wants the students to think for themselves; but ultimately, the teacher must have values of his own and state them—again, with quiet dignity.

Here are some other issues which grow out of science topics. These are Values Level issues, but it is important to stress that the student needs to know some science in order to deal with them. It may not always be the science taught in schools; but when that science is relevant, it will concern itself with values.

Values Issues

1. *Consumer Report* has called new cars, as they are delivered to new owners, "do it yourself" kits. What has been your family's experience with a new car? What did the engineers fail to engineer? What did you and your family do about the faults you found? What else could have been done?

2. How much chlorine or other chemicals are needed to keep a private swimming pool clean? Where would you draw the line on how often your neighbors could use your pool if you had one?

3. How did the races of man originate? Would you join a segregated swim club? Would you go as a guest to one? If you wanted to break the segregation at a swim club, how would you go about it?

4. Would you rather have wormy apples than use sprays which might be poisonous? What other alternatives are open to you?

5. Would crossbreeding to produce a new vegetable or fruit excite you? Which two fruits or which two vegetables would you like to see made into a new type?

6. What do the critics of the research linking cancer and smoking say? How would you answer them? When you're twenty-one, do you think you'll be a cigarette smoker?

7. How do human beings reproduce? Do you believe that every student in the twelfth grade should be given full birth control information before graduating from high school? Who should give this information?

8. Describe the fuel system on the antiballistic missile. Are you someone who would write a letter to the editor of your local newspaper on the antiballistic missile system? Would you put a bumper sticker on your car proclaiming your point of view?

9. Is toothpaste effective in fighting tooth decay? Nationally advertised toothpastes cost more than do private brands available at some drugstores and department stores. Which brand of toothpaste do you use? Would you use a cheaper, unadvertised brand? Should cities fluoridate their water supplies? Should they provide free dental care for families who can't afford to pay for care?

10. Are you someone who would never get on a motorcycle without a helmet? What else are you doing to stay alive longer?

11. If your community had a piece of swampland that could be left as is or drained and used for recreation, a jet port, or a place to dispose of junked cars, which would you prefer? On what would you base your decision? Do you think that this is the same choice that you would have made last year? If not, why have you changed your choice?

Sometimes a teacher begins with content and builds toward values issues. Sometimes he motivates subject-matter study by opening with a value-oriented inquiry. There is no one rule. A teacher knows his style and he knows his students. What is really important is that students do not become science-sophisticates without a deep awareness of the values issues underlying their abundant knowledge.

Imagine the impact upon a science class if a teacher brought in a study of the extensiveness of lead poisoning in slum children. Dr. Glenn Paulson of Rockefeller University has reported that there are probably twenty-five to thirty-five thousand lead-poisoned children in New York City alone.[1] They get the lead poisoning by chewing old paint and plaster in run-down housing. Lead poisoning is difficult to deal with because it has symptoms which are easily mistaken for other common childhood diseases, such as the flu. The shocking thing is that lead poisoning can do permanent neurological damage: it can produce severe mental retardation. It can cause this kind of damage to from one-fourth to one-half of the children who are victims of lead poisoning. It is also shocking that we still find lead poisoning so many years after the development of lead-free interior paints.

The students could look into the science of lead poisoning. They could get samples of old paint and plaster from slum housing and analyze them. They could investigate the incidence of lead poisoning in other environments. They could try to invent paints which use no lead. It could be all very objective, but, eventually, if one accepts the values approach, there has to be a third-level step which would involve *doing* something about the subject being studied. In the lead-poisoning example, for instance, students (whether from the slums or the suburbs) could act in the following ways:

1. They could survey what, if anything, their own local health and housing authorities are already doing to solve the problem.

2. They could write a letter and ask New York City to explain what it is doing about Dr. Paulson's findings.

3. They could get in touch with Dr. Paulson and offer to do some legwork on the incidence of lead poisoning in their own city or town.

4. They could write their congressmen and urge them to look into the problem and perhaps draft legislation to

combat the wasteful and almost criminal neglect of human life which occurs with lead poisoning.

5. They could march with signs in the slum neighborhoods and conduct a campaign to alert the mothers in the slums.

6. They could mimeograph leaflets printed in simple English and Spanish to be delivered door to door to slum dwellers.

7. They could push to get a local radio station to give them time to put on a program on the problem of lead poisoning.

Some ways of acting on lead poisoning will appeal to some students more than others. There are many ways for students to act on their values, because the problem isn't an easy one. As Dr. Paulson puts it, it is a problem of getting "the lead out of slum children's guts and politicians' pants." Students could help, if the third level kind of teaching were to become the norm in science classes across America.

There are an infinite number of topics in science that lend themselves to action projects. Here are just a few, with some suggestions for possible projects. Some should be undertaken only with competent supervision.

Conservation. Start a letter-writing campaign to make a forest area part of the National Wilderness System. Build bird feeders to encourage wildlife.

Soil erosion. Build check dams in the community. Petition the Public Works Commissioner to combat erosion the class has discovered in the community.

Air and water pollution. Check your statistics. Begin an antipollution campaign. Hold a public meeting.

Smoking. Make the facts available to the school and community. Start a Smokers Anonymous after-school club.

Seat belts. Publicize the facts. Learn how to install seat belts. Start a campaign. Set aside a day when the class will install seat belts, free of charge, for all drivers who will bring their cars and be willing to pay only the cost of the seat belts.

Electricity. Learn about overloaded circuits. Volunteer to inspect anyone's home, free of charge, for overloading.

Sanitation. Study public health hazards of improper garbage disposal. Cooperate with the sanitation department to prepare suggestions for householders and publicity in newspapers.

Antilitter campaign. Cooperate with a fire department in putting on a demonstration project.

And still other topics that could easily lend themselves

to study and some action projects are: atomic radiation and fallout, the antiballistic missile system, drugs, population control, transportation, gardening, calories and weight watching, exercise and health, proper diet, chemical and biological warfare, race and racial myths.

Youth has demonstrated that it wants to play a part in improving our society. What better place to start than in the science classroom?

We have argued for an approach to science teaching that would focus upon values. We have witnessed scientists who had too little sense of responsibility for their art and craft for too long. It seems incomprehensible to us that science teaching should remain so stubbornly value free. Just the opposite is needed if science is to help us survive. We need science with responsibility. We need science with a willingness to grapple with the complexities of social issues. Science cannot afford the luxury of "business as usual" in this day and age. The great advantage that science has as a foundation for values is that science itself is so "culture free." The laws of science hold true anywhere and everywhere and for any people in the world.

It is indeed a question of values. Lifting subject matter beyond facts and concepts to the values level can help, for where science touches upon people's lives, values pertain. Where there is a lack of values, our community life festers and sours. Where there is confusion of values, we work at cross purposes, and our problems become exacerbated. History must not record that science teachers ignored the values issues and stuck to their facts and concepts. To do so would be to remain crudely prescientific and perhaps prevent us from having a future at all.

NOTE

1. *The Newsletter*, Society for Social Responsibility in Science, June 1969, p. 2.

Teaching Environmental Education with a Focus on Values

by Clifford E. Knapp

"Should I ride my bike to school instead of riding in a car or bus that pollutes?"

"Should I wear a sweater when I'm cold instead of turning up the heat and using more fuel?"

"Should I refuse to drink beverages bottled in nonreturnable containers because of the disposal problem?"

"Should I stop burning trash and leaves at home because this pollutes the air?"

These may be some of the many questions students ask themselves when they consider the environment and what to do about improving it. Environmental decision making is difficult, especially when students see conflicting attitudes and practices within the older generation. For example, some adults warn against using plastic garbage bags because they create disposal problems. Other adults recommend plastic garbage bags to reduce pests and odors. What should students *do* when taking out the garbage at home? What should they do when faced with the many environmental inconsistencies around them and the necessity of making choices themselves?

Questions of "right and wrong" and "should and should not" involve values. Because these issues are often complex and confusing to students, they need opportunities to think about the values issues involved and to learn to make difficult values choices on their own. The traditional ways of helping children develop values—by setting examples, persuading, limiting choices, and establishing rules—have not always worked. Students live only a small part of their lives under our control. They need to develop their own values and to learn a valuing process that will serve them when there is no one around to make decisions for them.

According to a relatively new theory of "values clarification," teaching the valuing process entails three important steps. First, the teacher should provide opportunities for students to express their ideas, feelings, and experiences concerning environmental topics. Time must be provided in the curriculum for the expression of values. Second, these expressions related to environmental issues and concerns should be accepted nonjudgmentally. If they are not, the student will soon learn to keep his true values to himself in order to avoid criticism. Third, the student should be encouraged to examine his position on specific environmental issues in more detail as well as to explore other aspects of the problem.

There are many values-clarification techniques available to the teacher for eliciting student ideas, feelings, and experiences and for encouraging deeper examination of them. These techniques are based upon the belief that valuing involves seven processes.[1]

SEVEN VALUING PROCESSES

Choosing

1. Valuing involves choosing freely, not as the result of peer or authority pressure. *What beliefs and personal behaviors have you developed concerning the environment that are truly your own, not the result of external pressures?*

2. Valuing involves considering alternatives before a choice is made. *What alternatives did you consider before determining how you would help improve the environment?*

3. Valuing involves carefully examining the consequences of each alternative. *Did you consider the consequences of the various ways to combat environmental pollution?*

Prizing

4. Valuing involves being proud of your choice (not boastful pride, but feeling-good-about pride). *Are you proud of the ways you selected to ease the pollution problem?*

5. Valuing involves sharing your convictions with others. *Have you publicly affirmed your belief in what you chose to do to protect the environment?*

Acting

6. Valuing involves acting according to your choice and not just having good intentions. *What have you actually done within the past week to reduce pollution?*

7. Valuing involves acting repeatedly and incorporating the behavior into your life pattern. *Did you incorporate these antipollution behaviors into your life on a regular basis?*

Teachers can weave these seven valuing processes into many student learning activities. The following teaching strategies are designed to help students clarify their values about the environment while they are learning the seven valuing processes.

STRATEGIES FOR CLARIFYING ENVIRONMENTAL VALUES

Value Sheets

A Value Sheet consists of a thought-provoking statement or quotation followed by a series of value-eliciting questions for the students to respond to. Value Sheets can also be composed of questions based on a film, play, or other experience that has been shared by the students. The following are two examples of a Value Sheet.

EXAMPLE:

People like to make money. If more profit can be made by polluting the earth, people will pollute. If more profit can be made by replacing an old machine, it will be thrown away. Increased profit has been the main reason for our high standard of living in the United States. Everybody is for making the environment a better place until it costs them more money. If pollution control causes a person to lose his job or causes him any inconvenience, he is not for it.

To think and write on:

1. Do you agree with the author's point of view about people and what they seem to value most?
2. Can you think of five things you value even more than money? List them.
3. What percentage of your allowance (income) would you be willing to give to improving the environment?
4. If you had to give up five electrical appliances or machines in your house to cut down on pollution, which would be the five easiest to do without? How would you feel if a new law was passed requiring you and your family to reduce electricity usage by one third? Would you do this without a law?

EXAMPLE:

Our society depends upon man's ability to change the natural environment.

To think and write on:
1. How has man changed the natural environment in your community? (For example, has he planted lawns, built roads, cleared land for shopping centers, etc.?)
2. Which changes in the environment do you think were good and which were bad for your community? Consider both short-term and long-term effects.
3. If you could make a change in your community's environment, what would you change? What would the consequences be?
4. Is this something you'd like to work on? What would your first steps have to be?

Picture without a Caption

Have each student write a caption to a picture depicting an environmental problem. The caption may reveal the student's values about particular environmental problems. Divide the students into small groups and provide an opportunity for them to share their captions. Ask them if they learned something about their environmental values and those of others in the classroom.

Role-Playing

Describe a situation which presents different viewpoints on an issue, and have the students assume the roles of the individuals involved. Role-Playing can point out a need for further study of an issue in order to better understand the facts.

EXAMPLE:

The following letter was written to a college newspaper in 1970.

To the Daily Egyptian:

When spring arrives this year, an indefensibly cruel scene will be reenacted on the coasts of the Northwest Atlantic and Gulf of St. Lawrence. Every spring and summer, thousands of baby seals are brutally slaughtered by Canadian and Norwegian hunters. The single purpose of these mass killings is to collect seal pelts which are made into fur clothing.

Whatever dubious justification exists for killing innocent creatures solely for their fur, there certainly can be no defensible excuse for the manner in which these seals are murdered. The hunters club and skin them, in many cases while they are still conscious. Last spring alone, 260,000 baby seals were killed in this way. The United States government, on whose soil this barbarism is taking place, has failed to put an end to the manner in which these animals are being destroyed.

> *Sue Carruthers*
> *Graduate student*
> *Government*

Have students play the roles of the letter writer, a seal hunter, a United States government official, and officials from Canada and Norway.

EXAMPLE:

At a city council meeting, an ordinance to ban the sale of nonreturnable beverage containers is to be voted upon. Before the vote is taken, the mayor reads letters received from three concerned citizens.

Dear Mayor:

As a consumer, I urge that the council defeat the proposed ordinance that would ban the sale of nonreturnable beverage containers in the city. Many of my favorite drinks are not available in anything but throwaway bottles and cans. It would be an inconvenience for me to drive to the next town to buy them there. Besides, this is supposed to be a "free country." This law would take away my freedom to buy the beverages I like in my hometown.

> *Signed,*
> *Bert Crust*

Dear Mayor:
  Please tell the city council to vote for the ordinance to ban nonreturnable beverage containers. As you know, we have a litter problem in the city, and the ban would reduce it considerably. Besides, it costs less to buy drinks in returnable containers. Our city should be a leader in doing something about our nation's refuse problem.

                                        Signed,
                                        Betty Smith

Dear Mayor:
  As a member of the Chamber of Commerce, I would like to voice my opposition to the proposed law to ban the sale of nonreturnable bottles and cans. Many people in our community will drive to neighboring towns to purchase nonreturnables. Our businesses will suffer from the ordinance, and some people will lose their jobs and be inconvenienced. Please vote no on this issue.

                                        Signed,
                                        Philip Harding

  Role-play the city council meeting, having the students take the positions of the letter writers and other interested citizens.

Contrived Incidents

  The teacher can create situations which stimulate discussion of controversial environmental issues.

  For example, the teacher can take the students on a short walk on the school grounds during which the teacher casually throws a piece of paper on the ground and walks away. The teacher could also break a limb from a tree or write on the school building with chalk. A guest speaker could be invited into the classroom to disagree with the teacher on an environmental issue. After the incidents, the students can discuss their thoughts and feelings.

Devil's Advocate

  The teacher can develop plausible reasons defending various pollution practices and attempt to justify that position to the students.

EXAMPLE:

  The teacher could state reasons why a chemical factory *should be allowed* to continue to dump waste into a river.

Some plausible reasons could be:

    1. It keeps the cost of the chemical products low.

    2. The industry could not compete with other chemical industries if it had to build expensive waste treatment facilities.

    3. Rivers have been used to dispose of wastes for centuries.

    4. Most of the public doesn't really care if the dumping continues.

After the short talk justifying certain kinds of pollution, the teacher should encourage discussion on the topic.

Values Continuum

The teacher can construct an environmental Values Continuum and place it on the chalkboard. The students go to the board in turn and place a mark on the line indicating their position. Have them indicate some of the reasons for selecting their position.

What is your position on these value lines?

Returnable Ron |————————————————| **No-Deposit Norris**

He uses only returnable containers and will not eat or drink anything that comes in a throwaway container.

He uses only nonreturnable containers because he thinks that returnables are too much trouble to take back.

Bike-Riding Betty |————————————————| **Motoring Mable**

She doesn't use any vehicles that pollute the air and therefore rides her bike to work forty miles away each day.

She uses motor vehicles every chance she gets. She even retrieves the evening paper by taking the car down the driveway of her home.

Pure-Air Paul |————————————————| **Pollution Polly**

He is so opposed to air pollution that he takes short breaths so he won't add as much carbon dioxide to the air.

She is so uncaring about air pollution that she burns cigarettes for incense.

Let-Live |——————————————————————| Pesticide
Larry | | Pete
He is so against any   He uses pesticides so
type of pesticide that   freely that he sprays his
he allows mosquitoes to   house and backyard
bite him rather than   daily to get rid of
spray them.   insects.

Open-Ended Questions

An Open-Ended Question is written on the chalkboard, and
the students are asked to respond in writing. Student
responses may indicate some of the values which they
believe to be important.

EXAMPLE:

1. If I had the power to correct one environmental
problem, I would choose....
2. The best way to reduce noise in my community is to....
3. The school grounds could be made more beautiful by....
4. I would rather live with a little pollution than....
5. All of the attention paid to pollution in the newspapers and
on television is....
6. The laws regulating pollution should be....

Time Diary

The student is asked to keep a record of how he spends his
time for one week. A Time Diary is a chart listing what a
person does every hour or half-hour during the week. It
should be stressed that this is a private diary that the
teacher will not read. After completion of the diary, students
are asked to respond to such questions as:

1. What have you done this week, if anything, that might
have contributed to pollution?
2. What have you done this week, if anything, that might
have made your environment a better place in
which to live?
3. How many hours did you spend in activities which involved
the use of electricity? If you wanted to, how could you
reduce this amount of time next week? Do you want to?
4. In general, are you proud of (do you feel good about)
how you used your time this week?

Autobiographical Questionnaire

The teacher can construct questions which will examine the

students' behavior in regard to environmental pollution.
Have you ever:

1. thrown refuse on the ground or in the water?
2. picked up litter from the ground?
3. burned trash outside?
4. reported a violation of a fish or game law?
5. donated time or money to an environmental organization?
6. fixed a leaking water fixture immediately?
7. asked your mother to change her laundry detergent to a less harmful one?
8. written a letter to the editor protesting a misuse of the environment?
9. written a letter to a government official expressing your position on an environmental issue?

Students write, then talk about, any time(s) they have performed these activities. In this way, students hear from their peers alternatives for environmental action which they might want to build into their own lives.

Values Voting

The teacher asks questions which require students to take a stand on issues by raising their hands. The purpose of voting is to direct students' attention to problems that they may not have thought much about. The teacher should vote, too, showing that he/she has an opinion.

1. How many use lead-free gas in your family car?
2. How many have ever thrown a piece of paper on the ground and left it?
3. How many have passed litter without picking it up?
4. How many have purchased nonreturnable bottles during the last week?
5. How many have refused to buy something because it had excess packaging?
6. How many have refused to have purchases placed in a paper bag at the store in order to conserve paper?

Rank Order

Words or statements are placed on the chalkboard and the students are asked to rank them in order of their preference. Rank ordering can lead to discussions of why different students have varying preferences. Here are examples of rank ordering.

1. Given a small budget to spend on the litter problem in your

community, how would you rank the following proposals to spend the money?

    a. Purchase litter containers.

    b. Place no littering signs in strategic places.

    c. Hire someone to pick up litter.

2. If you had the money to purchase machinery to recycle only one type of material, how would you rank the following in importance in your community?

    a. paper

    b. glass

    c. aluminum

3. Your city owns one thousand acres on the edge of town. How would you rank the following land uses? (After the ranking ask, "What other alternatives would you suggest?")

    a. Lease the land to a strip mining company with the understanding that the city would share in some of the profits and the company would reclaim the land.

    b. Sell the land to a large department store for development of a shopping center.

    c. Lease the land for grazing.

Coded Student Papers

The teacher of students can code papers with pluses or minuses indicating what the writer is for (plus) or against (minus). The papers can be written by the students, and the teacher can do the coding instead of assigning a letter grade. The students can also code each other's papers to indicate where they agree and disagree with the author. This technique is also useful in analyzing environment articles which appear in newspapers and magazines. Students can more clearly determine the writer's values and understand why a certain position is taken on an issue.

EXAMPLE:

Place pluses next to words or phrases that you agree with and minuses next to words or phrases that you disagree with.

A Conservationist's Lament

The world is finite, resources are scarce,
Things are bad and will be worse.
Coal is burned and gas exploded,
Forests cut and soils eroded.
Wells are dry and air's polluted,

Dust is blowing, trees uprooted.
Oil is going, ores depleted,
Drains receive what is excreted.
Land is sinking, seas are rising,
Man is far too enterprising.
Fire will rage with Man to fan it,
Soon we'll have a plundered planet.
People breed like fertile rabbits,
People have disgusting habits.
Moral:
    The evolutionary plan
    Went astray by evolving Man.

    The Technologist's Reply

Man's potential is quite terrific,
You can't go back to the Neolithic.
The cream is there for us to skim it,
Knowledge is power, and the sky's the limit.
Every mouth has hands to feed it,
Food is found when people need it.
All we need is found in granite
Once we have the men to plan it.
Yeast and algae give us meat,
Soil is almost obsolete.
Men can grow to pastures greener
Till all the earth is Pasadena.
Moral:
    Man's a nuisance, Man's a crackpot
    But only Man can hit the jackpot.
                    — Kenneth Boulding

ADDITIONAL VALUES-CLARIFICATION ACTIVITIES

Read the following story, and then list the names of the characters according to whom you liked the most and whom you liked least. Discuss the lists after completing them. Try to describe some of the values you think each man may hold. Have the students discuss how the situation could be resolved.

The Ajax Paper Company was dumping poisonous chemicals into a stream, causing the fish to die and the water to become smelly and polluted. Mr. Pedigrew, president of the company, knew that the fishing, swimming, and tourist businesses were suffering, but pollution control would have cost the company a lot of money. The company employed about half of the town's residents, and doing something about the problem would mean that most of them might have to be fired. Mr. Chambers, chairman of the town's Chamber of Commerce and long-time friend of Mr. Pedigrew, wanted to bring more tourists to the area, but didn't want to report the pollution because of the already high unemployment in the area. Mr. Chambers wanted instead to develop another amusement park to attract more tourists as well as to provide more jobs. Mr. Barnum, owner of the only amusement park in the area, feared the competition of another amusement attraction and reported the polluting paper company to state environmental control officials. The company was closed down and the employees were put out of work. Mr. Townsend, mayor of the town, sympathized with the families of the unemployed workers and wrote a letter to the state to try to reopen the paper company even though it would still pollute the stream. Mr. Moneybags, owner of a large summer resort, became so angry with the mayor's attempt to reopen the paper company, that he withdrew his support for a community park that the mayor was promoting, making it impossible to complete the project.

Make a survey of how foods are packaged for sale. Bring in samples of packaging which seem to be excessive and wasteful. Why do manufacturers sometimes use packaging which appears to waste materials? How much refuse could be eliminated if products were packaged differently? Display your findings on posters. What would happen if people didn't buy products that had excess packaging?

Electricity is derived largely from burning fossil fuels which pollute the environment and are in relatively short supply. Life on earth can be improved and the supply preserved by using less electricity. Have the students make a list of those electrical conveniences that they could use less or eliminate entirely.

Conduct a panel discussion or debate concerning the question of whether drilling for oil under water should be continued in certain areas. Also discuss placing oil pipelines above ground as some oil companies propose to do in Alaska. Consider the viewpoints of the oil companies, ecologists, local citizens, and government officials.

Have each student design a vehicle for a family to use in the city. They should consider such factors as air pollution, size of the vehicle, how to park it, and where it should travel in the city. How does each design reflect the student's values?

Conduct a classroom discussion about the pros and cons of completely eradicating a particular pest. If students assume opposing viewpoints, the discussion will serve to help clarify their values about the environment. Examine specific insects or bugs such as the mosquito, Japanese beetle, elm bark beetle, bag worm, tick, flea, chigger, aphid, blister beetle, and boll weevil. Examine plants such as poison ivy, ragweed, and poison sumac. Which ones will affect the ecology of an area least if they are completely eradicated? Does the whole class agree that a particular plant or bug is a pest?

Discuss Ogden Nash's poem "Song of the Open Road."

> I think that I shall never see
> A billboard as lovely as a tree
> And unless the billboards fall,
> I'll never see a tree at all.

Did the poet really mean that he'd never see a tree as long as billboards are there? If he were a businessman who depended upon the tourists who saw the sign, would he feel the same way? Write a poem about billboards from a businessman's point of view.

CONCLUSION

These, then, are some ways to help students develop their own environmental values and internalize the seven valuing processes.

But what about the teacher's values? Here are some questions the teacher might look at to assess some of his/her own educational and environmental values:

1. What are some environmental problems existing in your community?
2. Do you know of some effective means for dealing with these problems in your community?
3. Which of these problems would provide opportunities for meaningful involvement of the students in your class?
4. Which should be given the most emphasis in your curriculum: local, regional, state, national, or world environmental problems?

5. Are you optimistic or pessimistic about the future quality of the environment?

6. Which environmental values of your students should you attempt to influence and which should you not attempt to change?

7. What influence do you have on the environmental values of your students?

8. Are different viewpoints in environmental controversies discussed in your class?

9. Which instructional techniques are used in your class to teach about environmental problems (games, role-playing, field trips, newspapers, guest speakers, films, slides, books, periodicals)?

Teaching environmental education with a focus on values is no easy job. But the possibilities open to the teacher in this area are exciting, numerous, and varied. And, if we *don't* teach environmental education with a focus on values now, the next generation may not be around to do it for us.

NOTE

1. For a more complete treatment of the values theory on which this article is based and for other values-clarification teaching strategies, see: Louis E. Raths, Merrill Harmin, and Sidney B. Simon, *Values and Teaching* (Columbus, Ohio: Charles E. Merrill Publishing Co., 1966); Sidney B. Simon, Leland W. Howe, and Howard Kirschenbaum, *Values Clarification: A Handbook of Practical Strategies for Teachers and Students* (New York: Hart Publishing Company, Inc., 1972); Merrill Harmin, Howard Kirschenbaum, and Sidney B. Simon, *Clarifying Values Through Subject Matter: Applications for the Classroom* (Minneapolis: Winston Press, Inc., 1973).

The Search for Values with a Focus on Math

by Merrill Harmin, Howard Kirschenbaum, and
Sidney B. Simon

Reprinted with permission from *The National Elementary Principal*.
Copyright 1970, National Association of Elementary School Principals.
All rights reserved.

This is a crazy world we live in. We realize just how crazy
it is when we notice those clever advertising lies, read the
bewildering newspaper headlines, and witness the obvious
contradictions between what adults preach and what adults
do. We notice how frequently our political leaders act with
easy duplicity and how seldom our citizens find joy when
they achieve affluence. We try to reconcile the suffering,
rioting, and even killing, with technology, culture, and—
occasionally—wisdom.

Somehow today's youth seem especially aware of those
ills and as a consequence have more difficulty than we did in
giving our society their allegiance. Whereas earlier
generations slipped through a stage of idealism into an
acceptance of the existing order, more and more of today's
youth are not accepting their society. In simplest terms, it
would seem that traditional values are just not very
palatable to vast numbers of today's youth.

The result, it seems to us, is that more and more of our
young people are becoming valueless, aimless, empty of
commitment. That is a frightening state to be in, for it
is not easy to live in aimless drift, feeling that life has no
purpose. This sometimes leads to psychological damage (a

feeling of self as a meaningless unit) and sometimes to more
visible damage (a frustrated acting out of rage against the
institutions that helped produce such emptiness). Much of
this is behind the recent student outbursts. Note the negative
tone of those outbursts: Students seem so much more aware
of what they are against than of what they are for.

What has all of this to do with mathematics? Well, we
believe that teachers—regardless of what subject matter they
are teaching—can help young people make some sense out of
the confusion that surrounds all of us. Every teacher can
help students find commitments and a positive sense of self
in society. This we call teaching for values clarification, and
we believe strongly that there are few educational objectives
more vital.

In general, the way to help students clarify their values is
to give them practice in grappling with values issues so they
can work through the many conflicting pressures they
receive from society and can develop their own skills for
evaluating and resolving those pressures.

There are many mathematically based problems that may
be used to give students this sort of practice in dealing with
values issues. Let's look at a number of examples. Some of
these examples, we should point out, are more appropriate
for some groups of children than for others, either because
of the difficulty of the mathematics or because of the
relevance of the subject matter. We've purposely included a
wide range of suggestions in order to indicate the many
possibilities.

Word Problems with Value Implications

If mathematics lessons would include a few word
problems which touch on value issues and if these issues
were discussed briefly either before or after the computations
were performed, the search for value clarity would be
advanced. Look at these word problems, for example.
Problem One:

Bill bought a stingray type bike for $35. Three years later,
he sold it for $15. While he owned the bike, he spent $9 on
repairs. How much did it cost Bill to use his bike each year?
What percent of the purchase price did he lose when he sold it?

Value questions: Under what conditions would you tell a
buyer everything that was wrong with something you were

trying to sell him? What if he didn't ask? Would you lower
the price to someone who was really poor? If you didn't sell
your old playthings, what else might you do with them?
Problem Two:

Look at this chart showing the number of fires this year in
various parts of our city. This second chart lists the number
of houses and apartment buildings (called "dwellings") in
each fire district. How many dwellings in each district did
not have a fire? How many dwellings in each district did have
a fire? What percentage (or fractional part) of the dwellings
had fires? Make a graph showing the districts that had the
most fires, the second most, and so forth.

Value questions: Do you know how the fires started? Were
the buildings in poor condition? Were people careless? How
close have you ever come to setting fire to your house or
apartment? What did you learn from that narrow escape?
Have you ever put out a fire? What was it like? How did you
feel? Little children set a lot of unnecessary fires. What
would you do to prevent them from playing with fire? Would
you like the job of a fireman? How do you know?
Problem Three:

June works an hour once a week washing the kitchen floor
for her mother. She also dries the dishes every evening, but
that takes only 15 minutes a night on the average. She
spends about 30 minutes a week picking up her clothes and
playthings. How much time does June spend in working
around the house each week? Each year? What proportion of
her work time does she spend drying dishes?

Value questions: Do you think that June should be paid for
her housework—for all of it, part of it, or none of it? If she
is paid for her housework, then do you think June should
help to pay for her food and clothing? If you have your own
children, how will you handle chores around the house? What
can you do to improve the way work is done around
your house?
Problem Four:

The average hot lunch in the school cafeteria costs 45¢,
including milk. If you buy lunch outside of school, you can
buy a hot dog for 25¢; a wedge of pizza, 20¢; a bag of potato
chips, 10¢; soda pop, 10¢; ice cream on a stick, 12¢; candy
bars, 6¢; apples, 2 for 25¢; and oranges, 11¢ each.

Make up a list of the various combinations of food you can

buy outside of school for 45¢. How much would it cost to bring a sandwich and a piece of fruit from home? What does it cost for a typical week if you eat in school, if you eat outside of school, if you bring a bag lunch from home?

Value questions: Where do you usually eat lunch now? Have you tried one of the other alternatives? If you could save $1 a week on lunch, how would you spend that $1? If you were given $1 a week more for lunch money, how would you spend it? Could you go without lunch one day to save more? Would you be just as happy if someone invented a pill which would give you the same food value as a lunch? Explain. What other purposes does lunch serve in your life—besides giving you food?

Value discussions such as these hold students' attention. But is this kind of work really mathematics? How about the time it takes away from regular classroom study of math?

These are the questions we hear most frequently when we suggest that values issues be woven into mathematical word problems. Our reply is that students need to learn how to deal with complicated values issues. Indeed, there can be terribly serious consequences for not knowing how to confront the values problems which surround our lives. We say that if a teacher is willing to take a little time away from pure mathematics (no more than he feels comfortable about), he will be providing an important service to his students and perhaps to society. We also point out that teachers who use this kind of an approach usually find that their students are happier in class and in a better frame of mind for their more formal work in mathematics. They enjoy the change of pace that occasional values discussions provide.

Many other value-laden word problems can be constructed. Each problem, of course, should utilize appropriate mathematical skills and should involve values issues which are relevant to the children and which they can deal with at a suitable level. Here are a few examples of such topics. Each topic is accompanied by a very brief indication of the mathematics related to the topic which might be formed into a word problem and then, in parentheses, by some illustrative value questions which could be discussed.

Planning a birthday party. Given a certain number of guests, how much food will be needed? How much will it cost? What proportion of time might be spent in eating, playing games, and so forth? (Value questions: How do you decide who to invite to your party? Should you ever invite someone who doesn't have many friends? What would happen if someone came to your party without a gift? What is the purpose of giving a gift?)

Mail-order buying. Examine a mail-order catalogue and then figure out the shipping charges and insurance costs for the things you would like to buy. Consider differences between express and parcel post costs and between shipping many things together and shipping them separately. (Value questions: How important are material things to you? If you didn't spend the money for the mail-order goods, what else could you do with it? How do you decide what you want to buy? Do you usually want the things your friends have?)

Writing letters to the city council. If each member of the class writes a letter to all of the council members, how many letters will be sent in all? How much will the postage cost for these letters? (Value questions: Is it important to express your ideas to elected public officials? What other ways besides letters might people use to communicate with public officials? How can you make your voice heard? What do you think are the best ways to express your views? Why?)

School statistics. Looking at the appropriate tables, find out how many adults in our country have not finished high school. How many have not finished elementary school? Make a graph showing the changing proportion of adults in the United States who had not finished high school as reported each decade since 1920. (Value questions: What do you think some of the reasons might be for people not wanting or not being able to finish high school? How important is education to you? What problems might you have in getting all of the education you want? What might you be able to begin doing right now to solve these problems?)

These are only a few suggestions of the kinds of word problems which a teacher can develop to explore a variety of mathematical problems that have value implications. Teachers who are interested in this technique will find the daily newspaper an excellent source of facts and figures that relate to values issues.

Personalized Mathematics Problems

One reason students may not become interested in math

problems is that the situations described in textbooks often
generate an air of unreality. An urban youngster, for
example, is unlikely to be captivated by the problem of how
many bushels of wheat Farmer Jones can produce. On the
other hand, if a student can work with figures and situations
which are related to his own experience and daily life, the
chances are that he will become quite involved and be more
motivated to solve problems accurately.

With this in mind, some teachers have their students keep
Time Diaries and Budget Diaries. The Time Diary is simply
a chart with a column for each day of the week, divided into
half-hour blocks. *All* activities (eating, sleeping, talking on
the telephone, watching TV, doing homework, hanging
around, and so forth) are included.

The Budget Diary, of course, is an accurate record, down
to the penny, of where the student's money comes from and
where it goes. Students are asked to keep these records
up-to-date and to bring them to class every day. Problems
utilizing the student's own statistics are easy to frame and
naturally lead to values issues. Here are some examples of
problems and values questions which could be drawn from
children's Time Diaries and Budget Diaries. Again, the
values issues are in parentheses.

1. What percentage of your waking hours is spent with
others? What percentage is spent alone? (Do you like this
balance? Is it right for you? For everyone? Why do some
people always need people around them? In what ways do you
spend time differently from other children?)

2. What fraction of your time is spent doing things you
really and truly enjoy? (How can you make this fraction
bigger? Is your goal in life to enjoy yourself? If not,
what is it?)

3. Using the total time you slept last week as an average,
how many hours per year do you sleep? What is the ratio
of your sleeping time to the time you spend watching TV?
(Do you get enough sleep to satisfy you? What activities
might you cut out if you wanted more time to sleep? What
is the best time of day for you to do difficult things? How
does not getting enough sleep affect your behavior?)

4. On the average, how much free time a day do you have?
What percentage of this time is spent watching TV? (How do
you handle conflicts with other members of your family over

what to watch? The last time your television wasn't working,
what did you do with your free time?)

5. If you put 20 percent of your monthly income into a
savings account and received 5 percent interest compounded
quarterly, how much would you have in five years —
assuming your income remains the same? (How much do you
actually save a month? Is there anything you want so
much that you are saving for it? Do you think your savings
habits are good?)

6. What percentage of your income do you spend primarily
for the benefit of others? (When you are older, what
percentage of your income would you like to donate to worthy
causes? What are some causes you simply wouldn't give a
penny to? Do you ever send anonymous gifts? When was the
last time you were given too much change when you
bought something? What did you do?)

7. A researcher reported that when a family gets into
financial trouble, the last thing that changes is its standard
of living. (If your income were cut in half, what things would
be the first to go out of your budget? What would be the
last to go?)

Extra Assignments with Values Implications

Some teachers use out-of-class assignments that combine
thinking about values issues with mathematics experiences.
If a teacher can thus stimulate value thinking (without
being judgmental), students typically get themselves
involved in value discussions and thoughts, even if no class
time is allocated for that purpose.

The following examples will suggest the kinds of
assignments students might be given for out-of-class work.
In every case, of course, it is important that the teacher be
sure that the assignments will be appropriate to the students.
The values questions in these examples are placed in
parentheses.

1. Take a poll of students' attitudes toward several things
that you think are important. Then put your findings in graph
form. (Discuss your reasons for selecting these attitudes to
survey, and comment on your findings.)

2. Using U.S. Census reports, find the per capita income
of white and nonwhite persons in rural and urban areas in
your section of the country. (Present your data and discuss

what you think might be done to eliminate any inequities you uncover.)

3. Find advertisements that illustrate faulty logic and unfounded claims. Look especially for advertisements which use percentages and phrases such as "More people use Brand X." (Discuss the role of advertising in influencing what you buy.)[1]

4. Imagine that you have a million dollars to use any way you wish to improve your school. How would you spend it? Be specific. Obtain facts from the principal, business office, and so forth. (Keep in mind that how you spend money usually indicates what you value.)

5. Observe a water faucet at home which is leaking or which you allow to drip slowly for a few minutes. Try to estimate how much water is wasted in a given amount of time. What is the cost per month? Per year? (Whose water is it? Would you repair a leaky faucet for a neighbor?)

6. Look at the supermarket advertisements in your newspaper. Make up a list of basic groceries used in your home and see which would be the cheapest place to buy these items. (Would it be worth going to that store to buy these things? Explain.)

7. Here is a flyer from a discount store listing several sale items. Pretend that you are a checker. How much change would you have to give a person if he bought each of these items and gave you a five dollar bill? A twenty dollar bill? (Do you think you might be able to buy some of these items less expensively in a Goodwill or Salvation Army store? Would you rather pay less in one of these stores or would you prefer to buy in a regular discount or department store? Why?)

8. Compare the annual cost of subscribing to various magazines you like to read with the cost of buying them each month on the newsstand. (What magazines do you read? How do you decide what to read? Do you think you will want to read different magazines when you are older?)

9. Figure out how much several different brands of cereal cost per ounce. Compare the cost per ounce when you buy each of these cereals in different-sized boxes. (What do you eat for breakfast? How do you decide what to eat? Would you be willing to prepare breakfast for the family? What

would you need to do in order to prepare breakfast? Why should you do this? How do you act on mornings when you don't have breakfast?)

These assignments might well be modified with more or less mathematics and with more or less stimulation of value-oriented thought. With a little experimentation, a teacher will soon find a form that suits him and the students he is teaching. Most students seem to enjoy this kind of exercise even when it is assigned in addition to regular school work.

Summary

It should be clear that we believe that students need to learn more than subject matter. They also need to learn how to think through the values confusion that so characterizes our age, and they need to find more effective ways of relating to the world around them. Those who do not learn these things are likely to suffer from apathy, blind conformity, or irrational rebelliousness; those are the most frequent alternatives to clear personal values.

Values-clarifying practice *can* be woven into mathematics lessons. We suggest the construction of word problems that lead to values discussions, efforts to personalize the data of mathematics study, and the use of out-of-class assignments that combine values and mathematics.

It must be emphasized that the purpose of these exercises is not to get students to accept the teacher's values. On the contrary. Students already have plenty of adults telling them what to think. But students get very little help in learning the skills necessary for choosing on their own from among the many conflicting values they hear about.

Nonprofessionals typically argue for a particular set of values; only a professional educator is likely to master the strategies necessary to help students learn to think for themselves in this confusing realm. This does not mean, however, that the teacher must be silent about his own values. Not at all. It is wise to show students that teachers face the same values issues as do students, and when a teacher states his position, he should say that his value judgment is merely one alternative among many and that it is offered only for further consideration.

Clearly, our objective is not to have students pretend to

hold values that they will not, in fact, live by. Our aim is to help students develop skill and confidence in dealing with values confusion — and that takes lots of practice. All around will be the pressures to join a conforming or a dissenting majority. Our dream is of students who march to their own drummers. Mathematics teachers who appreciate the significance of this goal can take some time to help students search for that drum beat.

NOTE

1. For a discussion of ways students can analyze advertising see: Sidney B. Simon and Phyllis Liberman, "Analyzing Advertising: An Approach to Critical Thinking," *National Elementary Principal* 46, no. 16 (September 1966).

Teaching Home Economics with a Focus on Values

by Howard Kirschenbaum

Reprinted by permission of the author and the Adirondack Mountain Humanistic Education Center, Upper Jay, New York 12987.

How much of what we teach permanently penetrates our students' lives?

How many students read Shakespeare after high school? How many write poetry or letters to the editor after graduation? How many of our students ever use a quadratic equation again, or think more logically after taking geometry? How many look through a microscope, or analyze a solution, or even employ the scientific method in their own lives? How many ever read, speak, or write that foreign language again? How many wear seat belts as they had to do in driver education?

What's worth teaching? How do we justify our curricula to our students or to ourselves? What do we say when someone looks us in the eye and asks: "What difference have you made in the lives of your students?"

In the home economics area there is no excuse for not being able to answer honestly: "A big difference!" The subject matter of home economics is filled with issues and skills that could deeply penetrate the lives of students. The problem is that we so often get caught up in "covering" the curriculum—the facts, concepts, and basic skills—that we never get to the most exciting part of the subject matter. This part we call the *values level.*

The values level is that aspect of the subject matter which deeply touches students' lives and relates to their concerns. On the values level, students grapple with new alternatives for thinking and behaving. Teachers ask students to look more closely at how what *they say* corresponds to what *they do.* Students publicly affirm where they stand on important issues and hear opposing points of view. They come to understand themselves better — what they prize and cherish, what they are for and against, what their priorities are.

How does this values level work? What does it look like? Home economics teachers developed the following examples of teaching with a focus on values.*

Unfinished Sentences

One teacher used Unfinished Sentences with her students. Each student completed aloud any one of the sentences. Then the class continued its discussion on child development.

> 1. If I have a child, the thing I will emphasize most in helping him (her) grow up is....
> 2. One thing my parents (parent) helped me with which I hope to help my own child with is....
> 3. One mistake my parents (parent) made with me which I hope I won't make with my children is....
> 4. One thing I would like to give my children which money can't buy is....
> 5. One part of my personality I'm going to have to work on in order to be a good mother (father) is....
> 6. I would like to have...children because....

The facts, concepts, and skills relating to child development are important. But this teacher also had her students personalize the subject matter for their own lives.

Sensitivity Modules

One class was discussing how to keep a family budget.

*The author is extremely grateful to the following teachers whose ideas, examples, and words form the substance of this article: Lucy Minahan, home economics teacher, Pittsford (N.Y.) High School; Frances M. Dicintio and Karen Peterman, home economics teachers, Goodyear Jr. High, Akron, Ohio; Rose Ann Lowe, English teacher, Central-Hower Sr. High, Akron, Ohio.

That led to the topic of material possessions and just how much money was necessary for happiness. This led to wondering what it was like to be poor. The teacher asked the students to select one of the following Sensitivity Modules and to actually do it:

1. Live for three days on the amount of money a welfare mother in your state receives to feed a son or daughter closest to your own age.

2. Turn down the heat in your own house some night in January or February, and spend the night in a cold house.

3. Go to a Goodwill Industries or Salvation Army store and see how many school clothes you can buy with fifteen dollars for a family of four children.

4. Compare the prices of the same brands and models of record players, TV sets, and transistor radios at your local stores with those on display at a credit store in the inner-city area nearest you. Make the same kind of comparison in grocery stores.

5. Wear old clothes and sit in the waiting room of the state employment office. Listen, observe, and talk to some of the people near you. Read the announcements on the bulletin board, etc.

Rank Order

A home economics teacher writes: "I listed three alternatives or choices on the chalkboard for the students and let them rank them 1-2-3 according to their feelings.

"You are a high school senior. What is the worst thing that could happen to you? (Rank order these three possibilities with the worst first.)

    a. to not graduate from high school

    b. to be thrown out of your home

    c. to be involved in the drug culture

"My students got involved immediately in thinking about their goals and future. They talked about their lives and what they valued. How important is a diploma? What exactly would the drug scene do to me? How do I see my family?"

Here are some other Rank Orders, used by home economics teachers in Akron, Ohio:

1. Which of the following do you regard as least harmful? (Rank these from least to most harmful.)

    a. marijuana (one "joint" a day)

    b. tranquilizers or pep pills (two a day)

    c. cigarettes (a pack a day)

    d. liquor (two drinks a day)

2. If you had twenty dollars to spend in a large department store, where would you be most likely to spend the money? It must all be spent in one department. (Rank the departments from most likely to least likely.)

    a. clothes department

    b. records, entertainment department

    c. cosmetics, beauty department

3. In your leisure time, which would you most like to do? (Rank from most to least.)

    a. listen to favorite records or TV programs

    b. participate in a family activity you enjoy

    c. go shopping with friends

4. To you, what is the most important reason for sewing? (Rank from most to least.)

    a. to economize

    b. to express your personality

    c. to increase your wardrobe

The discussions following these Rank Orders were lively, fun, and thought-provoking. Each student was forced to weigh his or her classmates' alternatives, and everyone could get involved.

Proud Whip

Another teacher writes: "Students need to evaluate their good actions as well as their less desirable ones. This values strategy gives them the opportunity; each student expresses publicly actions of which he or she is proud. They want others to know about it. Students may volunteer or be requested to express something, or they may pass."

Following are examples of students' Proud Whip statements:

    I am proud that I helped my family by....

    I am proud of my project because....

    During my (year, semester, grading period) in

      home economics, I am proud that I....

    I am proud that my parents think that I....

    I am proud that I spent money (for, on, to)....

    I am proud of my friend (name) because....

Chairs

A teacher writes: "When a person is vacillating between two very strong choices in his or her life, the two-chair strategy can be very helpful.

"Judy was very worried and preoccupied with the question of whether to marry at Christmas vacation or wait until June, after she graduated. She got two chairs, one to represent Christmas and one for June. While sitting in the Christmas chair, she explained why she wanted to get married during Christmas vacation. She got up and sat in the June chair in order to tell the Christmas chair why it would be better to wait until June. Judy went back and forth between the chairs until all the reasons and feelings were expressed.

"I taught Judy the strategy of using two chairs. She then went on to act it out in front of her fiance. His task was to be a loving and caring listener while she literally did all the work of finding out where she stood. Students need to be taught such skills to help them grapple with the confusion and conflict in their complex lives."

A single values-clarification strategy rarely solves a particular values problem or dilemma. It would be naive, for example, to expect the Chairs technique to instantly clarify Judy's dilemma and give her *the* answer. What the strategies do accomplish, however, is to initiate, continue, and further the process of values clarification. Once students begin thinking for themselves, there is no stopping them. Values discussions frequently spill over into other classrooms, as indeed they should, for there are values issues connected with every subject area taught in our schools. Values discussions also tend to carry over into the home.

The teacher must have a real faith in the *process* of values clarification. There are no right and wrong answers in these exercises. There is no guarantee that all students will share the same opinion or share the teacher's opinion. But in a very real sense, each person lives in his own world, and each person must build his value system on the basis of his own experiences. With the values-clarification approach, students, teachers, and parents share their experiences and learn from one another as they become more closely in touch with the values that will govern their lives.

Home economics teachers are in a unique position to help young people develop and live by those values.

Personalizing Foreign Language Instruction

by David E. Wolfe and Leland W. Howe

Reprinted by permission of the American Council on the Teaching of
Foreign Languages from *Foreign Language Annals*, vol. 7, no. 1,
October 1973, pp. 81-90. Copyright ©1973 by the American Council on
the Teaching of Foreign Languages.

As a content area in public schools, foreign language is in
trouble. Fewer students are studying foreign languages.
There may be several reasons for this trouble: 1) fewer
students are choosing to go on to college and therefore do not
need a language as a prerequisite for a college degree; 2)
many colleges are dropping the language requirement from
their degree programs; and 3) there is a growing feeling
among students that a foreign language and all the work
entailed in learning it is irrelevant to their current
concerns and problems. Regardless of the reason, if foreign
language teachers do not begin to think differently about the
role of foreign languages in the curriculum and as a result
begin to teach differently, they may soon be without jobs in
public schools.

Students, parents, and educators are calling for more
humane schools; many of them want to put an end to the
factory system kind of schooling that treats children and
young adults as products to be molded into shape and
packaged for the world of business and industry. The cry is
for schools which provide personalized teaching and learning
and in which the primary responsibility of the teachers is to
attend to the concerns and needs of the students, to help

them become better decision makers and better functioning human beings. Teachers increasingly are beginning to read and listen to such people as Abraham Maslow, Carl Rogers, and Arthur Combs, who for some years have been writing about a new educational psychology that goes beyond the mechanistic approaches of behaviorism and has, as its central focus, the human being—his "self," his perceptions, his beliefs, and his values. The goals of this new "humanistic" education, according to Maslow, are 1) to help the student achieve his full potential, 2) to help the student discover his own identity, 3) to help the student become a self-directed learner who makes wise choices about his own learning, and 4) to help the student meet his basic psychological needs for security, belonging, dignity, love, respect, and self-esteem.[1]

How can the teaching and the learning of a foreign language contribute to these humanistic goals? Certainly they cannot if teachers continue to try to cover the book—to be on Chapter 22 during the second week of February. The "coverage syndrome" is characteristic of "factory education." With the pressures of getting the students through the material, the teacher has little time for the concerns or interests of the students because these often seem to divert attention from the skills to be acquired or the content to be covered. Students in such classes, therefore, feel as though they are being processed, and it is this feeling that the students of the 1970s overwhelmingly reject.

ROLE OF FOREIGN LANGUAGES

Foreign languages have a distinct role to play in the humane curriculum. In addition to satisfying a utilitarian need if students wish to travel or live in a foreign country, the study of a foreign language can be a sensitizing experience for students. Herein lies a central function of languages in the school curriculum. A foreign language can be used as a means for students to "get outside" themselves and, from a new perspective, examine their lives, their values, and their ways of thinking. This new perspective is that of a different culture and its way of conceptualizing, thinking about, and verbalizing things through its own language. Thus, language can serve the same purpose as do the humanities—

philosophy, art, literature, and music. It can provide
students with mirrors in which they can study themselves —
who they are, where they are going, where they want to go,
and how they can get there.

Languages, if they are to provide sensitizing experiences
for students, will have to be approached in a manner
considerably different from the simple coverage of the book,
drill and recitation, programmed instruction, or the other
approaches that constitute the bulk of instructional
pedagogy in the conventional contemporary school. Indeed,
foreign language teachers will need to learn new teaching
strategies and techniques that involve using the language to
help students talk about and, from the perspective of this
language, examine their own beliefs, attitudes, values,
interests, and concerns.

The purpose of this article is to delineate some strategies
and techniques for using language as a sensitizing
experience to the students' own values, beliefs, and life-
styles. The writers have translated the strategies into two
languages — French and Spanish — using a step-by-step
format in which the purposes, procedures, and follow-up
activities are outlined in sufficient detail for the classroom
teacher to use them as they are or adapt them for his
own use. The aim is to help students find answers to the
questions, Who am I? and What do I want to be?

These strategies can become games or gimmicks if they do
not have any framework that has a goal. Used out of context,
they can become nonpurposeful "time killers." Their power
will be diminished if the teacher does not know the values
or goals of humanistic education. Therefore, caveat emptor.

VALUES GRID

The Values Grid is an activity that helps the student
discover the steps he must take in order to develop stronger
and clearer values.[2]

Procedure

Distribute a copy of the Values Grid to the students.

Choose some pertinent current issues with the students; for
example, la guerre en Indochine, la ecología, la légalisation
des avortements, las elecciones presidenciales, la discipline
dans cette école.

Ask the students to write next to these issues two or three key words that summarize their ideas on the issue. The seven numbers heading the columns on the right-hand side of the paper represent the following questions:

1. ¿Está *orgulloso(a)* de su punto de vista?
   Est-ce que vous êtes *fier* de votre point de vue?
2. ¿*Afirmó publicamente* su punto de vista?
   Avez-vous *affirmé publiquement* votre point de vue?
3. ¿Ha formado su opinión sobre otras *alternativas*?
   Avez-vous choisi votre avis parmi d'autres *alternatives*?
4. ¿Ha formado su opinión después de *mucha consideración* sobre los pros y contras?
   Avez-vous fait votre choix après avoir *considéré* le pour et le contre?
5. ¿Ha formado su opinión *libremente*?
   Avez-vous choisi votre avis en toute *liberté*?
6. ¿Ha *manifestado* sus creencias?
   Avez-vous *agi,* ou *fait* quelque chose selon vos croyances?
7. ¿Ha manifestado su opinión *varias veces*?
   Avez-vous agi *plusieurs fois* selon vos croyances?

These seven questions can be written on the chalkboard or projected by the overhead projector. The students write the key words (those in italics) at the top of each column. These seven questions are then answered in relation to the issue. If there is a positive response, a check is marked in the appropriate box. If there is no positive response, the box is left blank.

Values Grid

Issue	1	2	3	4	5	6	7
1. Les avortements							
2. La ecología							
3. La discipline							
4. Las elecciones							
5. La guerre							
Etc.							

Follow-Up

After checking the boxes, the students may form small
groups to discuss one of the issues, their position on it, and
how it did or did not meet the seven valuing processes.
(The more check marks there are for each issue, the stronger
the value tends to be for the individual.) The students
must know that they are being asked not to defend their
beliefs, but to evaluate the means by which they arrived at
their convictions and the strength of their beliefs. The students
can also discuss orally before the class or write a short paper
about the experience and what they learned about themselves.
They should be encouraged to keep logs and compare their
first entries with those of a future date.

TWENTY THINGS YOU LOVE TO DO

This strategy allows the students to ask themselves if they
are really getting out of life what they want.[3] Are the lives
they are leading based on what they want, or do they wait
for fate to decide for them? In order to help students discover
who they are and to help them build the kinds of lives they
want to live, teachers must help them discover their values
and desires. This strategy serves that purpose.

Procedure

Distribute sheets of paper to the students and have them
number from one to twenty down the middle of the paper.

Instruct them, "Háganme el favor de escribir las veinte
cosas que más les gusta hacer en su vida." "S'il vous plaît,
écrivez les vingt choses que vous aimex mieuz faire dans
votre vie."

To encourage the students to get started, the teacher
might say, "Estas cosas pueden ser sencillas o importantes.
Si prefieren, piensen en las estaciones del año y en las
cosas que les gusta hacer." "Ces choses peuvent être simples
ou importantes. Si vous voulez, pensez aux saisons de
l'année et aux choses que vous aimez faire pendant ces
saisons." The first time this strategy is attempted, the
students may have difficulty in knowing where to begin. It is
appropriate for the teacher to offer one or two suggestions
from his own life by saying, "Me gusta dar un paseo
después de cenar," "J'aime bien aller aux matchs avec
mon ami(e)."

The teacher also, perhaps publicly on the chalkboard, draws up a list of twenty things he likes to do. Some students will have difficulty in finding twenty things they like to do; others may be able to list many more. It is important to tell the students, "Si vous en avez moins de vingt ou plus de vingt, ça ne fait rien." "No importa si ha escrito más de o menos de veinte." This activity alone may take ten to fifteen minutes to complete, depending on grade and language level.

When the students have finished, tell them to write the following symbols, letters, or numbers in the left column of their papers. (Depending on the language competence of the students, the teacher will have to choose carefully or edit the following suggestions.)

1. ¡Ponga un $ si la cosa cuesta más de $3-5 hacerla!
   Mettez un $ si la chose vous coûte plus de $3-5 à faire!
2. ¡Ponga una S si prefiere hacer la cosa solo(a)!
   Mettez un S si vous préférez faire la chose tout(e) seul(e)!
3. ¡Ponga una P si prefiere hacer la cosa con otras personas!
   Mettez un P si vous préférez faire la chose avec d'autres personnes!
4. Las letras PL están colocadas al lado de las que tiene que planear.
   Les lettres PL sont mises à côté de celles qui doivent avoir un plan.
5. ¡Ponga N-5 al lado de las que no habría hecho hace cinco años! (N = no)
   Mettez NP-5 à côté de celles que vous n'auriez pas faites il y a cinq ans. (NP = ne ... pas)
6. Al lado de las cinco más importantes, escriba del 1-5. Uno para la más importante o más preferida.
   Ecrivez les numéros 1-5 à côté de celles qui sont les plus importantes. Le numéro un sert pour la plus importante ou la plus aimée.
7. ¡Indique el día o la fecha la última vez que hizo la cosa indicada!
   Indiquez la dernière fois que vous l'avez faite en écrivant le jour ou la date.

It is clear that some of these steps can be used at all levels; others can be used only after certain grammatical points have been learned. A guideline for teachers to

remember is that they never should go beyond the point
at which the students would be frustrated by the instructions.
The procedure can be altered to Fifteen Things You Love
to Do, or Ten Things You Love to Do. Experience has
shown that some students may not have more than ten things
they like to do. This activity may continue for two to
three days depending upon the age group and the amount
of time each day the teacher wishes to spend on it.
Therefore, the students should keep Values Notebooks to
which they can refer for future classroom use and which
allow them to see how their interests may change or
broaden during the year.

Follow-Up

Have the students write short compositions (100-150 words)
or make oral presentations based on one of the activities they
like to do best. The following questions may serve as
guidelines for students: With whom? When (what time)?
Where? Under what conditions?

Have two or three students write their lists on the board,
eliminating those items that are too personal. (The teacher
may also write his list on the board.) This second step can be
followed by the Public Interview (explained later in the
article).

Other Procedures

¡Ponga una I si la cosa le es íntima!

Mettez un I si cette chose est intime!

¡Ponga una T para las cosas que los otros pensarán son
    típicas!

Mettez un T pour les choses que les autres penseront sont
    tipiques!

¡Ponga una M para las cosas que quiere mejorar!

Mettez un M pour les choses que vous voulez (faire)
    mieux ou améliorer!

Ponga una F para las cosas que no estarán en su lista cinco
    años de ahora!

Mettez un F pour les choses qui ne seront pas sur votre liste
    cinq ans dès aujourd'hui!

VALUES VOTING

This strategy is a simple but quick means to let students
publicly affirm their convictions.[4]

Procedure

Read aloud a series of questions always preceded by
¿Cuántos de vds. ...? or Combien parmi vous...?

Examples:

1. ¿Cuántos de vds. van a la iglesia? ¿A cuántos les gusta ir?
2. ¿Cuántos de vds. ven la televisión más de tres
horas al día?
3. ¿Cuántos de vds. piensan que a los "teenagers"
les sea permitidos comprar su propia ropa?
4. Combien parmi vous vont voter pour le même parti
politique que leurs parents?
5. Combien parmi vous croient qu'il faut tricher de
temps en temps?

At first, students may all vote alike or the way they think
the teacher wants them to vote. As they learn that no
punitive action is connected with their choices, they tend
to be more discriminating in their voting. The teacher
should also vote, but should wait a second or two after
the class has committed itself in order to avoid influencing
the students' choices. Students raise one hand for being in
favor, two hands for being strongly in favor. They indicate
negative votes by putting thumbs down—one hand for
be'ng against, two hands for being strongly against. They
fold their arms to show they are undecided; their taking
no action means they pass.

Encourage the students to submit their own questions.
The teacher should use these questions on subsequent days.
Motivate the students to ask their questions in the foreign
language (orally) or write them on three-by-five-inch cards.
Values Voting can be used as a feedback device for the
teacher. For instance, ¿A cuántos les gusta la novela que
estamos leyendo? Combien parmi vous aiment écrire une
petite composition le lundi? This brief information can help
a teacher alter activities that students find unproductive or
uninteresting.

Students vary in their preferences for learning activities.
Some will not understand the question and will not vote on it.
It is suggested that the question first be read in the target
language and then be translated for those who did not
understand. The voting questions may also be written on
clear plastic sheets and shown with an overhead projector.
The questions are covered with a sheet of paper, revealed one
at a time, and read aloud. This method allows eye- and ear-

oriented students to understand the question. The questions can also be reproduced on a ditto machine so that every student has a copy. As many as twenty or thirty voting questions can be duplicated in this manner. On any specific day the teacher may randomly select five or ten questions or select a student to direct the activity.

This technique can be used at the beginning of the class in lieu of the "warm-up." It tends to lose its value after five or ten minutes. Depending on the desires of the students, Values Voting can be followed by discussion of one or two of the questions so that students can tell why they voted for or against an issue.

RANK ORDER

Rank Order gives the students practice in choosing among alternatives and in publicly affirming, explaining, or defending their choices.[5]

Procedure

Prepare several questions based on the vocabulary and structures that the students know. The questions are worded so that students have to make a value judgment.

Give two, three, or four choices for each question. At first, younger students or beginning pupils may have to be given only two choices. It may be the first time they have ever been given alternatives, or the linguistic comprehension load may be too much the first or second time and, therefore, they may not be able to retain all of the options given. As students develop more maturity in selecting or listening ability, the number of alternatives is increased.

Read the question and choices and ask several students to give their rankings. A student should always be given the opportunity to pass by saying, "No quiero responder," or "Je ne veux pas répondre." After six or eight students have responded, the teacher gives his ranking. As with Values Voting, discussion may follow so that students may give their reasons for their responses. At this time participation is open to all, regardless of prior participation. The teacher may also duplicate the questions and the alternatives and distribute them. All students should write their rankings, and six or eight should share theirs with the class.

Sample Rank Order questions:

1. ¿Dónde quisiera pasar el sábado?
   - **a.** en la playa
   - **b.** en el parque
   - **c.** en un almacén
2. Comment apprenez-vous le mieux?
   - **a.** en écoutant le professeur
   - **b.** en petits groupes
   - **c.** en étudiant seul(e)
3. Imaginez que vous êtes un Noir! Dans quels pays voudriez-vous vivre?
   - **a.** aux Etats-Unis
   - **b.** au Sénégal
   - **c.** en France
4. ¿Que prefiere hacer después de cenar?
   - **a.** préparar mis tareas
   - **b.** ver la televisión
   - **c.** llamar por teléfono a un(a) amigo(a)

The teacher may ask students to prepare other Rank Order questions and alternatives in order to bring a different focus to the process. This strategy also can be used to motivate students for a lesson—on a dialogue, a reading passage, a literary work, or a news event. For example, a recent news item may tell of a dictator as having taken over a country. Using the guidelines outlined above, the teacher may ask, "Si tuviera que vivir en un país de habla española que tiene un dictador, en cuál viviría vd. (**a.** en España **b.** en Cuba **c.** en la Argentina)?"

Students may not have enough information to vote thoughtfully, and they may follow up this question with a research project on one or all three countries by reading articles in English or Spanish or by interviewing native speakers of these countries if they are available in the community. After completing the project, they report to the class and another vote is taken. Using the target language, students should give reasons for changing or not changing their votes.

UNFINISHED SENTENCES

This strategy helps the students discover and explore some of their attitudes, beliefs, actions, convictions, interests, aspirations, likes, dislikes, goals—in short, their values indicators.[6] Students often emerge from this activity with growing awareness of their developing values.

Procedure

Provide the students with a list of Unfinished Sentences. These can be presented on the overhead projector or duplicated so that students can keep them in their logs.

Have the students keep written records of their stand with the date indicated. The records serve as reminders of the ways their beliefs and goals may change.

Large or small group oral work is an excellent follow-up activity. For teachers interested in ideas for ways to have more personal oral work of a small group nature in individualization of language learning, most of the strategies in this paper are appropriate.

Examples:
1. Los sábados me gusta...
   Le samedi j'aime...
2. Si tuviera veinticuatro horas que vivir yo...
   Si j'avais vingt-quatre heures à vivre...
3. Me siento bien cuando...
   Je suis à mon aise quand...
4. No quiero que mis niños...
   Je ne veux pas que mes enfants...
5. Lo que busco en la vida es...
   Ce que je cherche dans la vie c'est...
6. Antes yo era...
   Autrefois j'étais...
7. Nunca he querido...
   Je n'ai jamais aimé...

The teacher may also use Unfinished Sentences as feedback by saying, "La cosa que me gustó más de esta unidad es...." Or after reading about French influence in West Africa, the teacher may say, "Je ne savais pas que...."

This technique is similar to one offered by George Brown entitled "Sentences Completion Form: Who Am I?" Brown suggests that the students, after completing the sentences, list five single words that they can associate with themselves now.[7]

PUBLIC INTERVIEW

A Public Interview allows a student to have the undivided

attention of the class for ten minutes and to affirm and explain publicly his stand on various values issues.[8] A positive side result of the interview is that students rethink about or discuss what they have said outside of class. Experience shows that this strategy is particularly favored by students.

Procedure

Ask for volunteers to be interviewed about their beliefs, values, feelings, and actions.

Have a volunteer sit at the front of the class while the teacher interviews him from the back of the class.

Explain the following ground rules and make sure students adhere to them. The teacher may ask the student-volunteer any question about any aspect of his life or values. The student must answer honestly. The student has the option of passing on any question he does not wish to answer by saying "No quiero responder." The student ends the interview at any time by saying, "L'entretien est fini," or "La entrevista está terminada." The student then may ask the same questions of the teacher. The same ground rules apply except that the teacher may not pass on a question unless the student did.

Ask questions that are based on known vocabulary and structures. Sometimes it will be necessary to teach an additional vocabulary item or two. However, students should be encouraged to stay within their linguistic limits.

Sample interview questions:

1. ¿Va vd. a la iglesia? ¿Le gusta ir? ¿Qué aprende vd.?
2. Si vd. fuma, ¡díganos por qué!
3. Si pudiera tener cualquier edad, ¿Cuál le gustaría tener?
4. ¿Vd. se pelea con sus hermanos? ¿Por qué se pelean? ¿Por qué se pelean sus padres y vd.?
5. ¿Por qué cree vd. en Dios?
6. ¿Qué marca de pasta dental usa vd.? Cómo llegó a usarla?
7. ¿Cuál es su curso preferido en la escuela, y por qué?

I URGE TELEGRAMS/LETTERS TO THE EDITOR

These two similar strategies give students the opportunity to make a statement about something that is personal to them.[9] Moreover, public affirmation is one of the processes in developing values.

Procedure

For the I Urge Telegrams strategy, give the students four-by-six-inch cards or, for greater realism, blank Western Union telegraph forms.

Have the students choose a real person (in the country where the language under study is spoken) and write a telegram to that person beginning with "Insisto en que vd. ..." or "Je tiens à ce que ..." in fewer than twenty-five words. Students should be encouraged to send the telegram to that person.

For the Letters to the Editor strategy, have the students write letters to the editor of a newspaper or magazine in the country where the language is spoken.

Have carbon copies made, read to the class, and posted for all to see. A request is made of the editor to send copies of any printed letters that actually appear. These letters are then clipped to the carbon copies of the original letters.

A recent event that might have impelled students of French to write a letter to the editor happened in Quebec Province, Canada. The Minister of the Interior allegedly was going to allow open season on the wolf population because the wolves were a menace to farmers who had domestic animals. Students also might be interested in writing a letter to a French newspaper protesting or defending nuclear weapons testing. In addition to affirming a belief publicly, students also learn cultural differences of letter writing. The students read their telegrams or letters to the class, giving their reasons for their feelings and explaining how they arrived at that position.

THE FALL-OUT SHELTER PROBLEM

This is a simulated problem-solving exercise that is more suited for fourth or fifth level classes or intermediate college conversation courses.[10] It raises a host of values which the student must attempt to work through in a rational manner. It poignantly illustrates how our values differ and how we often have trouble listening to people whose beliefs are different from our own.

Procedure

Divide the class into groups of five to seven students.

Describe the situation to the students. Your group comprises members of a department in (Bonn, Mexico City, Paris) which has responsibility for disaster planning. Suddenly World War III breaks out, and atomic bombs are dropping everywhere. An emergency call from a bomb shelter center informs you that there are ten persons requiring shelter and there is a supply of food and water sufficient for only six people for the three-month waiting period required for elimination of the radiation hazard. Within the next half hour you must decide which six persons are to go into the shelter. No decision at the end of this time period means that all ten will die. The following facts are the only information available about the ten persons.

Spanish List:
1. Señora de 23 años, encinta.
2. Policía con pistola.
3. Indio revolucionario en su segundo año de estudios médicos.
4. Cura de 54 años.
5. Chica de la universidad.
6. Bio-químico.
7. Escritor de 42 años.
8. Campesino de 31 años.
9. Atleta olimpiaco: excelente en todos deportes.
10. Actriz, cantante, bailarina.

French List:
1. P...du "Moulin Rouge," enceinte.
2. Gendarme avec pistolet.
3. Etudiant africain, assez révolté, deuxième année à la Faculté de Médecine.
4. Auteur/historien fameux, 42 ans.
5. Savant en bio-chimie.
6. Petit fonctionnaire, 30 ans.
7. Curé d'un petit village, 50 ans.
8. Jeune fille lycéenne.
9. Danseuse, cantatrice.
10. Athlète arabe, très fort en tous sports.

Have students discuss in the target language the pros and cons about keeping the six people.

Give time warnings of fifteen, ten, five, and one minutes.

Ask the groups to give their lists for their choices.

The teacher may then ask, "How well did you listen to the

others?" "Did you let others influence your decision?" "Were
you so stubborn that the group could not reach a decision?"
"What does your selection say to you about your values?"
A short position paper can be written for follow-up.

THE PERSONAL LIFE MAP

This technique may be used to show how students can
understand and express their feelings.[11]

Procedure
Instruct the students to close their eyes and draw
imaginary maps on their eyelids.

Explain that for each student the left side of the map is
where he is now in his life — his feelings and his awareness of
himself. The right side of the map is where he wants to go
in his life. In the middle there are obstacles that block him
from where he wants to go. The student is to determine
whether anything can be done about these obstacles now.
If not, he is not to change them but to be aware of them
and how he feels about them.

Have students use the target language to share their
experiences orally with the class or have them write brief
papers (100-200 words). Such papers should not be graded,
only corrected. The content should not be corrected to avoid
destroying the value-clarifying effect of such an assignment.

THE HERE AND NOW WHEEL

The Here and Now Wheel allows the students to express
their inner feelings in one word. Often these inner feelings
help to explain overt behavior.

Procedure
Have the students draw circles and divide them into four
or five pie-like sections.

Have the students write in each of these sections one word
that identifies their feelings. In a beginning class this activity
can be completed in English to identify some of the words
the students will need to know in the foreign language. These
words are left on the board for a few days until the students
no longer have need of them.

Ask volunteers to take one of their "feelings" words and formulate a sentence. For example, "Ahora estoy *enojado* porque acabo de sacar una mala nota en un examen de inglés." Or, "Je suis *ennuyé* parce que je n'aime pas cette classe." For variety, this technique can be used at the beginning of the class for one week, in the middle for the next week, and at the end for the third week. It can also be used at the beginning and end of the same class session. Students can see how their feelings can change over a period of time or within the short span of one class session. The wheel can be dittoed with the day of the week written above each wheel. Students can see how feelings can vary from day to day. It is important to remember not to penalize students for giving their true feelings. The information obtained can help the teacher to understand why students behave as they do and to gain information about things the teacher is doing in class and how they affect the students. Some sample words students may need to know are cansado(a), enojado(a), triste, contento(a), aburrido(a), feliz, orgulloso(a), hambriento(a), heureux(se), fatigué(e), ennuyé(e), malade, fâché(e).

Some Final Thoughts

These strategies are only a few of the many that can be developed and used to make the teaching and learning of foreign languages more humane and personally involving for the student. It is important to stress again, however, that these are not games to be played in the classroom by the uninitiated teacher. One does not develop a humane and personally involving classroom overnight by simply playing a few values games. The trust level in the classroom must be sufficiently high before students will risk sharing the kind of personal information called for in many of the strategies. Trust builds in a classroom when students are encouraged to risk only a very small amount at first and when they find that what they have to say is well received and accepted by both the teacher and other students. The teacher may find students reluctant, or even resistant, to participate in the strategies in the beginning. However, when students find it is safe to share their feelings and thoughts, involvement is likely to soar.

It is important to keep several guidelines in mind: 1)

Participation should always be voluntary. 2) Students must
listen to each other and respect the rights of others to differ
in their views. 3) The content of the strategies should not
be used for grading purposes. If the teacher follows these
three guidelines and seriously cares about and respects
the opinions of the students, the strategies should work well
in the classroom....

NOTES

1. Abraham H. Maslow, *The Earther Reaches of Human Nature* (New York:
The Viking Press, 1971), chapter 13.
2. Sidney B. Simon, Leland W. Howe, and Howard Kirschenbaum, *Values
Clarification: A Handbook of Practical Strategies for Teachers and Students*
(New York: Hart Publishing Company, Inc., 1972), p. 35.
3. Ibid., p. 30.
4. Ibid., p. 38.
5. Ibid., p. 58.
6. Ibid., p. 241.
7. George I. Brown, *Human Teaching for Human Learning: An Introduction
to Confluent Education* (New York: The Viking Press, 1971), p. 61.
8. Simon, Howe, and Kirschenbaum, *Values Clarification*, p. 139.
9. Ibid., p. 262, p. 264.
10. Ibid., p. 281.
11. Brown, *Human Teaching for Human Learning*, p. 36.

The Use of Selected Value-Clarifying Strategies in Health Education

by Jack D. Osman

Reprinted with permission from the *Journal of School Health*, December 1973.

The purpose of this study was to explore the feasibility of using selected value-clarifying strategies in a health education course for future teachers. The study was further designed to develop, modify, describe, and evaluate these selected strategies. Subpurposes included: 1) identifying the potential advantages and possible limitations of values clarification for health education; 2) assessing student success in the valuing process; 3) providing opportunities for students to learn the process of valuing; and 4) assisting the student in reducing the gap between speech and actions.

It was theorized that if a consistent application of value-clarifying strategies based on the seven criteria of valuing could help reduce the gap between what people know and what people do, it would seem that values clarification might be an effective learning-teaching process to use in health education.

College juniors and seniors preparing to be secondary teachers who were enrolled in the investigator's sections of Health Education 301 at The Ohio State University during the spring quarter of 1971 comprised the study population.

Students were instructed in the usual course content but with a focus on the seven levels of valuing: 1) choosing

freely, 2) choosing from alternatives, 3) choosing after
thoughtful consideration of the consequences of each
alternative, 4) prizing, being happy with the choice,
5) publicly affirming the choice, 6) acting on the choice, and
7) acting repeatedly as a pattern of life.[1]

Twenty value-clarifying strategies were modified, altered,
or designed to assist students in two or more of the levels
of valuing. Half of the following value strategies were used
more than once during the quarter. (Most of these strategies
are described in *Values and Teaching*[2] or *Values Clarification:
A Handbook of Practical Strategies*.[3]

Value Sheets
Thought Cards (Sheets)
Rank Order
Weekly Reaction Sheets
Values Continuum
Public Interview
Twenty Things You Love to Do
Personal Coat of Arms
I Learned Statements
I Urge Telegrams
Values Grid
Autobiographical Questionnaire
Here and Now Wheel
Who Comes to Your House?
Success Symbols
Forced Choice Ladder
IALAC Sign Story
Partner Risks or Sharing Trios
Privacy Circles
I Wonder Statements

The following are examples of value strategies used during
this study.

Value Sheets

The most frequently used (twenty-two times) and probably
the most versatile value strategy is the Value Sheet. It
consists of a provocative, often controversial statement, or
stimulator, designed to stir up strong feelings. Ideas for
Value Sheets often come from essays, quotations, definitions,
poetry, or song lyrics. If the quote or statement does not
stimulate the student positively or negatively, it will make a

weak Value Sheet. The design of this strategy prohibits neutrality.

Each student receives a dittoed sheet containing the provocative statement. Following the stimulator, a series of three to six "you-centered" questions is asked. "What is *your* reaction?" "What are the implications here for *your* own life?" Try to avoid "why" questions. Questions must never be moralizing; they should not have an implied right or wrong answer.

This series of directed questions helps the student focus his thinking on the values problems raised by the statement. The purpose of the questions is also to help carry each student through the value-clarifying process of choosing, prizing, and acting in a nonthreatening but systematic manner. Students are instructed to think about each question before responding in writing. Writing reflects more critical thinking than speech. Students are encouraged to write their sincere thoughts about the statement, not what they think the teacher wants to hear.

The investigator found many uses for Value Sheets. They served as motivating devices for new topics or concise unit summaries. Value Sheets were often used as one of the discussion options in a Partner Risk situation. On a few occasions they were used in small and large group discussions. Regardless of the size of the discussion group, Raths, Harmin, and Simon state:

> The important consideration in the use of value sheets is that each student has an opportunity to grapple with the questions *before* getting involved in any discussion that might tempt him to avoid thinking for himself and listen passively to others.[4]

The Value Sheet strategy is usually inappropriate for discussions. Value-centered discussions often lead to arguments. Participants tend to become defensive and closed-minded in such discussions. These conditions are the very opposite of those most conducive to values clarification.

The most frequent and perhaps the most effective use of the Value Sheet was to have each student respond to the questions, in writing, privately and deliberately. The Value Sheet was shared with no one. In this manner, the student was not swayed to accept the group consensus or the ideas of the teacher.

In addition to the above uses, students always had the
option of turning in the completed Value Sheets.
Nonjudgmental but clarifying responses were sometimes
noted in the margins before the instructor returned the sheets.
This procedure enabled the investigator to gain insight into
the thought patterns of the students and feedback about
particular Value Sheet stimulators. Raths, Harmin, and
Simon also note several other ways in which Value Sheets
can be used.

Depending upon the nature of the Value Sheet stimulator
and/or the extent or depth of the "you-centered" questions,
value theory could be accomplished on all seven levels. The
investigator generally chose stimulators which related to the
course content and occasionally ones which had an emotional
flavor. Samples of several Value Sheets are listed here.
EXAMPLE:

The Beginning Teacher

Greeting his pupils, the master asked:
   "What would you learn of me?"
And the reply came:
   "How shall we care for our bodies?"
   "How shall we rear our children?"
   "How shall we work together?"
   "How shall we live with our fellowman?"
   "How shall we play?"
   "For what ends shall we live...?"
And the teacher pondering these words sadly walked
away, for his own learning touched not these things.

—Source Unknown

To think and write on:
   1. What would you do under these circumstances?
   2. In what ways could you identify with the teacher?
   3. What are you doing to prepare yourself to answer these
   kinds of questions?

EXAMPLE:

A Caution to Everybody

Consider the auk;
Becoming extinct because he forgot how to fly, and
could only walk.
Consider man, who may well become extinct
Because he forgot how to walk and learned how to fly
before he thought.

—Ogden Nash

To think and write on:

    1. What, if anything, does this poem say to *you*?

    2. React to Robert M. Hutchins' statement: "Whenever I feel like exercise, I lie down until the feeling goes away."

    3. If *you* choose not to engage in regular activity, list several reasons why.

    4. If *you* have a regular pattern of activity, list several reasons why *you* continue it.

    5. Find someone else in class whose beliefs (about activity) are different from *yours*. Without trying to persuade the other person to your point of view, discuss your behavior with the intent of understanding.

EXAMPLE:

Self-Concept

    The concept of self serves as a censor for one's perceptions. An individual does not perceive what is actually in his physical and social environment. He perceives those aspects that relate to, enhance, and maintain the self. According to Rogers, as an individual moves toward a more positive view of self, he becomes more open to his experience. That is, he can be less defensive and does not have to distort what he perceives. He is able to perceive his world more realistically. The more unworthy an individual feels, the more defensive he has to be, and the more he has to distort his perceptions to maintain the person he thinks he is. The more unworthy an individual feels he is, therefore, the more difficult it is to change his self-concept.

    Combs says that "it is people who see themselves as unliked, unwanted, unworthy, unimportant, or unable who fill our jails, our mental hospitals, and our institutions." He describes the individual who has a positive view of self as one who expects to be successful, as one who behaves courageously, is less disturbed about criticism, is free to pay more attention to events outside the self, behaves unselfishly, does not have to be concerned about whether he is conforming.

                         —Travis L. Hawk

To think and write on:

    1. How does *your* self-concept measure up to the above statements?

    2. As a future teacher of students or a parent of children with poor self-concepts, list at least three things that you can do to help strengthen the students' or children's self-concepts.

3. Relate the above two paragraphs to drug abusers. Explain why you feel this way.

EXAMPLE:

Give Them the Flowers Now
Closed eyes can't see the white roses,
Cold hands can't hold them, you know;
Breath that is stilled cannot gather
The odors that sweet from them blow.
Death, with a peace beyond dreaming,
Its children of earth doth endow;
Life is the time we can help them,
So give them the flowers now!

Here are the struggles and strivings,
Here are the cares and the tears;
Now is the time to be smoothing
The frowns and the furrows and fears.
What to closed eyes are kind savings?
What to hushed heart is deep vow?
Naught can avail after parting,
So give them the flowers now!
— Leigh M. Hodges

To think and write on:

1. Without long thought or even complete sentences, what are your present thoughts about this poem? What does it say to *you*?

2. When was the last time you gave someone "flowers"? Explain.

3. Have you ever felt guilty after the death of a loved one — that perhaps you withheld some "flowers" from him?

4. React to the statement: "There are possibly more 'hang-ups' in our country with personal depth than with personal sexuality."

5. What are the implications in this Value Sheet for your own life?

6. Contract with yourself, in writing below, the living person who will be the recipient of your "flowers." By when? How often? Date and sign the contract.

Thought Cards

A Thought Card, or Thought Sheet, is a statement written to reflect something the student is really for or against; it could reflect the quality of living or thinking of the preceding week; it could state deep beliefs, interests, goals, or fears of the students. It could be about anything at all — the weather, world situations, parents, religion, school, etc.

Students are told that one Thought Card written on a 3 x 5 index card is due each Monday. It is to be the ticket of admission to class. The card can be of any length, style, or form. Poetry, prose, drawings, lyrics, quotes, etc., are all acceptable. If the students were thoughtless that week, the cards should so state.

Students are further informed that the signed Thought Cards would be read only by the instructor. Selected cards would be read aloud to the class each week without mentioning the names of the writers. In this way students would be exposed to numerous ideas and to the thinking of their classmates, motivated to try new styles of Thought Cards, and stimulated for the ensuing discussion. If a student did not want his particular Thought Card to be read aloud, he was instructed to write "Please do *not* read aloud" across the top of the index card. Each student's privacy is always to be maintained.

When the instructor feels that a favorable class atmosphere prevails, the Thought Cards can be used in various ways. However, this is only done with the prior knowledge of the students. When appropriate, students can be asked to share their Thought Cards in a Partner Risk situation (a strategy in which individuals share personal thoughts on selected topics), but they should also be given other, less personally threatening, options from which to choose.

Toward the middle of the quarter, students can discuss their Thought Cards in groups of threes or fours. Several students may choose not to participate in these group discussions. Near the end of the semester, students should be given the opportunity to read their own Thought Cards aloud to the class. This technique identifies the writer and usually creates excellent discussions.

An interesting variation of the Thought Card is to ask students to write their Thought Cards based on one of the topical considerations for the week. This helps students focus their thinking (and discussion) around the course outline.

Samples of student Thought Cards are listed below. As

the interested reader can note, the students' Thought Cards, collectively and/or individually, can teach powerful health lessons.

"I dislike school because it teaches me to fit in the present society without questioning its values."

"Good mental health is having a realistic distance between what you are and what you want to be."

"I can't stand white people being nice to me just because I'm black. Treat me just as you would any other human being."

"Never let school interfere with your education."

"Many teachers I've had teach to students as if their minds were empty chalkboards, waiting to be scribbled up with useless bits of information."

"Be a liberal, have friends left and right."

"In the middle of the word life there's a big word — if."

"If I had all the money I've spent on beer and cigarettes returned to me, I'd have a small fortune."

"What are those with all the hair trying to prove? Does it take intelligence to grow hair?"

"Why can't I ever tell people no?"

"Having sex without enthusiasm is like eating grapefruit without sugar."

"Sex seems so meaningless and trivial...afterwards."

"If sex was dirty, it would probably be spelled with four letters instead of three."

"I am curious as to the difference between sex and sexuality."

"To touch, to feel, is the greatest experience that two people can encounter. Why is this looked down upon by society?"

"Everyday I become more and more aware our senses have been restricted, especially the sense of touch. We do not feel free to hold hands, to hug, to kiss, and so we waste inadequate words where contact would have said it all."

"We met Ronnie yesterday while on a picnic. He wandered around from group to group while his mother sat in the car and her boyfriend fished. Ronnie said he was three years old, but I think he was a little older. He asked if we felt funny when he was around. He said he would like to kill himself but he didn't know how. When we left, I hope Ronnie had met two new friends."

"One is not supposed to smoke, be overweight, eat high cholesterol foods, etc. But are a few extra years of life worth it if one so fears death that he gives up all pleasures and vices to avoid it? Is not this fear of death paranoid? Are those who campaign against these vices simply replacing physical illness with mental illness?"

Evaluation of the Study

Evaluation of the study was accomplished in four phases. The first evaluative instrument used was Shostrom's Personal Orientation Inventory (POI), a measure of self-actualization.[5] The paired interpretation of two scales in this instrument was used to assess the process of student valuing. This instrument was administered during the first and last weeks of the quarter. A statistically significant difference at the .01 level was determined by the t-test between the means of the paired scales. Lack of a control group prohibited the interpretation of this finding as being attributable to the experimental procedure. The use of the POI was found to be relatively sensitive to changes over a ten-week period and, therefore, may be a feasible measure of the valuing process.

A Course Valuing Scale was developed and administered by the investigator during the last week of the quarter to determine in a percentage rating the opportunities and/or encouragement for each of the seven levels of value theory. The collected data indicated that well over 50 percent of the course time provided students with the opportunity and/or encouragement to become involved in the valuing process.

A scale to assess the degree to which students become involved in the valuing process as a result of the experiences in the course was completed during the last week of the quarter. Almost 50 percent of the students rated themselves as having become more involved in the valuing process since the course began. More than 80 percent expressed a greater awareness of their values. Almost half of the eighty-eight students stated that their speech had become more consistent with their actions as a result of the experiences in this course.

A Student Satisfaction Scale was designed to determine the efficiency, effectiveness, and satisfaction of each strategy through a five-point continuum rating. Seventeen of the twenty strategies received good to very good ratings in each of the three categories. The three strategies receiving fair to poor ratings were the same ones which the instructor felt were not implemented properly. Student responses to the open-ended comments gave further insight into the merits and limitations of each strategy.

In summary, the stated results of this investigation combined with the feedback of students throughout the quarter, interpreted and analyzed in relation to the teaching experiences of this investigator, lead to the conclusion that the use of selected value-clarifying strategies in a health education course for future teachers is not only feasible but also personally satisfying and professionally edifying.

NOTES

1. Louis E. Raths, Merrill Harmin, and Sidney B. Simon, *Values and Teaching* (Columbus, Ohio: Charles E. Merrill Publishing Co., 1966), p. 30.
2. Ibid.
3. Sidney B. Simon, Leland W. Howe, and Howard Kirschenbaum, *Values Clarification: A Handbook of Practical Strategies for Teachers and Students* (New York: Hart Publishing Company, Inc., 1972).
4. Raths, Harmin, and Simon, *Values and Teaching*, p. 85.
5. Everett L. Shostrom, *Manual for the Personal Orientation Inventory* (San Diego: Educational and Industrial Testing Service, 1966).

Teaching the Valuing Process in Sex Education

by Floyd D. Rees

Reprinted with permission from *School Health Review*,
March-April 1972, pp. 2-4.

How can we as teachers help young people use their sexuality in a mature and responsible manner, in ways that will not be harmful to themselves or others? Truly, here is the real challenge and, also, the opportunity in teaching sex education.

As teachers we must never forget that human sexuality is involved with interpersonal relationships, the psychosocial aspects of sexuality. The teacher must become involved in helping young people develop a rationale for their behavior in these kinds of relationships.

Over and over again the teacher observes young people using their sexuality in immature ways. The young girl plays at sex, for which she is not ready, because fundamentally she wants love; the immature boy plays at love, for which he is not ready, because he wants sex. Often we observe a young individual treated as a mere object for another's physical pleasure. Using another human being as an impersonal sexual conquest must be considered immature, and yet it is happening all the time. Too many of our adolescents are acting irresponsibly in the use of one of the most powerful physical drives. Consequently, the great challenge to the teacher is to help the student build a code of behavior within his life, a rationale for his actions that will reflect a mature use of his sexuality.

Basically, young people are interested in discussing the use of their sexuality and the development of sexual values. This has become evident to me in speaking with many groups of students over the years and, also, through teaching sex education. While young people do have the usual biological questions, soon the conversation begins to reflect value questions—the "should I" or "shouldn't I" type of inquiry, along with that important "why" or "why not." Our youth are perplexed; they desire dialogue in this area. There are many questions they would like to discuss. The sex education program must give them the opportunity for this type of discussion, along with its main concomitant, interpersonal valuing.

The teaching day is alive with value-oriented questions and decisions. No matter what a teacher's area of specialization, he cannot teach without being confronted with situations that reflect values. This is especially true in sex education if the subject matter is not solely of an anatomical or physiological nature. Today the trend is away from concentrating upon reproductive physiology. A modern program deals with material involving the psychosocial aspects of human sexuality. Reproductive physiology in all its ramifications is important, but it is only a piece of the pie, not the whole pie itself.

Today, as teachers in modern sex education programs, we must work with students in arriving at value decisions. Traditionally, some teachers have tried to dictate value decisions to their students. With this technique, the teacher makes the decision and then attempts to impose it upon the student, hoping the student will adopt the teacher's value.

However, in today's changing society it is imperative that the teacher and student cooperate with one another in arriving at a decision, using the valuing process.

Since a value is a standard of preference, a criterion for judging the relative worth of a thing or an idea, it is personal in nature, and the process by which it is formulated is a personal process. A person's values are simply the personal standards or criteria he uses in decision making, and for that reason should not be dictated by another individual.

The basic way a person arrives at his values is by means of the thinking process. Consequently, the development of reflective thinking has been a major goal of American

education for many years. The sex education program offers
an opportunity for the achievement of this goal through
the valuing process.

The Confusion of Pluralism

Before the valuing process is described, it is important that
we look at some of the confusions young people are faced
with in a pluralistic society, where the positions people take
concerning sexual morality tend to be many and varied. This
variety has caused a great deal of confusion among our youth,
for many do not know where they should stand or why.
Basically, the confusion arises from observing three different
types of sexual morality prevalent in our society.

The absolutistic position reflects the traditional Christian
teachings of morality by commandment. Followers believe
God has spoken; they do not feel obligated to test or prove
anything, only to believe and obey. Reliance is upon the
supernatural rather than the empirical. The absolutistic
position is often called by our youth the "old morality."

The second type of sexual morality young people seem
confused about is the relativistic position. For the relativist,
sensory experience is the only measurable reality. He deals
with the natural world rather than the supernatural; the
approach is pragmatic. The advocates of this position see
right and wrong not as eternal verities, but rather as wise or
foolish actions that can vary according to time, place, and
circumstance. This is essentially situation ethics, except that
the relativist requires more logic and, also, precise testings of
empirical data by means of the scientific method. Here the
dictum is from science rather than from the supernormal.

The third type of sexual morality that confronts youth is
based on the hedonistic point of view. The hedonist puts
personal pleasure first, either denying the existence of an
orderly universe or rationalizing his behavior in the belief
that he will escape any consequences. The basic ethic of the
hedonist is that the greatest pleasure is the greatest good.
To the hedonist, devotion to pleasure is a way of life. Many
of our youth refer to this approach to life as the "fun
morality." This is at the opposite end of the continuum
from the absolutistic position.

To further emphasize the need for the valuing process, and
adding to the perplexity of our youth, we find these positions

on sexual morality actually manifested in four basic sexual standards. The first, abstinence, which is based on the absolutistic position, forbids intercourse to both sexes before marriage. Next is the double standard, the Western world's oldest, which allows males to have coitus before marriage but not females. Shades of the relativistic position are in evidence here. The third, and one that is growing in popularity with young people, is called permissiveness with affection. This standard accepts coitus for both sexes when a stable, affectionate relationship is present. It is sort of a bed now—wed later approach: If two people believe they are in love, then they believe coitus is right. Here again we see some aspects of the relativistic position. The fourth position, permissiveness without affection, is one which accepts coitus for both sexes on a voluntary basis, regardless of affection. We see much of this type of relationship today in films and novels. The hedonistic position is at the basis of this standard.

Youth at the Crossroads

All of these positions and standards reflect some of the difficulties our young people face in choosing personal standards for their sexual behavior. However, a modern sex education program can help them develop a responsible rationale for their behavior. This can be accomplished if teachers are truly educators rather than indoctrinators. The educator will not present his students with a set of prepackaged formulas and conclusions, but will aid them in the thinking process. He will challenge them to reach their own conclusions, especially in areas of controversy.

The responsible teacher will provide reliable data, and show students how to find sound data themselves, in order to reach their own decisions in an objective and unbiased way. This approach reflects the basic values underlying the scientific method, as well as the process of reflective thinking, both of which are taught in varying degrees from the earliest grades.

Incorporating the scientific method with reflective thinking is called valuing or value teaching. The general philosophy of this approach is that the teacher and student work together to arrive at a value decision.

Basic Components of Valuing Systems

Today, there are a number of approaches being presented in

the literature of professional education which reflect the valuing process. These have many things in common. Here are the basic criteria that most valuing systems contain:

1. The teacher presents important concepts and aids the students in researching and gathering reliable data, knowing that the student's values will be formulated from various experiences plus the collected information.

2. The student carefully analyzes and reflects upon his experiences and the collected data, ferreting out the various available alternatives.

3. Next, the student reflects upon the consequences of the alternatives, attempting to synthesize the various choices available. This is done in relation to what the young person feels is important in his life, what is prized and believed in. Finally, certain choices are made, and from these, values are formulated.

4. During the whole process, opportunities are given to the student to talk with peer groups about the value decisions made, stating the possible consequences from his choices; as well as verbalizing his basic beliefs in relation to the value(s) involved.

It must be emphasized that the whole process of valuing is an ongoing activity, taking place as the student experiences many different types of learning activities. Each step in the process must be accompanied by interesting activities and teaching techniques, some of which will be listed later.

5. As the student takes part in a variety of learning activities and begins to reflect upon his basic beliefs and to formulate his values, the teacher gently prods him with questions as to why he believes as he does. The teacher asks, "Why are you for this? Against that? Why did you make the choice you did?" The idea here is to motivate the student to think and rethink his position, to reflect upon the choice he has made, the value he has formulated.

In this process it should be observed that the main role of the teacher is one of a motivator, an educator, not an indoctrinator. The teacher is attempting to get the student to analyze, verbalize, and reflect upon the problems he faces in our sexually complex society. The teacher must motivate the young person to formulate a rationale for his behavior, one that will be meaningful to him and, it is hoped, will ultimately help him use his sexuality in a responsible manner.

Psychologically Permissive Climate

If the teacher is going to get his students to verbalize their
beliefs, ideas, and values, a psychologically permissive climate
is very important. That is, the student must feel free to state
his beliefs and ideas freely, without feeling that he will
be penalized for holding them. He must feel free to research
all angles of a problem, to look at both sides of the coin, to
talk about the alternatives and consequences involved openly
and without fear of academic reprisal by the teacher. Without
a psychologically permissive climate, the valuing process
cannot function properly and will ultimately fail.

An up-to-date sex education program has a dialogue-
centered classroom, and this is essential to the valuing
technique. Reflecting this basic approach are some teaching
procedures that lend themselves to the valuing process and
its motivation: 1) panel discussions; 2) debates between
students; 3) debates between invited adults; 4) audiovisual
aids such as films, film strips, records, tapes; 5) talks by
community leaders; 6) reports by students; 7) division of
class into small discussion groups, with group leaders
reporting back to the class as a whole; 8) committee work by
students with final oral and written reports; 9) independent
research; and 10) role-playing.

The Ultimate Challenge

Valuing is the heartbeat of sex education! Without this
process the program slowly dies, suffocated by the
indoctrination of the teacher's preconceived, prepackaged
ideas. Surely, our young people deserve more. They must be
allowed to formulate their own values, which, ultimately,
will be the ones they live by.

The success or failure of this whole process is up to the
classroom teacher, for it is he who must meet the challenge of
valuing. He must motivate a program that will be exciting
for his students, one that will eventually aid all of society.
Time is running out, we have played ostrich long enough, the
heartbeat of many of our sex education programs is barely
audible. Let's give our programs a lifesaving transfusion
through valuing.

Values in Religious Education

INTRODUCTION

In our experience, organized religions are among the groups most receptive to values clarification. At first our own narrow perspective caused us to be surprised. We guessed that religious groups would be resistent to change and most threatened by the possibility of departures from traditional values. Actually, as in any institution, this is often the case. But the religious organizations seem to have two factors operating which usually override their historical conservatism.

First, the old ways of teaching values—moralizing, persuading, reward and punishment, and the like—are not working very well these days. Young people seem to be moving away from the church, and the various religions are reaching out for new ways of involving youth in the religious community and helping them see the relationship between religion and their own lives. Values clarification has been perceived by many as an effective means of accomplishing this.

Beyond the pragmatic level, a second reason for religion's attraction to values clarification is its consistency with what almost all religions believe—namely, that real faith is ultimately freely given and cannot be imposed by one person upon another. Values clarification, with its emphasis on free choice, fits in precisely with this view, suggesting that one goal of religious education might be to provide young people with opportunities to thoughtfully contrast and compare their religion with others and, finally, to choose a belief system that has personal meaning to them.

The articles in this section provide both a theoretical and practical approach to bridging the gap between values clarification and religion.

How Can We Teach Values?

by John H. Westerhoff III

From *Colloquy*, January 1970. Used by permission.

Every once in awhile, you find a book that you cannot put down. You find yourself quoting it over and over again. *Values and Teaching*, by Raths, Harmin, and Simon, is that sort of book. Every parent and teacher ought to read it. The following thoughts taken from that book should tell you why.

Almost every parent and teacher shares a concern for his children's values. Values are the bases upon which persons decide what they are for and against, or where they're going and why. The lives of persons with clear values have direction and meaning.

It is only natural that we try to communicate our own values to children and youth. We talk about setting an example or pointing toward good examples. We try to persuade or convince a child, through dramatic or emotional pleas, that this or that set of values is the one for him to follow. We set rules and regulations, we reward or punish to mold his behavior in certain "right" directions. We present certain values as having a religious base and use the authority of religion as a persuader. We appeal to conscience, that still voice that we assume is in the heart of everyone.

With deep concern, we moralize and lecture about charity,
courtesy, honor, perseverance, and other values we think
important.

But deep within us, we know the futility of all such
approaches. Just as you cannot give a child a faith, you
cannot give him values. They cannot be injected like a
vaccine. A child is a person; we dare not rob him of his
freedom. You can influence, offer guidance, and confront him
with decisions, but little more. Still, you can enable a person
to clarify his own values and thereby evolve a permanent set
for his life. That's what *Values and Teaching* is about.

But we are getting ahead of our story. The whole problem
of values has become complex. Life in the United States is
richer with choices and opportunities than ever before. New
means of communications in the home introduce children to
values different from those of his family. As a family travels
about, it is confronted with a growing number of divergent
values. But choices and opportunities are often confusing
for children to comprehend. This is one reason why it is more
difficult today for a child to develop a clear value system.
The family, the community, the school, and the church used
to create a homogeneous environment where values seemed
self-evident. Today, we live in pluralistic communities.

The communication media, the family, the country, and
the schools no longer give a single view. They suggest to a
child that there are many, many different ways of living.
What is right and what is wrong, what is true and what is
false, what is good and what is bad, what is just and what is
unjust, what is beautiful and what is ugly, are in debate in
a pluralistic community. A child of today confronts more
choices than the child of yesterday. He has many more
alternatives. This is not necessarily bad, but it makes the
passing on of values much more difficult than it was
in the past.

It is in the context of experience that a person grows and
learns. Out of this context come certain general guides to
behavior. These give direction to life and may be called
values. Since values emerge from a person's experience, we
would expect that the experience of confronting a variety of
value systems would make his problem difficult. But his
problem is compounded by the gap between what his parents
and other adults say and what they do. He hears us say that

certain values are important, but he sees us live by others. As he is exposed to our inconsistencies, it becomes increasingly difficult for him to develop a clear set of values of his own.

Often, a child grows up wondering if anything is right or good, if anything matters. He is apt to believe that one way of life is just as good as another and no particular way of living really matters. To live with such thoughts is to end up being apathetic, flighty, inconsistent, uncertain, a drifter, an overconformer, an overdissenter, a role-player, a person who finally is not able to function as a full human being in society because he doesn't have any values by which he is willing to live and die.

Yet a value system remains a person's most important possession. We need to find a way amidst all our problems to enable persons to develop strong values. *Values and Teaching* suggests a way of helping people to clarify their unexpressed values as a step toward developing a final value system.

Raths, Harmin, and Simon begin by establishing a series of criteria for values. The first criterion is this: A value must be chosen freely. If something is a guide to one's life, whether or not an authority is watching, it must be a free choice. If there is coercion, the result is not likely to stay with you out of range of the source of that coercion.

A second criterion suggests that a value is always chosen from among alternatives. Obviously, there can be no choice if there are no alternatives from which to choose. It makes no sense, for example, to say that one values eating. One really has no choice in the matter. What one may value is certain types of food or certain forms of eating, but not eating itself. Only when a choice is possible do we say a value can result.

Third, impulsive or thoughtless choices do not lead to values. For something to guide one's life meaningfully, it must emerge from a weighing and an understanding. Only when the consequences of the alternatives are clearly understood can one make intelligent choices. A value therefore results from a choice made after thoughtful consideration of the range of alternatives and the consequences involved.

Fourth, when we value something it has a positive quality for us. We prize it, cherish it, esteem it, respect it, hold it dear. We are happy with our values. A choice, even when we have made it freely and thoughtfully, may be a choice we are not happy to make. We may choose to fight in a war, but be sorry that circumstances make that choice reasonable. In our definition, values flow from choices that we are glad to make.

Fifth, when we have chosen something freely after consideration of alternatives, when we are proud of our choice, glad to be associated with it, we are likely to affirm that choice when asked about it. We are willing to affirm publicly our values. We may even be willing to champion them. If we are ashamed of a choice, if we would not make our position known when appropriately asked, we are not dealing with values but with something else.

Sixth, when we have a value, it shows up in aspects of our living. We spend money on a choice we value. We budget time and energy for our values. Nothing can be a value that does not give direction to actual living. The person who talks about something but never does anything about it is not speaking of his values.

Last, when something reaches the stage of a value, it is likely to reappear on a number of occasions in the life of the person who holds it. It shows up in different situations at different times. We would not think of something that appeared once in a lifetime and never again as a value. Values tend to have a persistency and assume a pattern in our lives.

Collectively, these characteristics define a value. It is important to understand this definition of a value so we can proceed with the process by which we can enable people to clarify their values. This process becomes particularly important in a world that is changing as rapidly as ours. Each person should develop habits of continually reexamining his purposes, aspirations, attitudes, feelings, and the like if he is to find the most intelligent relationship between his life and the surrounding world, and if he is to make a contribution to the creation of a better world. The development of values is a personal, lifelong process. If we could learn the method by means of which we look at life and clarify what we value, then we could have a system by which we could live purposefully in a pluralistic world. Raths, Harmin, and Simon offer us such a process.

The way is simple and fun. First, encourage children to make choices and to make them freely. Second, help them discover available alternatives when faced with choices. Third, help them weigh alternatives thoughtfully, reflecting on the consequences of each. Fourth, encourage them to consider what it is they prize and cherish. Fifth, give them opportunity to make public affirmation of their choices. Sixth, encourage them to act, behave, and live in accordance with their choices and, last, help them to examine repeated patterns of behavior in their lives. In this way one can encourage the process of valuing. The intent is to help children to clarify what they value; this is very different from trying to persuade them to accept some predetermined set of values. It affirms the crucial importance of values, but it also holds that human beings can be thoughtful, wise, and that values will come when persons use their intelligence freely and reflectively to define their relationships with each other and an ever-changing world. It is a process based upon a religious understanding of man.

I'm sure many of you can think of objections to this process; for instance, that children appreciate being told what to do and believe, or that you can't trust children to choose the values that would serve them best, or that children are not old enough or experienced enough or wise enough to choose values for themselves. Raths, Harmin, and Simon intelligently confront all these in their book.

Their answers are based upon a sound theological understanding of man and a sound understanding of the learning process. We'll all have to do some soul-searching before we are ready to accept their proposal. But I think of the lines in the television play *Plenty of Rein*, by Clair Roskam, which go:

Narrator: When does the time come, then, to let go and say their destiny is in God's hands and not yours?

Keith: When they're wise enough to make the right choices.

Narrator: Then somewhere they have to learn to make significant choices for themselves and bear the responsibility for them.

Edna: Even if they're wrong?

Narrator: We all have our right to failure. When does the time come when your concern is excessive, and your protection is overprotective? When do your children have to learn to flex the muscles of their own judgment, even if they take the wrong course and it breaks your heart? The time must come because if they can't stand against you and against the crowd on positions they take for themselves, then how do they become men and women? How do they become anything more than well-behaved children?

Keith: Then what are parents for?

Narrator: To guide, to teach—remembering always that your children's destiny is not at any point in your hands, but in the hands of God. If you have realized this, then it seems to me you'll never have to face the question of when to let go. The hardest part of being a parent must be the initial decision—what it takes is faith.... Sometimes it has to be said, "This child is an individual soul, the co-equal of mine." Sometime it has to happen. A child struggles for his independence and his maturity, and his right to make even wrong choices. Ultimately he must put his faith and trust, not in his parents, but in God. And for a parent this may be very hard and very painful. But to protect his child too long—that must be to stand between the child and God. For even as the parent bears alone the responsibility for his life and his choices before God, so is the child born with that privilege and that burden.

Those Old-Time Values

by Rod Brownfield

Reprinted with permission from the *Catechist;* copyright 1972 by Pflaum/Standard.

Not so long ago, most of us believed that values were fixed and immutable, the eternal verities. It was that way, certainly, if one were a good American, even more so if one were a good Catholic. We valued God, country, cleanliness, work and its rewards, motherhood, forty hours, the underdog, J. Edgar Hoover, the common good, General Motors, individualism, justice, the Legion of Decency, progress, and whatever Sister said...though not necessarily in that order.

Most of us can remember when it was just that way. But the hard rock of our values has been chipped away by Lee Harvey Oswald, the atom bomb, Vietnam, Vatican II, minority rights, Auschwitz, the Munich Olympics, wiretapping, women's lib, inflation, the Pill, pollution, television, X-rated movies, abortion laws, priests in prison, Nixon in Peking... though not necessarily in that order.

Once one only had to invoke the Constitution or the Ten Commandments for everyone and everything to fall back into its proper place. But everything decent—that is, American and Christian—now seems in disarray, disheveled, in conflict, out of whack, near chaos. Where have all the ancient, honored values gone?

The truth is: So many of our values were of a terribly thin
fabric, if values at all. Many of our values simply were
habitual attitudes, props supporting the status quo,
customary ways of avoiding uncomfortable involvements. Or,
quite often, we were victims of our own chauvinism(s) —
national or religious or cultural or sexual; we were bigots
who found security and pleasure in parading our wealth of
shared ignorance. Oh, we did have values. Good and bad.
And sometimes our priorities ran in favor of the less worthy
sort. It still happens, only the value content changes —
according to sales goals, the rigors of final exams, the
nearness of an election, the remoteness of home and mother,
the thoroughness of the Internal Revenue Service, the social
tolerance of prejudice, the pecking order for promotion, the
distance of the target, peer pressures of the ubiquitous
Joneses.

However right or wrong the values we once cherished, we
did value values. Perhaps we still do. But in this age of
programmed obsolescence, values seem to come into being
rapidly and to perish even more quickly. Many historical
observers of our Western culture and civilization are telling
us that today our values and priorities are in shambles.
Our culture itself is said to be tottering, close to collapse.
Institutions of every sort, traditional guardians of all
that is good and worthy, seem at a loss to safeguard the very
values that they are pledged to promote and to protect. This
is a time of confusion in values. This is an age of cynicism
if we can accept Oscar Wilde's definition of a cynic as one
who knows the price of everything (no small task today)
and the value of nothing.

But what does all this hand-wringing and wailing have to
do with religious education? Quite a lot. Christianity
espouses a system of values rather clearly set forth — though
less extensive than popular theology and pious tradition
would suggest. This Christian value system, however, does
not exist in a vacuum. It exists within a historical framework,
within the limits of cultural institution, adjacent to other
value systems, other human involvements, other human
needs. Thus the Christian system always is in competition
for attention and for adherence.

Then too, in America today, the Christian value system is
somewhat disadvantaged. It is diminished by its very

respectability in the pantheon of America's pluralistic value systems; it often seems today to be bland stuff, even passé. It must compete with the brilliance of the physical sciences (though recently their dazzle has dimmed). It must compete with the profit motive, with politics, with pop art and pop culture, with the invasion of Eastern mysticism, with the dicta of the behavioralists, with the posh pronouncements of the ad men. But most of all, Christian values must compete with Christian institutions, with their fading grandeur and with their deadening trivia.

Religious educators concerned with Christian values need to be aware of what might be called "value impact." A set of values comes into existence in a historical and human context. If these values are clear and apparent, contributive to human good, productive in the lives of those who espouse them, then mountains move and empires tumble. Christianity with its values system certainly has generated that kind of impact. It burst into time and space, altered human awareness, invigorated a dying culture, civilized barbaric tribes (at least superficially), enriched the arts, and promoted the human spirit and human dignity. And then it became comfortable, established, an institution; something of its vitality diminished; its motivating drive waned; its own values were compromised in its institutional concern for power and prestige. Christianity, in brief, began as a powerful religious movement encompassing a value system that was a way of life; it has become a complex institution burdened by law and custom, generally respected in its advanced age, but nostalgic for its youthful fidelity to primary values.

These core values, the real stuff of Christianity, are there still. Layers of institutional crust can be peeled away to expose the pristine quality of the values taught—but more, *lived*—by Christ Jesus, his Apostles, and the early Christian community: a rich faith in a loving God and in a risen Lord, communal concern for one another, a covenant of sharing, a promise of peace and healing to the poor and the sick and the oppressed.

These values are potent still. But their power is never realized in the incantation of word formulas; the power flows in human deed. Thus, in religious education, Christian values are transmitted more in the conduct and attitude of the

teacher than in all the texts, audiovisual materials, and
student programs. If values are clear and apparent in the
life of the teacher, value education is possible. If his teaching
presence is permeated by his values, they will have an impact
on students in a way that needs few words. Exposure to
values lived is so much more attractive than imperatives
imposed.

But living his values before twenty to thirty impressionable
young persons places demands on the teacher. First, he must
be able to distinguish core values from secondary and even
superficial values, which may not be values at all. For
example: The teacher must so evidence a real relationship
with Christ Jesus in the Eucharist that he forgets small
matters such as drill in folding the hands just so or in
keeping one's eyes downcast or in reciting the correct
prayer when returning from the Communion station. Good
manners are a poor substitute for a real sense of sharing
the life of Jesus.

Small things camouflaging as values are a time bomb. Come
adolescence, the young person begins to sift and sort the
superfluity of data presented over the years as the essential
stuff of religion, as necessary to life now and hereafter.
(And if the young person is not sifting and sorting, then
he is not maturing; and if he is not maturing, then there is
no hope of his becoming a fully participating member of the
Christian community.) Too often the data the young person
must sort have been presented as if everything were of the
same value weight; worse, it may have been offered as if
every single piece were essential to the whole — all or nothing.
This jerry-built structure imposes a crisis in crisis-ridden
adolescence. Chunks of data, when scrutinized, conflict
with personal experience or later and better information.
Fragments fall, the whole structure teeters. Who, really,
created the crisis? Not the young person.

There is this too in teaching religious values: In the past,
religious educators, like others in authority, have violated
the essential condition of a genuine religious life — freedom.
God freely invites man to share in his life. Man's response,
in turn, must be chosen freely. Life with God is never a
shotgun wedding. And yet, so often in religious education —
and in Christian life — the option to choose freely is not there.
Rather, imperatives are imposed. "You shall...or else."

The unexpressed axiom seems to be: The individual Christian, however knowledgeable, however well-behaved, however faith-filled, simply cannot be trusted to make the right judgments; he must be told what to do, what to think, what to cherish. Conformity is more desired than free commitment. Following scriptural norms, this is a false value. No one can be coerced into sharing God's life. How is it that God invites us to the feast of life, but the church demands, under threat of ultimate penalty, that we be present in the banquet room—yet we do not have to eat?

Permitting anyone—child, adolescent, adult—to choose to respond freely to God's generosity is ever a risky business, threatening; the invited person can say no. All value choosing involves this threat, this risk. But the threat is larger in the life of the person invited; he must have the opportunity to choose, or he may never perceive the value of himself, the reality that God so loves him and cherishes his friendship. Command his obedience, and you have rendered the individual faceless, the gracious Lord of life a tyrant.

Somehow, value teaching needs to conform to the value structure of Scripture. If God cherishes human worth, then so must the religious educator. If God values free choice, so must the religion teacher. If the will of God can be defined as the good of man—individually and collectively—then human good is the highest priority, and the teacher must be sure that his every teaching act reflects the same concern expressed in God's will. Here, as always, the priority is: First things first—that is, maximum opportunity for man to seek union with a God who seeks union with man. Dare the teacher inhibit in any way the relationship between God and those whom He loves? Dare the teacher impair or impede the growth of that relationship?

Christian teaching is—or ought to be—prophetic. The work of the prophet is to deliver God's message, not to edit it or to shape it to conform to the messenger's own viewpoint. The message, if truly God's, is always straightforward and emphatic; its value content is directly applicable. And always the message is sent when shoddy and superficial and selfish values confuse and pollute real values. Thus the prophet, thus the message. The message is to strip away the crust of nonsense, to return freshly to the clear invitation of God to life. The message is meant to realign priorities. It seems evident, in this time of value confusion, that we need prophets.

But, alas, the prophet finds himself in conflict with other voices, other priorities, other power sources. (If all were going right in the relationship between God and his people, why the prophet?) This clash between God's desire for human good and the status quo is the reason the prophets of Scripture so often tried to beg off God's call. No prophet was ever popular. Rather, the prophet risked—and usually realized—rejection, harm, even death.

If the teacher is prophet, he assumes the role knowing full well that the message is God's own, not his. And despite some degree of risk, he knows he is filled with power, filled with the Spirit of God, the Spirit of Truth. And because he is a Christian teacher, he knows everything proceeds from one central value teaching: God is love, love is everything. Every other value flows from this life principle. Thus, Saint Augustine said: "Love, and do what you will." Jesus more specifically set the value priority this way: Love God, love your neighbor, love yourself. (Without some awareness of being loved or lovable, love of God and love of neighbor are all but impossible.)

One thing is clear: No teacher of Christian values can do the job well unless he is aware of and comfortable with the full Christian value system, unless he is sorting and structuring his own values and their priorities. He must be aware of what exactly is at the core of Christian faith-life, what contributes to his own growth toward God, what helps him to act, what moves him closer to community with his fellow Christians. And too, he must sort out and diminish those superficial beliefs (more likely superstitions) and actions (or nonactions) that retard or prevent growth toward God and community.

A very fine circumstance for the teacher to test, clarify, and realign his Christian values would be in community with his fellow religion teachers. Some sort of programmed coming together of teachers ought to be deliberately inserted into the school-year plan. Without this opportunity to live his own values in community, the Christian teacher may never test and live those values that he professes. And it would be doubtful, short of this testing or some other, that he is ready, really, to work with young Christians and their need for values.

Three Ways To Teach Church School

by Sidney B. Simon

From *Colloquy*, January 1970. Used by permission.

So much teaching, even colorful, dynamic, and flamboyant teaching, never gets beyond the "facts" level. I remember a college physics professor who stunned his audience one day. In a crowded, tiered lecture hall he suspended a giant steel ball on a thin cable. He dragged the ball up to the top row, held it against his nose with the cable taut, and let it go. Then he stood there, waiting, while the ball reached the end of its arc and headed back toward his nose. The class gasped as the ball approached, closer and closer, ready to knock him over. Of course, the law of physics prevailed and the ball stopped just short of clobbering him in the head. The class learned a fact: A pendulum loses inertia with each swing. That fact would appear on a true and false question on the midterm exam. It was an important but isolated fact and in a sense a "so what?" fact. Despite the sheer drama of his teaching, this professor was still operating on the facts level, the lowest of the three levels of teaching.

The second and higher level is the "concepts level." Here, a series of facts is linked and generalizations drawn from them. At the concepts level, there are fewer multiple-choice and short-answer tests. A teacher is more likely to use essay questions to evaluate the learning. This is obviously more complex teaching and more exciting learning. As a parent, I would be quite happy if all of my children's teachers moved beyond the facts level and taught at the concepts level. (The millennium, however, is many light years away. Another law of inertia and one my physics instructor didn't understand.)

Concepts-level teaching is very good teaching, but there is still a more desirable kind of teaching at a third level. It may be the most important level of all. It is what I call values-level teaching. It directly involves a student in examining his own values. It asks many "you-centered" questions and insists that the student confront issues suggested by the content. These issues should involve him in choices which are relevant to his day-to-day life.

Can this third level of teaching be done with the typical content of a typical church school course? I would answer with a resounding yes. Not only can it be done, it must be done if we are to make of church school more than a once-a-week platter of platitudes.

TWO EXAMPLES

The Trimphant Entry into Jerusalem (Mark 11:1-19; Luke 19:28-40)

Facts Level:
1. What instructions did Jesus give his two disciples?
2. Did it go just as Jesus said it would go?
3. What was the reaction of the Pharisees to the large crowd of Jesus' disciples who were praising him?
4. How did Jesus answer the Pharisees?

Concepts Level:
1. What is the meaning of Jesus riding into the city of Jerusalem on an ass?
2. What were the people who threw palm branches before him expecting to have happen?
3. What are the important distinctions between the Pharisees and the disciples?

Values Level:
1. Would you have been able to turn over the tables of money changers in the temple? Wasn't this violent and destructive of private property? Is this anything like the cases of students who force deans out of their offices? Or like the cases of persons who burn draft board files? Have you ever participated in an act that destroyed

property? Name a time when you feel you could do so.

2. The disciples seemed to have no embarrassment about demonstrating their beliefs in public. How easy is it for you to announce to anyone what you believe when it is unpopular or you might be punished for doing so? Have you ever participated in a demonstration for civil rights or to end the war in Vietnam? Why? What kind of demonstrations do you think are acceptable? When should people participate in a demonstration?

These values questions are merely suggestive. Other teachers might be interested in using the story to get at a whole different range of values questions. Important, however, is the idea that the third level of teaching always focuses on the "you" and is relevant to the student's life. There should not be any effort made to have every student come out with a single set of "right" values. Values are very complex and very personal; there are no "right" values.

Saint Francis of Assisi

Facts Level:

1. What was Saint Francis' real name? Where and when was he born?

2. What were the events which led up to his turning over his old life?

3. What were his father's reactions?

4. What kind of clothes did Saint Francis wear? What did they represent?

5. How did Pope Innocent III react to all of this?

6. Why is Saint Francis almost always pictured with birds nearby?

7. Did he die of leprosy?

Concepts Level:

1. How far apart were the lives of the poor and the rich in the early thirteenth century when Saint Francis lived?

Saint Francis claimed that he was married to "Lady Poverty." Why was this such an unorthodox statement for a man of God to make at that time? What else was unorthodox about Saint Francis?

2. Pope Innocent had a real dilemma in dealing with Saint Francis. What were the issues surrounding the pope's problem?

3. How do you explain the rapid spread of the Franciscans?

4. Saint Francis literally worked himself to death, and even upon dying he thanked his Lord. Can you explain that?

5. What was Saint Francis' contribution to the church and why did he earn a place in its history?

Values Level:

1. How near do the poor live to you? How much concern should you have about their poverty? Have you ever done anything about it? Can anything be done? By you? If not you, by whom?

2. Do you know your own father well enough to know his reaction if you were to do what Saint Francis did? Explain.

3. Saint Francis was able to get through to the pope. What would you try to get the pope to accept if you were able to reach him? Would your writing a letter do any good? Explain.

4. Many men today also work themselves to death. Many others have ulcers, or smoke or drink too much because of their work. What does that say to you about your own life? What are you going to do about it?

Almost any subject matter can be viewed at the three levels discussed in this article. If we examine the teaching in our church schools, I am afraid we will find entirely too much on the first level. Facts are important. You can't build concepts without them. You can't make values choices without first examining as many alternatives as possible, and alternatives grow out of facts. What is needed, though, is more effort to go beyond the facts level. And beyond the concepts level. We need more content to confront students where they live. As we do, we turn church schools into something much more viable and relevant. It could also help us teachers to clarify our own values. Not bad, for a Sunday morning. Even sleeping late couldn't feel as good.

Value Clarification: New Mission for Religious Education

by Sidney B. Simon, Patricia Daitch, and Marie Hartwell

Reprinted with permission from the *Catechist;* copyright 1971 by Pflaum/Standard.

What They Are Saying to Themselves	What They Say Out Loud
I'm confused about what faith really means for me.	*Mark:* What is the story of Thomas about anyway? I mean, what are we supposed to get out of it?
Let's stick to the story.	*Teacher:* Well, it has something to do with the nature of faith. What did his experience teach Thomas?
	Mark: It showed him that Christ really did exist and would come to him even though he had doubted.
You haven't guessed my answer yet. Try again!	*Teacher:* Yes, but is that the most important part of the story?

Jane: At the end Christ says, "Blessed are they who have not seen and yet have believed."

Teacher: Good, and how would you tie that into the story?

Do people — do I — really feel that way?

Jane: That you have more faith if you can believe even though you haven't seen.

Mike: Yeah, faith is not dependent upon physical reality.

Let's not get carried away. This is 1971, not the year one. Things are different for me.

Carol: But wait a minute. I think Thomas was sharp. Today he would be a brilliant scientist. He just wanted to get the facts in before he made a decision.

Help!

Teacher: Good point. But is a scientist necessarily without faith?

Our Observations: There is an honest teacher-pupil relationship; very open and apparent. The teacher opens a door for exploration, but unfortunately only in an intellectual way, relating to the story instead of to the student. The kids support and help each other. There is a good classroom atmosphere.

This is not a bad classroom discussion. There are, however, important issues being implied and sometimes raised that are not being dealt with. The students are trying to use the story as a point of departure to discuss and explore their own beliefs, doubts, and attitudes. The

teacher does not seem willing to deal with these issues.
She steers the discussion back to the concepts as they
relate to the story and as the story relates to doctrine.

This maneuver is unfortunate, for her classroom contains
some of the most important elements for beginning the
process of discovering values: 1) the atmosphere is
supportive rather than critical; 2) despite the teacher's
evident manipulation of the discussion towards her own
preconceived idea of what is true and appropriate, there
is an open atmosphere that tolerates different views;
and 3) the students are interested in their values, and
they understand that content stories can lead into value
programs.

Had the teacher asked a different sort of question, she
would have steered the discussion to meet the needs and
concerns of her students. She might have asked questions
similar to these:

1. What are three things you believe in, with absolute faith,
though they may never be tested or proved?
2. Have you ever trusted someone's judgment only to
discover that you have been made a fool? How did you feel?
What did you do about it?
3. What have you learned in science this year that supports
your faith in God? How does it support your belief?
4. Who is the person in your life you trust the most? Why?[1]

These questions deliberately address themselves to serious
values issues being raised—issues that are not irrelevant to
the subject matter, but are at the heart of it. Students
should and do grapple with them. Whether or not this is a
careful and open process is the decision of educators....

But why should a teacher deliberately steer or allow a
discussion to range into the area of value exploration? In
these days of great confusion and conflict, when it is
difficult for people to find meaning for their lives, most
students will benefit from value-clarifying experiences.
*Values are the basis on which a sense of worth and identity
is shaped and cultivated.*

A student's self-concept is often small and uncertain, but
it can be strengthened by the value-clarifying process.
When the process becomes an inherent facet of an
individual's life, he is more purposeful, more able to make

choices and moral decisions, and more able to develop meaningful relationships with others. Certainly this is well within the province of religious education....

The basic assumption of this series is that all men have values and beliefs that guide and control their moral actions. We believe, then, that one role of religious education is to help a student examine his life and to help him to shape and to build a personal set of values....

The most natural and obvious place to look for this connection is in the life of Christ Jesus himself. One of the reasons that Christ's message had such impact was that he had a set of clear and unselfish values and that he acted on those values consistently and openly. He preached brotherly love and equality before God. More important, in practice he befriended prostitutes and lepers as well as the poor. He even included in his most trusted group of followers a generally hated tax collector, recognizing Levi's potential for good.

Jesus did not hesitate to speak to high officials with the same candor and conviction that he used with the general populace — a trait that won him the awe and respect even of those who would be his enemies. The Pharisees and Sadduccees (as in Matthew 22) tried on numerous occasions to find inconsistencies in Christ's preaching or practice but without success.

All of this contributed to Jesus' credibility. In effect, he built a secure and steadfast value system that was constantly and publicly affirmed. He was — and is — an ideal behavioral model for all men.

Jesus did not only say that you *should* forgive others the wrongs they do to you or that you *should* recognize the equality of all men. He did what he preached. Thus his message was absolutely clear.

That message is no less clear for contemporary man. Not only Christ's words, but his very life-style has meaning for us. It is one thing to sit at home and agree that something *should* be done about pollution, that we *ought* to love our neighbors, that we *should* make an effort to elect and to support honest government officials. It is quite another thing to take positive and constructive action on these beliefs. This imperative, of course, is important for

Christians as private citizens. But it is especially important for teachers who serve as *models* as well as *instructors* in Christian life.

But what implications does this have for teaching values in the schools? We want to suggest that an important distinction must be made between *belief* and *action*. Having a good moral sense of right and wrong is important. It also is important to act out these attitudes.

We make this distinction in terms of value indicators and actual values. An attitude or belief does not become a clarified value until it is acted upon, publicly and regularly. These are demanding criteria. Thus it seems evident that most people have very few values. Our theory states that people with very few values tend to be conforming, apathetic, inconsistent, and often very ambivalent — all of which seems quite logical when you realize the extent to which values do guide a man's life.

While it is the ultimate goal of our program to develop strong values, it would be a mistake to discount totally the importance of value indicators. They are an essential part of man's moral character. A firm system of beliefs must be developed before action *can* be taken. Furthermore, each individual must make decisions about which beliefs he can act upon.

A person who has a strong system of beliefs will be better able to develop active values when the need arises. A very simple example: The child who truly believes that honesty is the best policy will be less likely to shoplift if the opportunity to do so presents itself. A child who grows up believing in the commandment to "love your neighbor" is more likely to accept people and customs different from those of his own family....

Students no longer will accept single definitions of standards of behavior, values, and mores when they are presented as dogma. The media have provided them with the many alternatives, each presented in an attractive and inviting way. How can we help our students to discover which of the alternatives is best for them?...

Value inquiry is based on a very specific pattern.

Step 1 — *Elicit* information and spontaneous responses from students about themselves.

Step 2 — *Accept* their responses genuinely. The object is to get the students to reveal themselves without fear of being judged.

Step 3 — *Push* the student toward more honesty and more commitment. Ask questions that will encourage him to examine more closely what he has said about himself.

Step 4 — *Accept* whatever comes out of Step 3 if you want that kind of honesty to continue.

But aren't there any absolute values that we can teach our students? Many of our readers undoubtedly ask this question.

We would allow that there are certain absolutes essential to Christian education: belief in God, the Resurrection of Christ, the Holy Spirit, and the veracity of the Ten Commandments, to name a few. But there are really far fewer immutable and absolute values than most of us realize. What students need most is not a list of the values of today but a process for finding new expressions of values that are yet to come. This is what value training is all about.

NOTE

1. For the theoretical background for these questions, see: *Values and Teaching* by Louis E. Raths, Merrill Harmin, and Sidney B. Simon (Columbus, Ohio: Charles E. Merrill Publishing Co., 1966).

Values in the Family

INTRODUCTION

The first article in this section, "The Split-Level American Family," documents the changing nature of the American family—its gradual loss of influence over the development of young people and the simultaneous gain in influence by television and by the peer group. We think it is a thought-provoking piece, but the question remains: What are families to do about this gradual erosion of their influence in the lives of their children?

Some families throw up their hands in despair and hope that the churches or schools will somehow teach their children how to live in a complex world. But many, if not most, families are not satisfied with such a laissez-faire attitude. In the late 1960s and 1970s, there has been an enormous rise in popularity of various adult and inter-age educational programs such as "Parent Effectiveness Training," "Conjoint Family Therapy," "Family Communications Workshops," "Family Encounter Groups," and the like. These structured programs are designed to build more effective human relationships in the family—relationships in which parents, while no longer dictating the lives of their children, can still be of help and support to them in their overall development.

Values clarification, too, can be used in the context of the family. In the four articles by Kirschenbaum and Simon presented in this section, numerous practical alternatives are offered to parents and children for helping each other in their individual search and in the family's search for satisfying values.

The Split-Level American Family

by Urie Bronfenbrenner

Children used to be brought up by their parents.

It may seem presumptuous to put that statement in the past tense. Yet it belongs to the past. Why? Because *de facto* responsibility for upbringing has shifted away from the family to other settings in the society, where the task is not always recognized or accepted. While the family still has the primary moral and legal responsibility for developing character in children, the power or opportunity to do the job is often lacking in the home, primarily because parents and children no longer spend enough time together in those situations in which such training is possible. This is not because parents don't want to spend time with their children. It is simply that conditions of life have changed.

To begin with, families used to be bigger—not in terms of more children so much as more adults—grandparents, uncles, aunts, cousins. Those relatives who didn't live with you lived nearby. You often went to their houses. They came as often to yours, and stayed for dinner. You knew them all—the old folks, the middle-aged, the older cousins. And they knew you. This had its good side and its bad side.

On the good side, some of these relatives were interesting people, or so you thought at the time. Uncle Charlie had been

to China. Aunt Sue made the best penuche fudge on the
block. Cousin Bill could read people's minds (according to
him). And all these relatives gave you Christmas presents.

But there was the other side. You had to give Christmas
presents to all your relatives. And they all minded your
business throughout the years. They wanted to know where
you had been, where you were going, and why. If they didn't
like your answers, they said so (particularly if you had told
them the truth).

Not just your relatives minded your business. Everybody in
the neighborhood did. Again this had its two sides.

If you walked on the railroad trestle, the phone would ring
at your house. Your parents would know what you had done
before you got back home. People on the street would tell you
to button your jacket, and ask why you weren't in church
last Sunday.

But you also had the run of the neighborhood. You were
allowed to play in the park. You could go into any store,
whether you bought anything or not. They would let you
go back of the store to watch them unpack the cartons and
to hope that a carton would break. At the lumber yard, they
let you pick up good scraps of wood. At the newspaper office,
you could punch the linotype and burn your hand on the
slugs of hot lead. And at the railroad station (they had
railroad stations then), you could press the telegraph key
and know that the telegraphers heard your dit-dah-dah
all the way to Chicago.

These memories of a gone boyhood have been documented
systematically in the research of Professor Herbert Wright
and his associates at the University of Kansas. The
Midwestern investigators have compared the daily life of
children growing up in a small town with the lives of
children living in a modern city or suburb. The contrast
is sobering. Children in a small town get to know well a
substantially greater number of adults in different walks of
life and, in contrast to their urban and suburban agemates,
are more likely to be active participants in the adult settings
that they enter.

As the stable world of the small town has become absorbed
into an ever-shifting suburbia, children are growing up in a
different kind of environment. Urbanization has reduced
the extended family to a nuclear one with only two adults,

and the functioning neighborhood—where it has not decayed
into an urban or rural slum—has withered to a small circle
of friends, most of them accessible only by car or telephone.
Whereas the world in which the child lived before consisted
of a diversity of people in a diversity of settings, now for
millions of American children the neighborhood is nothing
but row upon row of buildings inhabited by strangers. One
house, or apartment, is much like another, and so are the
people. They all have about the same income and the same
way of life. And the child doesn't even see much of that, for
all the adults in the neighborhood do is come home, have a
drink, eat dinner, mow the lawn, watch TV, and sleep.
Increasingly often, today's housing projects have no stores,
no shops, no services, no adults at work or play. This is the
sterile world in which many of our children grow, the
"urban renewal" we offer to the families we would rescue
from the slums.

Neighborhood experiences available to children are
extremely limited nowadays. To do anything at all—go to a
movie, get an ice cream cone, go swimming, or play ball—they
have to travel by bus or private car. Rarely can a child
watch adults working at their trades. Mechanics, tailors, or
shopkeepers are either out of sight or unapproachable.
A child cannot listen to gossip at the post office as he once did.
And there are no abandoned houses, barns, or attics to break
into. From a young point of view, it's a dull world.

Hardly any of this really matters, for children aren't home
much, anyway. A child leaves the house early in the day, on a
schoolbound bus, and it's almost suppertime when he gets
back. There may not be anybody home when he gets there.
If his mother isn't working, at least part-time (more than
a third of all mothers are), she's out a lot—because of social
obligations, not just friends—doing things for the community.
The child's father leaves home in the morning before the child
does. It takes the father an hour and a half to get to work.
He's often away weekends, not to mention absences
during the week.

If a child is not with his parents or other adults, with whom
does he spend his time? With other kids, of course—in school,
after school, over weekends, on holidays. In these
relationships, he is further restricted to children of his own
age and the same socioeconomic background. The pattern was

set when the old neighborhood school was abandoned as inefficient. Consolidated schools brought homogeneous grouping by age, and the homogenizing process more recently has been extended to segregate children by level of ability; consequently, from the preschool years onward the child is dealing principally with replicas of the stamp of his own environment. Whereas social invitations used to be extended to entire families on a neighborhood basis, the cocktail party nowadays has its segregated equivalent for every age group down to the toddlers.

It doesn't take the children very long to learn the lesson adults teach: Latch onto your peers. But to latch he must contend with a practical problem. He must hitch a ride. Anyone going in the right direction can take him. But if no one is going in that direction just then, the child can't get there.

The child who can't go somewhere else stays home and does what everybody else does at home. He watches TV. Studies indicate that American youngsters see more TV than children in any other country do. By the late 1950s, the TV-watching figure had risen to two hours a day for the average five year old, three hours a day during the watching peak age of twelve to fourteen years.

In short, whereas American children used to spend much of their time with parents and other grownups, more and more waking hours are now lived in the world of peers and of the television screen.

What do we know about the influence of the peer group, or of television, on the lives of young children? Not much.

The prevailing view in American society (indeed in the West generally) holds that the child's psychological development, to the extent that it is susceptible to environmental influence, is determined almost entirely by the parents and within the first six years of life. Scientific investigators—who are, of course, products of their own culture, imbued with its tacit assumptions about human nature—have acted accordingly. Western studies of influences on personality development in childhood overwhelmingly take the form of research on parent-child relations; the peer group or other extraparental influences are scarcely being considered.

In other cultures, this is not always so. A year ago, at the International Congress of Psychology in Moscow, it was my privilege to chair a symposium on "Social Factors in Personality Development." Of a score of papers presented, about half were from the West (mostly American) and half from the Socialist countries (mostly Russian). Virtually without exception, the Western reports dealt with parent-child relationships; those from the Soviet Union and other East European countries focused equally exclusively on the influence of the peer group, or, as they call it, the children's collective.

Some relevant studies have been carried out in our own society. For example, I, with others, have done research on a sample of American adolescents from middle-class families. We have found that children who reported their parents away from home for long periods of time rated significantly lower on such characteristics as responsibility and leadership. Perhaps because it was more pronounced, absence of the father was more critical than that of the mother, particularly in its effect on boys. Similar results have been reported in studies of the effects of father absence among soldiers' families during World War II, in homes of Norwegian sailors and whalers, and in Negro households with missing fathers both in the West Indies and the United States. In general, father absence contributes to low motivation for achievement, inability to defer immediate for later gratification, low self-esteem, susceptibility to group influence and juvenile delinquency. All of these effects are much more marked for boys than for girls.

The fact that father absence increases susceptibility to group influence leads us directly to the question of the impact of the peer group on the child's attitude and behavior. The first—and as yet the only—comprehensive research on this question was carried out by two University of North Carolina sociologists, Charles Bowerman and John Kinch, in 1959. Working with a sample of several hundred students from the fourth to the tenth grades in the Seattle school system, these investigators studied age trends in the tendency of children to turn to parents versus peers for opinion, advice, or company in various activities. In general, there was a turning point at about the seventh grade. Before that, the majority looked mainly to their parents as models, companions, and guides to behavior; thereafter, the children's peers had equal or greater influence.

Though I can cite no documentation from similar investigations since then, I suspect the shift comes earlier now and is more pronounced.

In the early 1960s, the power of the peer group was documented even more dramatically by James Coleman in his book *The Adolescent Society.* Coleman investigated the values and behaviors of teenagers in eight large American high schools. He reported that the aspirations and actions of American adolescents were primarily determined by the "leading crowd" in the school society. For boys in this leading crowd, the hallmark of success was glory in athletics; for girls, it was the popular date.

Intellectual achievement was, at best, a secondary value. The most intellectually able students were not those getting the best grades. The classroom wasn't where the action was. The students who did well were "not really those of highest intelligence, but only the ones who were willing to work hard at a relatively unrewarded activity."

The most comprehensive study relevant to the subject of our concern here was completed only a year ago by the same James Coleman. The data were obtained from more than 600,000 children in grades one to twelve in 4,000 schools carefully selected as representative of public education in the United States. An attempt was made to assess the relative contribution to the child's intellectual development (as measured by standardized intelligence and achievement tests) of the following factors: 1) family background (e.g., parents' education, family size, presence in the home of reading materials, records, etc.); 2) school characteristics (e.g., per pupil expenditure, classroom size, laboratory and library facilities, etc.); 3) teacher characteristics (e.g., background, training, years of experience, verbal skills, etc.); and 4) characteristics of other children in the same school (e.g., their background academic achievement, career plans, etc.).

Of the many findings of the study, two were particularly impressive; the first was entirely expected, the second somewhat surprising. The expected finding was that home background was the most important element in determining how well the child did at school, more important than any of all aspects of the school which the child attended. This generalization, while especially true for Northern whites, applies to a lesser degree to Southern whites and Northern Negroes, and was actually reversed for Southern Negroes, for whom the characteristics of the school were more important than those of the home. The child apparently drew sustenance from wherever sustenance was most available. Where the home had most to offer, the home was the most determining; but where the school could provide more stimulation than the home, the school was the more influential factor.

The second major conclusion concerned the aspects of the school environment which contributed most to the child's intellectual achievement. Surprisingly enough, such items as per pupil expenditure, number of children per class, laboratory space, number of volumes in the school library, and the presence or absence of ability grouping were of negligible significance. Teacher qualifications accounted for some of the child's achievement. But by far the most important factor was the pattern of characteristics of the other children attending the same school. Specifically, if a lower-class child had schoolmates who came from advantaged homes, he did reasonably well; but if all the other children also came from deprived backgrounds, he did poorly.

What about the other side of the story? What happens to a middle-class child in a predominantly lower-class school? Is he pulled down by his classmates? According to Coleman's data, the answer is no; the performance of the advantaged children remains unaffected. It is as though good home background had immunized them against the possibility of contagion.

This is the picture so far as academic achievement is concerned. How about other aspects of psychological development? Specifically, how about social behavior—such qualities as responsibility, consideration for others, or at the opposite pole, aggressiveness or delinquent behavior? How are these affected by the child's peer group?

The Coleman study obtained no data on this score. Some light has been shed on the problem, however, by an experiment which my Cornell colleagues and I recently carried out with school children in the United States and in the Soviet Union. Working with a sample of more than 150 sixth-graders (from six classrooms) in each country, we placed the children in situations in which we could test their readiness to engage in morally disapproved behavior such as cheating on a test, denying responsibility for property damage, etc. The results indicated that American children were far more ready to take part in such actions.

The effect of the peer group (friends in school) was quite different in the two societies. When told that their friends would know of their actions, American children were even more willing to engage in misconduct. Soviet youngsters showed just the opposite tendency. In their case, the peer group operated to support the values of the adult society, at least at their age level.

We believe these contrasting results are explained in part by the differing role of the peer group in the two societies. In the Soviet Union, *vospitanie*, or character development, is regarded as an integral part of the process of education, and its principal agent — even more important than the family — is the child's collective in school and out. A major goal of the Soviet educational process, beginning in the nursery, is "to forge a healthy, self-sufficient collective" which, in turn, has the task of developing the child into a responsible, altruistic, and loyal member of a socialist society. In contrast, in the United States, the peer group is often an autonomous agent relatively free from adult control and uncommitted — if not outrightly opposed — to the values and codes of conduct approved by society at large. Witness the new phenomenon of American middle-class vandalism and juvenile delinquency, with crime rates increasing rapidly not only for teenagers but for younger children as well.

How early in life are children susceptible to the effects of contagion? Professor Albert Bandura and his colleagues at Stanford University have conducted some experiments which suggest that the process is well developed at the preschool level. The basic experimental design involves the following elements. The child finds himself in a familiar playroom. As if by chance, in another corner of the room a person is playing with toys. Sometimes this person is an adult (teacher), sometimes another child. This other person behaves very aggressively. He strikes a large Bobo doll (a bouncing inflated figure), throws objects, and mutilates dolls and animal toys, with appropriate language to match. Later on, the experimental subject (i.e., the child who "accidentally" observed the aggressive behavior) is tested by being allowed to play in a room containing a variety of toys, including some similar to those employed by the aggressive model. With no provocation, perfectly normal, well-adjusted preschoolers engage in aggressive acts, not only repeating what they had observed but elaborating on it. Moreover, the words and gestures accompanying the actions leave no doubt that the child is living through an emotional experience of aggressive expression.

It is inconvenient to use a live model every time. Thus it occurred to Bandura to make a film. In fact, he made two, one with a live model and a second film of a cartoon cat that said and did everything the live model had said and done. The films were presented on a TV set left on in a corner of the room, as if by accident. When the children were tested, the TV cartoon turned out to be just as effective as the film using real people. The cat aroused as much aggression as the human model.

As soon as Bandura's work was published, the television industry issued a statement calling his conclusions into question on the interesting ground that the children had been studied "in a highly artificial situation," since no parents were present either when the TV was on or when the aggressive behavior was observed. "What a child will do under normal conditions cannot be projected from his behavior when he is carefully isolated from normal conditions and the influences of society," the statement declared. Bandura was also criticized for using a Bobo doll (which, the TV people said, is "made to be struck") and for failing to follow up his subjects after they left the laboratory. Since then, Bandura has shown that only a ten-minute exposure to an aggressive model still differentiates children in the experimental group from their controls (children not subjected to the experiment) six months later.

Evidence for the relevance of Bandura's laboratory findings to real life comes from a subsequent field study by Dr. Leonard Eron, now at the University of Iowa. In a sample of more than 600 third-graders, Dr. Eron found that the children who were rated most aggressive by their classmates were those who watched TV programs involving a high degree of violence.

At what age do people become immune from contagion to

violence on the screen? Professor Richard Walters of
Waterloo University in Canada and his associate, Dr.
Llewellyn Thomas, showed two movie films to a group of
thirty-four-year-old hospital attendants. Half of these adults
were shown a knife fight between two teenagers from the
picture, *Rebel Without a Cause;* the other half saw a film
depicting adolescents engaged in art work. Subsequently, all
the attendants were asked to assist in carrying out an
experiment on the effects of punishment in learning.

In the experiment, the attendants gave an unseen subject
an electric shock every time the subject made an error. The
lever for giving shocks had settings from zero to ten. To be
sure the assistant understood what the shocks were like,
he was given several, not exceeding the level of four, before
the experiment. Since nothing was said about the level of
shocks to be administered, each assistant was left to make
his own choice. The hospital attendants who had seen the
knife-fight film gave significantly more severe shocks than
those who had seen the art-work film. The same experiment
was repeated with a group of twenty-year-old females.
This time the sound track was turned off, so only visual cues
were present. But neither the silence nor the difference in sex
weakened the effect. The young women who had seen the
aggressive film administered more painful shocks.

These results led designers of the experiment to wonder
what would happen if no film were shown and no other
deliberate incitement were introduced in the immediate
setting of the experiment. Would the continuing emotional
pressures of the everyday environment of adolescents — who
see more movies and more TV and are called on to display
virility through aggressive acts in teenage gangs — provoke
latent brutality comparable to that exhibited by the older
people under direct stimulation of the movie of the knife fight?

Fifteen-year-old high school boys were used to test the
answer to this question. Without the suggestive power of the
aggressive film to step up their feelings, they pulled the
shock lever to its highest intensities (levels eight to ten). A
few of the boys made such remarks as "I bet I made
that fellow jump."

Finally, utilizing a similar technique in a variant of what
has come to be known as the "Eichmann experiment,"
Professor Stanley Milgram, then at Yale University, set up

a situation in which the level of shock to be administered was determined by the lowest level proposed by any one of three "assistants," two of whom were confederates of Milgram and were instructed to call for increasingly higher shocks. Even though the true subjects (all adult males) could have kept the intensity to a minimum simply by stipulating mild shocks, they responded to the confederates' needling and increased the degree of pain they administered.

All of these experiments point to one conclusion. At all age levels, pressure from peers to engage in aggressive behavior is extremely difficult to resist, at least in American society.

Now if the peer group can propel its members into antisocial acts, what about the opposite possibility? Can peers also be a force for inducing constructive behavior?

Evidence on this point is not so plentiful, but some relevant data exist. To begin with, experiments on conformity to group pressure have shown that the presence of a single dissenter—for example, one "assistant" who refuses to give a severe shock—can be enough to break the spell so that the subject no longer follows the majority. But the only research explicitly directed at producing moral conduct as a function of group experience is a study conducted by Muzafer Sherif and his colleagues at the University of Oklahoma and known as the "Robber's Cave Experiment." In the words of Elton B. McNeil:

> War was declared at Robber's Cave, Oklahoma, in the summer of 1954 (Sherif *et al.*, 1961). Of course, if you have seen one war you have seen them all, but this was an interesting war, as wars go, because only the observers knew what the fighting was about. How, then, did this war differ from any other war? This one was caused, conducted, and concluded by behavioral scientists. After years of religious, political, and economic wars, this was, perhaps, the first scientific war. It wasn't the kind of war that an adventurer could join just for the thrill of it. To be eligible, ideally, you had to be an eleven-year-old, middle-class, American, Protestant, well-adjusted boy who was willing to go to an experimental camp.

Sherif and his associates wanted to demonstrate that within the space of a few weeks they could produce two contrasting patterns of behavior in this group of normal children. First, they could bring the group to a state of intense hostility

and then completely reverse the process by inducing a spirit
of warm friendship and active cooperation. The success
of their efforts can be gauged by the following two excerpts
describing the behavior of the boys after each stage had
been reached. After the first experimental treatment of
the situation was introduced...

> ...good feeling soon evaporated. The members of each group
> began to call their rivals "stinkers," "sneaks," and "cheaters."
> They refused to have anything more to do with individuals
> in the opposing group. The boys...turned against buddies
> whom they had chosen as "best friends" when they first
> arrived at the camp. A large proportion of the boys in each
> group gave negative ratings to all the boys in the other.
> The rival groups made threatening posters and planned raids,
> collecting secret hoards of green apples for ammunition.
> To the Robber's Cave came the Eagles, after a defeat in a
> tournament game, and burned a banner left behind by the
> Rattlers; the next morning the Rattlers seized the Eagles'
> flag when they arrived on the athletic field. From that time on
> name-calling, scuffles, and raids were the rule of the day.
> ...In the dining-hall line they shoved each other aside, and
> the group that lost the contest for the head of the line
> shouted "Ladies first!" at the winner. They threw paper,
> food, and vile names at each other at the tables. An Eagle
> bumped by a Rattler was admonished by his fellow Eagles to
> brush "the dirt" off his clothes.

But after the second experimental treatment...

> The members of the two groups began to feel more friendly to
> each other. For example, a Rattler whom the Eagles disliked
> for his sharp tongue and skill in defeating them became
> a "good egg." The boys stopped shoving in the meal line.
> They no longer called each other names, and sat together at
> the table. New friendships developed between individuals
> in the two groups.
>
> In the end the groups were actively seeking opportunities
> to mingle, to entertain, and "treat" each other. They decided
> to hold a joint campfire. They took turns presenting skits and
> songs. Members of both groups requested that they go home
> together on the same bus, rather than on the separate
> buses in which they had come. On the way the bus stopped for
> refreshments. One group still had five dollars which they

had won as a prize in a contest. They decided to spend this sum
on refreshments. On their own initiative they had invited
their former rivals to be their guests for malted milks.

How was each of these effects achieved? Treatment One
has a familiar ring:

> To produce friction between the groups of boys we arranged
> a tournament of games: baseball, touch football, a tug-of-war,
> a treasure hunt, and so on. The tournament started in a
> spirit of good sportsmanship. But as the play progressed
> good feeling soon evaporated.

How does one turn hatred into harmony? Before undertaking
this task, Sherif wanted to demonstrate that, contrary
to the view of some students of human conflict, mere
interaction—pleasant social contact between antagonists—
would not reduce hostility.

> ...We brought the hostile Rattlers and Eagles together
> for social events: going to the movies, eating in the same
> dining room, and so on. But far from reducing conflict, these
> situations only served as opportunities for the rival groups
> to berate and attack each other.

How was conflict finally dispelled? By a series of strategems,
of which the following is an example:

> ...Water came to our camp in pipes from a tank about
> a mile away. We arranged to interrupt it and then called the
> boys together to inform them of the crisis. Both groups
> promptly volunteered to search the water line for trouble.
> They worked together harmoniously, and before the end of
> the afternoon they had located and corrected the difficulty.

On another occasion, just when everyone was hungry and
the camp truck was about to go to town for food, it developed
that the engine wouldn't start, and the boys had to pull
together to get the vehicle going.

To move from practice to principle, the critical element for
achieving harmony in human relations, according to Sherif,
is joint activity in behalf of a *superordinate goal.* "Hostility
gives way when groups pull together to achieve overriding
goals which are real and compelling for all concerned."

Here, then, is the solution for the problems posed by
autonomous peer groups and rising rates of juvenile
delinquency: Confront the youngsters with some
superordinate goals, and everything will turn out fine.

What superordinate goals can we suggest? Washing dishes and emptying wastebaskets? Isn't it true that meaningful opportunities for children no longer exist?

This writer disagrees. Challenging activities for children can still be found; but their discovery requires breaking down the prevailing patterns of segregation identified earlier in this essay—segregation not merely by race (although this is part of the story) but to an almost equal degree by age, class, and ability. I am arguing for greater involvement of adults in the lives of children and, conversely, for greater involvement of children in the problems and tasks of the larger society.

We must begin by desegregating age groups, ability groups, social classes, and once again engaging children and adults in common activities. Here, as in Negro-white relations, integration is not enough. In line with Sherif's findings, contact between children and adults, or between advantaged and disadvantaged, will not of itself reduce hostility and evoke mutual affection and respect. What is needed in addition is involvement in a superordinate goal, common participation in a challenging job to be done.

Where is a job to be found that can involve children and adults across the dividing lines of race, ability, and social class?

Here is one possibility. Urbanization and industrialization have not done away with the need to care for the very young. To be sure, "progress" has brought us to the point where we seem to believe that only a person with a master's degree is truly qualified to care for young children. An exception is made for parents, and for babysitters, but these are concessions to practicality; we all know that professionals could do it better.

It is a strange doctrine. For if present-day knowledge of child development tells us anything at all, it tells us that the child develops psychologically as a function of reciprocal interaction with those who love him. This reciprocal interaction need be only of the most ordinary kind—caresses, looks, sounds, talking, singing, playing, reading stories—the things that parents, and everybody else, have done with children for generation after generation.

Contrary to the impression of many, our task in helping disadvantaged children through such programs as Head Start is not to have a "specialist" working with each child but to enable the child's parents, brothers, sisters, and all those around him to provide the kinds of stimulation which families ordinarily give children but which can fail to develop in the chaotic conditions of life in poverty. It is for this reason that Project Head Start places such heavy emphasis on the involvement of parents, not only in decision-making but in direct interaction with the children themselves, both at the center and (especially) at home. Not only parents but teenagers and older children are viewed as especially significant in work with the very young, for, in certain respects, older siblings can function more effectively than adults. The latter, no matter how warm and helpful they may be, are in an important sense in a world apart; their abilities, skills, and standards are so clearly superior to those of the child as to appear beyond childish grasp.

Here, then, is a context in which adults and children can pursue together a superordinate goal, for there is nothing so "real and compelling to all concerned" as the need of a young child for the care and attention of his elders. The difficulty is that we have not yet provided the opportunities—the institutional settings—which would make possible the recognition and pursuit of this superordinate goal.

The beginnings of such an opportunity structure, however, already exist in our society. As I have indicated, they are to be found in the poverty program, particularly those aspects of it dealing with children: Head Start, which involves parents, older children, and the whole community in the care of the very young; Follow Through, which extends Head Start into the elementary grades, thus breaking down the destructive wall between the school on the one hand and the parents in the local community on the other; Parent and Child Centers, which provide neighborhood centers where all generations can meet to engage in common activities in behalf of children, etc.

The need for such programs is not restricted to the nation's poor. So far as alienation of children is concerned, the world of the disadvantaged simply reflects in more severe form a social disease that has infected the entire society. The cure for the society as a whole is the same as that for its sickest segment. Head Start, Follow Through, and Parent and Child Centers are all needed by the middle class as much as by the less economically favored. Again, contrary to popular

impression, the principal purpose of these programs is no
remedial education but the giving to both children and their
families a sense of dignity, purpose, and meaningful activity
without which children cannot develop capacities in any
sphere of activity, including the intellectual.

Service to the very young is not the only superordinate
goal potentially available to children in our society. The very
old also need to be saved. In segregating them in their own
housing projects and, indeed, in whole communities, we have
deprived both the older and the younger generations of an
essential human experience. We need to find ways in which
children once again can assist and comfort old people and, in
return, gain insight to character development that occurs
through such experience.

Participation in constructive activities on behalf of others
will also reduce the growing tendency to aggressive and
antisocial behavior in the young, if only by diversion from
such actions and from the stimuli that instigate them. But so
long as these stimuli continue to dominate the TV screen,
those exposed to TV can be expected to react to the influence.
Nor, as we have seen, is it likely that the TV industry will
be responsive to the findings of research or the arguments of
concerned parents and professionals. The only measure that
is likely to be effective is pressure where it hurts most.
The sponsor must be informed that his product will be
boycotted until programming is changed.

My proposals for child rearing in the future may appear to
some as a pipedream, but they need not be a dream. For just
as autonomy and aggression have their roots in the American
tradition, so have neighborliness, civic concern, and devotion
to the young. By reexploring these, we can rediscover our
moral identity as a society and as a nation.

Clarifying Values at the Family Table

by Howard Kirschenbaum

Reprinted by permission of the author and the Adirondack Mountain Humanistic Education Center, Upper Jay, New York 12987.

How would you describe the scene at your family dinner table? What is the room like? How does the table look? How many people usually sit at the table? Where do they sit? How long does the meal last? What is the conversation like? How would you describe the atmosphere? Which of the following situations occur too frequently to suit you?

Everyone talks, no one listens. Stories go uncompleted. Interruptions are frequent.

No one seems to have much to say. A heavy, sometimes tension-filled silence often hangs in the air.

One person dominates the conversation. The knowledge that he or she may begin a long lecture or interrupt at any time puts a damper on the conversation.

Everyone sits down and immediately begins eating. There's no sense of togetherness. It's each person in his own private world, except when passing the butter or answering a question.

The parents' conversation is witty and lively. The children listen obediently, but are rarely included in the conversation, except to occasionally answer a question posed by the parents.

Everyone begins eating so fast that there's no time
to appreciate the food—its cook, its smell, its taste, or
its very presence in a world where many are starving.

Every discussion turns into an argument. No one seems
to want to or know how to hear another person's point
of view.

The children dash away from the table as soon as they
are finished eating. They don't feel there is anything
worth staying for.

We see these situations often. Not in every home. Not all
the time in any one home. Yet often. Parents and children
rarely voice it, but they all want the family meal to be more
special than it is—more fun, more caring, more interesting.

No one technique can completely change a family's way of
relating to each other. Caring, helping, and listening cannot
be simulated or learned overnight. They are attitudes and
skills which take years to grow and deepen. Nevertheless,
there is something that families can begin doing *today*
which can help them grow together. It is a way to make the
family meal more lively and interesting, to help each member
become clearer about his own values and sense of identity.
It's called the Family Circle strategy.

The Family Circle is really a very simple procedure. First,
after all the food is placed on the table and everyone is seated,
everyone holds hands around the table. One member of the
family, *not necessarily a parent*, suggests a topic or question
that would be interesting or thought-provoking for each
person to think about and then to share with the others.
For example, the daughter might say, "Everyone think of the
nicest thing that happened to you today."

With eyes closed, still holding hands, each person ponders
the question or topic suggested. When a person thinks of
something he squeezes the hand of the person to his right
and to his left. After a half-minute or so, even if everyone has
not thought of something, people drop hands, open their
eyes, and proceed to help themselves to dinner. (Families who
want to say a formal prayer, in addition to the Family Circle,
can do so either before the circle topic is suggested or
before people begin eating.)

Then, one by one, each member of the family who wants to
shares his response to the question or topic that was raised.
Everyone should feel free to pass if he does not care to share

his thoughts, and no one should feel bad if he cannot think of something to say on a given topic. Some people speak up more easily than others, so it is often helpful to draw out the quieter members by asking, for example, "Susie, what was the nicest thing that happened to *you* today?"

Each person gets a turn as focus person. If Susie is the focus person describing her day, then Mother doesn't come in with a story of her own at this point. She and the others hear Susie out and ask Susie questions if they wish to. They don't argue or disagree with her either. If Susie just finished telling how a particular compliment she received about her clothes was the nicest thing that happened to her that day, another member would not chime in and say, "Ugh. That doesn't sound nice at all. That sounds like an insult to me." When a person is the focus person, his thoughts and feelings are listened to and accepted and that's all. Later on, there is time for disagreement or free discussion.

How long each person has the focus of the family depends a great deal on the question posed, the size of the family, the ages of the children, their growing ability to listen to one another, and how the family feels that night. Whether they take two minutes or fifteen minutes for their Family Circle, each family usually establishes its own flexible norms about time limits.

Once each member of the family who wants the focus has shared a response, the discussion can be more freewheeling. Members can say, "You know, Susie, the same compliment that made you feel good, I think, would have offended me because..." or "When you told your story, Jerry, it made me think of something that once happened to me...." Or the conversation can go in an entirely new direction.

Topics for a Family Circle are infinite. The only requirements are these:

1. They should be topics about which most of the family members are likely to have something to say.

2. They should be questions or issues for which there are no "right" answers.

3. Topics should be values-clarifying, thought-provoking, interesting, or just plain fun to consider.

To illustrate the variety of Family Circle topics, a list of fifty-two topics is provided below. However, some of the best questions and topics come out of the lives of family members.

Sample Family Circle Topics

1. What is one thing you really want to do tomorrow?
2. What is one thing you'd do differently if you did today over?
3. How would your life be different if you had a million dollars?
4. What is one thing you'd like to learn how to do?
5. What is one thing you'd like to learn how to do better?
6. What was one time you really disagreed with someone today?
7. Can you recall one of the best meals you've ever had?
8. What are your three favorite main dishes and your three favorite desserts?
9. What is a funny story you heard or a funny thing that happened to you recently?
10. What is something you'd like to do this coming weekend (Christmas, summer, etc.)?
11. What was the best thing that happened at school or at work today?
12. What was the worst thing that happened at school or at work today?
13. (When on vacation) What is your most vivid memory of a past vacation?
14. (When a guest is there for dinner) What is one thing you like or appreciate about our guest?
15. (When an old friend of the family is there) What is one fond memory you have involving our guest?
16. (When an old friend of the family is there) Can you recall when and how you first met our guest and what your first impressions were?
17. (Anytime, but definitely at Thanksgiving) Proceed several times around the circle, with each person saying, "I'm thankful for..." or "I'm thankful that..." and completing the thought.
18. (At any holiday) What is the meaning this holiday has for you?
19. (At any holiday) What is your best or most vivid memory of this holiday?
20. What is your earliest memory?
21. Who is the person or character you would most like to be, if you couldn't be yourself? (This person can be from history, fiction, the news, the entertainment or sports world, a cartoon,

your family or acquaintances, anywhere – real or imaginary, past or present.)

22. Who is the person (from any of the above sources) you *are* most like?

23. Who is the person you would least like to be like?

24. What is your favorite piece of furniture in the house?

25. What is your most prized possession?

26. What is your greatest success symbol?

27. What are some of the things you'd want to do if you discovered you had only one year left to live?

28. How would your life be different if you could have one, two, or three wishes come true right now?

29. Talk about your best friend and what you like about him.

30. What is some change you'd like to make in your life?

31. If you could live anywhere in the world for a year, where would you want that to be? (Why?)

32. What is some question you've been wondering about?

33. Talk about anything that's been bothering you.

34. Talk about where, when, and how you learned to ride a bicycle (to whistle, to play baseball, to kiss, to dance, to write, or to do anything else).

35. What is something you feel proud of?

36. Who is (was) the best teacher you have (had)? What do (did) you like about her or him?

37. What is a social issue which you feel very strongly about? What are some of your thoughts and feelings on this issue?

38. What three things which use electricity in the house could you do without most easily? What three things which use electricity would be the last you'd want to give up?

39. What is something interesting or important you learned, discovered, noticed, or relearned today?

40. What season of the year or kind of weather do you like most? (Least?)

41. What is one thing you like better about living in the country than the city (or vice versa)?

42. What is one thing you'd like to accomplish in the coming year?

43. Where is your favorite spot to be by yourself?

44. What is your favorite book (poem, TV show, kind of music, tree, flower, sport)?

45. Proceed around the table, and everyone say one word or phrase which expresses your feelings.

46. What would you like to be doing three (five, ten) years from now?

47. What is something you have in common with someone else at the table?

48. What is a quality children possess which you most wish adults would keep?

49. What do you associate with red (blue, green, yellow, or any other color)?

50. Which is your favorite piece of furniture (room, painting, or anything else) in this house?

51. What animal are you most like?

52. What is something you wish for that would help someone you know?

How often should the Family Circle be used? There is really no one answer to that. In some families, it can work almost every night, with many topics repeated frequently and many created by the family members for different occasions. Other families prefer to have a Family Circle once a week, or when guests come, or on holidays. There is no correct frequency; each family needs to discover its own best pattern by experimenting.

The family meal need not be like a battleground, a disaster area, or a morgue. It can be filled with interesting conversation in which members actually listen to one another. It can be a time when family members get to know one another better. It can be a time when values are clarified and important issues are considered.

Which would be the best Family Circle to try tomorrow in *your* house?

Dinner Table Learning

by Sidney B. Simon

From *Colloquy*, December 1971. Used by permission.

What would happen at your dinner table if each member of
the family were asked to draw his version of a Family
Coat of Arms? Supply each person with a shield-like design
divided into six sections, like this:

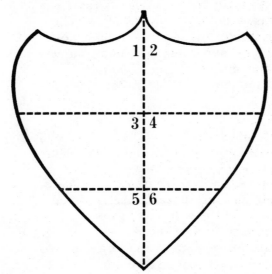

Children and parents can draw a simple sketch in each section. Use words only in section six. No awards will be given for art. The focus is upon values issues represented by each picture and what they say about what this family values.

1. In the first section, draw a picture which represents your view of your family's greatest achievement.

2. To the right of the first section, draw pictures to represent two things *you* are good at. Any two things.

3. Draw a picture showing your greatest failure in the past year.

4. Make a drawing symbolizing one issue, one value, about which you would never budge. It is one of *your* deepest commitments.

5. In the fifth section, draw a picture representing something you are striving to obtain. (It can be material goods, a personality trait, or an abstraction, etc.)

6. This is the only block on which to write words. Pick three words which you think should become the family motto. They can be three separate words or three words which make a sentence. They should be three words the whole family could believe in.

Each member then shares his coat of arms, one at a time, explaining why he drew what he drew. The discussion should help to clarify and strengthen certain ideas which will ultimately appear in the Family Coat of Arms—the six blocks representing a consensus of all the family members. The final task is to divide up the six blocks, with each member being responsible for at least one block, some doing two or more. Again, art is not the important idea. Values are. The final product is a group-built Family Coat of Arms.

Rank Orders

An easy but important and ongoing exercise to liven up the dinner table, and one which gets children and parents alike to look at moral decisions, I call Rank Orders.

Members of the family are given three items. Each person is asked to state his personal preferences. Here are some examples:

Which is the stupidest thing to do of these three?

a. To drive a car after an ice storm and scrape a hole only the size of a half-dollar to see through.

b. Always to ride a motorcycle without a helmet.

c. To start smoking cigarettes as a teenager.

Let me stress that there is no right answer to this Rank Order. Each person sees it from his own perspective. If the family can resist the easy temptation to moralize over a "right answer," a lot of searching and inquiring into each person's values can take place. And the search is fun and lively.

Another example:

Which would be the best job for you of these three?

a. To be a pickle inspector in a pickle factory, eight hours a day pulling damaged pickles off the conveyer belt.

b. To be a toll collector on a turnpike or thruway.

c. To be a wiper at the local car wash.

Sometimes the family begins to brainstorm new ideas for a Rank Order which grows out of ranking experiences like the one above. This example came in that way:

Which of these three things that might happen at Thanksgiving would bother you the most?

a. Having to work in the pickle factory all day on Thanksgiving.

b. If mother didn't cook and we sent out for a pizza for Thanksgiving dinner.

c. If she did cook the works, complete with pumpkin pie, chestnut stuffing, etc., and the family ate it in twelve and one-half minutes and then all rushed in to watch a football game and left her with the gravy slowly congealing on the plates.

Once a family gets the hang of Rank Orders, it can make them up about all kinds of issues: current events, family conflicts, hopes and goals, and priorities the family needs to establish about many things.

Twenty Things You Love to Do

Some evening, after the main course and before dessert, give each member a piece of paper and a pencil and ask each of them to number from 1 through 20 down the center of the piece of paper.

Ask each member to list twenty things, any twenty things, he or she loves to do in life. They can be as small as going for the mail or as big as celebrating Christmas. The only

criterion is that the person writing really loves doing it.
Try to be silent while people are thinking. Give them lots of
time to compile their list.

When everyone has completed his list, the lists need to be
coded by each individual. Here are some possible codings.
Each family can think of others.

1. Put a dollar sign by each item that requires an outlay of
at least three dollars any time you do it.

2. Place a P by each item which is more fun for you to do with
people and an A by each item which is more pleasurable
for you to do alone.

3. Put a 5 in front of any item which would not have been on
a similar list if you had done one five years ago.

4. Use the letters PL for any item which requires planning.

5. Put a D in front of anything you love to do which probably
would be disapproved of by most of the neighbors.

6. Finally, for each item on your list of twenty, record the
date when you did it last.

After the codings are finished, ask members of the family
to make what we call I Learned Statements. They are simply
sentences which go: "I learned that I..." or "I noticed that
I..." or "I relearned that I...."

One thing about the Twenty Things You Love to Do
exercise is that it can be done more than once. In fact, the
more a family begins to examine what it does, alone and
together, the more life changes and the more those things we
place on a list of items we love to do change, too. That is the
way it is with values. They are not locked in cement for life.
New data makes new values. And clarifying those values
generates a deeper awareness. One of the real outcomes
is that more of us refuse to settle for less than we want from
life. We don't kill time with aimless TV watching. We try to
live what we love. Knowing what we love is the first step.

SIMPLE "STARTERS" FOR FOLLOWING THE BLESSING

How nice it would be if there were more beautiful words
following the blessing than "pass the butter." Some families
include each member in sharing a small part of his life
before the food gets passed. For example, each member could
share the high point of his day. The person who can't think
of a high point has something to talk about, too: "What kind
of day is it when you don't have a high point?"

Another starter could be based on: "Were you in sharp disagreement with anyone today?" or "Who bestowed the most kindness upon you today?" or "What I Learned Statements could you make today?" or "When did you like yourself the most today?" or "How could the day have been better?"

A few other ideas could start the evening meal. Have each person send an I Urge Telegram. Some evenings the telegram could be to a national or an international figure. Other nights it could be sent to someone at school or at work. A third option is to send them to members of the family. The telegram is simply a form for saying to each other important things that need to be said. If the tone of the meal gets established so children realize that this is a significant time, they will not gag or joke about the telegrams they send. They'll do it with deep feeling.

A tender way of getting each member of the family to share something is to do three rounds of I Wonder Statements. They are simply open-ended answers to the phrases: "I wonder why..." or "I wonder how come..." or "I wonder what would happen if..." or "I wonder why I...."

What better time to keep alive the wonder in children than at the dinner table, right after the blessing and before the food is eaten?

USING A VALUE SHEET FOR A LONGER DISCUSSION

One of the most important strategies for clarifying values is a technique called the Value Sheet. People are asked to respond, usually in writing, to a highly charged, controversial statement. The writing is important. The discipline of putting thoughts on paper helps to clarify values. Value Sheets usually require you to write answers to four or five questions. All the questions are "you-centered." That is, they are questions which ask *you* to face up to where *you* stand on an issue. Finding out where *you* stand is one of the major objectives of value clarification. Read the article to everyone at the dinner table and get him to write out his answers to the five "you-centered" questions after the story.

We're Really Getting It Together, Man
"It's all a hassle, Man. The Establishment is forever trying

to jive you. Well, I'm through with being jived, with being hassled. I'm just going to stay here on this mountain, smoke a lot of dope, and really get myself together."

It's been five years since you've seen them. And now somehow you hear they've moved West and are close by. There is more to it than old friendship. More like kin they were.

*   *   *

When Tommy comes through the door, he nods at you and goes right on by. It had been a while. He didn't recognize you. So you follow him, looking hard at him when he turns around. It finally dawns on him who you are. "How are you, Man?" he smiles.

Then, without another word, he sits down at the console, pulls out a package of grass, and starts rolling joints. You look at him. He's wasted, gaunt; his eyes are kind of glazed-over remnants of faded blue. You finally get up to walk on. He is too spaced out.

He looks up, says, "You leaving? Come on back later and we'll rap." You say OK, but you have this feeling that you won't be doing that. Instead, you drive to where he and Laura live. Has she changed that much?

When you get there, you find out she has. You really don't believe what you see. Where once before was this beautiful, exciting woman there's now a drab little sparrow, living in a house without heat or water or electricity. Her clothes are rags. Her face is drawn and tight. Her eyes scare you.

*   *   *

But at least she's really happy to see you. And wants to talk: "Did Tommy do that?" she said, when you tell her of the scene at the station. "Wow, well, he's probably on cocaine. He stays stoked up all the time.

"I mean it's really beautiful for him, though. He glides through it all really well. He really works when he's stoned on drugs no matter how heavy they are. I can't handle it as much as he does. Like we both drop a lot of acid, but it's gotten where I don't need to but maybe every six weeks."

You hear her but you don't believe her. And you look at the filth and poverty and you ask her why. "Yeah, we're down to the wire, all right. But that's just for now.

"We're really getting it together, Man. I'm working with this great band and we're going to move to the city and Tommy's getting a job with this far-out station and..."

*   *   *

*You listen. You're hearing the same thing you had talked
about five years before. The same dreams. Laura keeps talking,
but it starts making less and less sense. She uses the
teenybopper terms "funky" and "out of sight" over and over.*

*It's a gray day with snow clouds hanging low over this
secluded mountain town. The flakes finally start falling as you
go back to pick up Becky.*

*"This is going to be a really far-out party," she tells you.
The party. Right. You'd forgotten.*

*She tells you where to drive, up the mountain, on a dirt
road that winds for eight miles. "Here's the place," she says,
pointing to a wooden shack.*

*   *   *

*You go inside. Already there are ten people, young men and
women, dressed in rags and tatters. They're already stoned.
You walk in but nobody makes any move to introduce you.
Becky lights up a joint, pours herself some wine, and sits
down on a bed in the corner of the two-room house.*

*You sit and watch, waiting for some kind of conversation to
begin. You look at Becky but she's spaced out, staring at the
coal oil lamp as it provides a faded yellow parchment
setting in the shack.*

*"Really far-out grass," a girl mumbles. "Yeah, really super
grass," somebody else says.*

*You sit in the corner for three hours watching them "get
it together." Looking at them "finding out where it's at."
Five years is a long time. It really is.*

Questions on "We're Really Getting It Together, Man":

1. List five immediate reactions you had to the story.
2. If the story is too anti-drug for you, tell why.
3. Tommy really seems to be fooling himself. How do you fool yourself sometimes?
4. Whom do you feel most sorry for in this story? Can you explain why you feel that way?
5. This is the hardest question for some people: What, if any, are the implications for your own life to be found in this Value Sheet exercise?

That is a Value Sheet. Any member can bring in the
statement or story part of a Value Sheet. Then the family
can rotate the responsibility for making up the questions
to clarify the values. Any subject matter will do. All it

need be is exciting, controversial, and full of values choices for the members of the family.

The Here and Now Wheel

A final game for the dinner table. I learned it from my colleague, Gerald Weinstein, at the University of Massachusetts. Each member draws a wheel and puts four spokes on it. On each spoke, each member lists exactly what he is now experiencing or feeling. It might be hunger or tiredness or anger or impatience or peacefulness. Each family member then writes two sentences about one of the spokes, one of the feelings. Expanding the feeling makes it more specific and more dimensional. These are shared around the dinner table. When family members get skillful at Here and Now Wheels, they are given the privilege of calling for anyone's Here and Now Wheel whenever a conflict develops or when one member in the family senses another member is going through something emotional which needs to be articulated.

I have shared a half dozen small ways of making the family dinner table a learning center. I have focused on the skills of values clarification since I believe that they are among the most important heritages parents can leave with their children.

I would suggest a few cautions if you are drawn to these ideas for clarifying values and want to try them out on your own families. Don't use these exercises to ram home a predetermined outcome. Don't moralize unnecessarily or your children will turn you off like a record player with its needle stuck in a groove. All of these exercises must be kept open-ended. Your own sense of wonder, discovery, and amazement should be kept alive. Values clarification is the name of the process, not value inculcation. With the incredible future ahead of us all, we must affirm the idea that few of us can really know what our children should value. We can't tell them what to value. We can't be there all the time to value for them.

On the other hand, we as parents should make the clearest statements we can about where we stand. We should do it not punitively, not with flattery, not with manipulation. We need to be open and less uptight as we come in touch with alternatives for our family values which may be more creative than the ones we picked up during our own upbringing.

Finally, we must give dignity to the family's search for its meaning. It is only as we teach a process, a way of negotiating the as yet unfathomable future, that we leave our children with an estate more valuable than stocks, bonds, jewels, or gold. We leave a way of making sense out of the confusion and conflict surrounding all of us. That way is called values clarification. There is an old Spanish proverb that goes, "The journey is more important than the inn." Take your own family on such a journey. And use the dinner table for the center of learning it is or can be.

Election Year and Dinner Table Learning

by Sidney B. Simon

From *Colloquy*, October 1972. Used by permission.

Dinner table conversations really need to be more than "Pass the peas," "Who has the ketchup?" and "Gerald, you're going to knock your milk over. Gerald, you knocked your milk over."

A presidential election year comes but once every four years, and if you keep your kids an average of sixteen years at a time, that means you're only going to get two real shots at getting them to think about elections, voting, and the like. (The four-year-old probably won't focus much on the topic and the eight-year-old most likely would have voted for the same candidate twice, so the attention is on those near twelve and the ones around sixteen.)

It is quite possible to conduct lively dinner table conversations concerning election issues. The members of the family could gain new respect for each other as they examine together some of the incredible ramifications of this great event, which appears with about the same frequency as leap year.

So much for introductions. Below are a series of simple strategies growing out of our work in values clarification. (See: *Values and Teaching* by Louis Raths, Merrill Harmin, and Sidney B. Simon. Columbus, Ohio: Charles E. Merrill

Publishing Company, 1966. Also *Values Clarification: A Handbook of Practical Strategies* by Sidney B. Simon, Leland Howe, and Howard Kirschenbaum. New York: Hart Publishing, 1972.)

Values clarification requires a few ground rules if you are going to make much progress out of trying them at your family dinner table.

Ground Rule One: State clearly, and also believe, that there are no *right* answers to most of the issues raised. (That's why we vote. If there were a right candidate, we would all vote for him. We don't. Witness what has happened to your favorite candidates in the past.)

If you are to be a sincere value clarifier, you will have to take delight in your family's diversity of opinion and focus with them on the *process* of *valuing* rather than upon one set of right values.

Ground Rule Two: Anticipate and accept a certain amount of ribald humor, flipness, cool-catness, etc., on the part of your children. The point is, don't get miffed or shocked if your own children think that the solution to Nixon is to assassinate him. They really don't mean that, and you would be just cutting off future talk if you made a large, moralizing attack on your children for their lack of respect.

OK, now let's look at a few of the values-clarification strategies. Most of the directions are self-explanatory. If you do have any doubts or confusion, refer to the books mentioned above which explain the rationale and the theory behind each of these exercises adapted for family dinner table seminars.

Values Voting

Values Voting has a game-like quality which makes it a very suitable starting place for using the dinner table to clarify some values about elections.

The facilitator can say something like this: "Family, I want to ask you ten questions about the whole election business just to give us a chance to see where some of our values are. There are no right answers to any of these questions, and we should have some fun seeing where we all stand.

"Next week, sometime, I'd like one of you to bring in ten questions to the dinner table, and we'll vote on your questions, too. Maybe we could make this a regular thing.

"Here's how we all vote. If you are *for* the issue in the question, simply raise your hand as in a normal vote. If you are *strongly* for the issue, wave your hand while it is raised. That will show your passion." (Every family needs a little passion.)

"If you are against the issue, vote with your thumb pointing down. You know, thumbs down. If you are passionately against it, move your thumb vigorously back and forth. A final way of signaling your vote is to fold your hands in front of your chest. That means, 'I don't know where I stand,' or 'I haven't made up my mind yet,' or 'I just don't care to reveal my stand. I pass.'

"OK, ready now? Here are ten values-voting questions about the election:

1. How many of you have ever been inside a voting booth?
2. How many of you think parents should take even preschoolers into a voting booth so they begin to get some awareness of the election process?
3. How many of you think it is a waste to vote for a candidate who has no hope of winning the election? That is, how many of you are against casting your vote for a protest candidate?
4. How many of you have ever worn a button supporting some political candidate?
5. How many of you have ever passed out literature for a candidate?
6. How many of you have ever rung door bells trying to get support for a candidate?
7. How many of you would give up your whole allowance one week as a contribution to the campaign fund of some candidate?
8. How many of you think it is worthless to vote?
9. How many of you would consider tearing down signs advertising a rival candidate?
10. How many of you would vote for a man who promised to bring an end to our involvement in the war in Indochina?"

After everyone in the family has voted on the list of questions — with varying degrees of interest and involvement, naturally — you can begin to search out which questions held the most possibilities for further talk. One or two questions often grip the whole family, and talk goes on merrily. Again, refer back to the ground rules and keep the discussion

going on an exploratory level. Don't let it get overly school-like.
Don't belabor it. Let it run its natural course, and if everyone
reverts back to ball scores, or whatever, that's OK, too.

However, if it works — that is, if people say it was fun
and that they would like to do something like that again —
then perhaps in a night or two you could move into the
second strategy, Rank Order.

Rank Order

This game is a variation on the voting questions strategy.
Here, your dinner table companions are given three items and
they are asked to set their priorities, to state their
preferences, one, two, and three.

    1. If these three men were alive and were running for
president, rank order how you would vote for them:
> **a.** Martin Luther King, Jr.
> **b.** Robert Kennedy
> **c.** Malcolm X

Perhaps you will have to explain a bit about who Malcolm X
was and what he stood for. That in itself would make dinner
exciting. You might find that you get into a large discussion
about assassination. Rank Orders are discussion starters.
At a lively dinner table, discussion roams far and wide when
this strategy is used.

Here's another:

    2. Rank order these three items. Which do you believe
political candidates should deal with the most?
> **a.** the energy crisis
> **b.** ecology
> **c.** racism

3. Which of these worries you the most in the conduct of
politics in the United States today?
> **a.** the president taking us to war without going
> through congress
> **b.** senators and congressmen requiring so much money
> to get elected that they become beholden to large
> business interests
> **c.** women, blacks, and other minorities being so badly
> underrepresented

4. As an individual, what is your ranking of these three ways
of helping the candidate of your choice?

      a. writing letters to the editor in support of him
      b. wearing a button with his name on it everywhere I go
      c. writing personal letters to adults I know asking them to vote for my candidate

5. Of these three sources of information about the election issues, which do you rank first?
      a. our hometown newspaper
      b. one of the big weekly magazines like *Time* or *Newsweek*
      c. the evening TV newscast

These Rank Orders are merely suggestive. Once you try a few, you will make even better ones, because you will know the issues your family is concerned about. Better yet, ask some of the children in the family to bring in Rank Orders for the next family dinner table learning session. They will bring in real winners.

Design a Button

Come to the table some night with some typical metal buttons over which you have stuck some self-stick blank labels. Give each person a felt-tipped pen and ask him to design a button arguing for something in the election he wishes to support or ban. Give everyone time to work. Then have each person read what his button says. Hopefully, each will wear his button to school or work the next day. Members of the family might also switch buttons for a day or two. Here are two buttons made up by my family:

STOP FIGHTING THE WAR,
START FIGHTING RACISM.

ERASE THE SPACE RACE.

I Urge Telegrams

Some evening, stop by the Western Union office and pick up enough blank telegrams for everyone in the family. Ask each person to send an I Urge Telegram to the candidate of his choice. He can send any message, but limit it to fifteen words and begin the message with, "I urge...."

Some of the issues raised at the dinner table for several nights may become heated. Inevitably, someone will send a telegram which says, "I urge you to drop dead." Laugh with it and give him another blank telegram.

Picture Without a Caption

Bring in a very provocative photograph from the newspaper
or from some magazine which shows a scene full of emotion
or action relating to an election issue. Get each person to look
at the picture closely and then write a caption for it.
The picture becomes a simple projective device for captions
which should generate a great deal of lively talk.

If Situations

It is useful to bring up controversial If Situations to get the
family thinking about values issues. For example:

> 1. If you were an American Indian, whom would you vote for?
> 2. If you were an unemployed technician at Boeing in
> Seattle, what would you want the candidates to be saying?
> 3. If you could get ten minutes on national TV, what would
> you advocate?
> 4. If one of the candidates were to be arrested for drunken
> driving...?
> 5. If no one went to the polls...?
> 6. If someone offered you a hundred dollars to change
> your vote...?

Where Do You Draw the Line?

Your family and each member in it probably has a place
where they draw the line. That is, a point you can't push
them beyond. It is fun to ask people around the dinner table
where they would draw the line on these issues.

> 1. Where would you draw the line on how young people
> could vote?
> 2. Where would you draw the line on the maximum each
> candidate could spend for his campaign?
> 3. Where would you draw the line on how truthful a
> candidate should be?
> 4. Where would you draw the line on how many senators
> should be women?
> 5. Where would you draw the line on cars being banned from
> the inner city as a pollution control?

Value Sheets

This is a standard values-clarification strategy. See
Values and Teaching for a whole chapter on Value Sheets.

Basically, these are provocative statements followed by
four or five questions to get people to think about and clarify
their values.

Someone should read the sheet out loud to the family at the dinner table. Then people should be asked in turn to respond to the questions. Below is a Value Sheet that should generate a good amount of discussion around your dinner table.

Value Sheet:

At the behest of western ranchers, the Federal Government has long engaged in a cruel, senseless, and wholly unnecessary destruction of wild animals.... The Department of the Interior has been spending eight million annually on "predator control." It has put out poisoned carcasses on the open range. It has used the "coyote getter" — a baited cartridge on a steel rod which shoots cyanide into the animal's mouth. From airplanes, it has scattered hundreds of thousands of lard-covered strychnine balls like deadly snowflakes. It is a thoroughly shameful, senseless, and savage business carried out not by crackbrained individuals but by an arm of the U.S. Government.

This hideous practice has resulted in the slaughter not only of coyotes but also of thousands of bobcats, mountain lions, badgers, foxes, opossums, raccoons, beavers, and porcupines. Every impartial scientist who has seriously studied this predator control program has condemned it as unnecessary, inhumane, and ecologically a disaster.

— The New York Times

1. What are the first three words that come into your mind on reading the above passage?
2. Are you interested in seeking out an opposing point of view on this subject so that you will be more competent to take a strong stand?
3. If this editorial had referred to private individuals, rather than the Federal Government, as perpetrators of "predator control" would your reaction be significantly different? Why or why not?
4. To what extent do you, as a United States citizen, feel responsible for the action described in the above passage? Explain.
5. Explain what, if anything, you plan to do as a result of having read the above.

This election year could provide a wonderful time for our families to grow closer as we look at some of the issues we will all have to live with for the next four years.

These eight strategies are merely suggestive of the kinds of things we can do before dessert is served. Family unity could grow from them. They have a way of getting us to reveal ourselves. As Sidney Jourard says, "No man can know himself until he discloses himself." Perhaps no family can really know its members until they are given time to search together. Martin Luther King, Jr., said it all when he said, "In order to live creatively and meaningfully, our self-concern must be wedded to other concerns." Let the election year be a time for clarifying our values about our country and its concerns.

The Listening Game

by Howard Kirschenbaum

From *Colloquy*, October 1970. Used by permission.

One morning recently, I overheard a conversation between two women on the 7:42 train. I sensed the women did not know each other well and had not spoken for some time. Yet they seemed friendly and were enjoying each other's company. Part of their conversation went like this:

"How is your daughter? She must be a big girl by now."

"Yes. She's graduating from high school this June."

"Isn't that nice. How is she doing?"

"Oh, fine. She's done well in school. But she's causing us some concern these days, I'm afraid."

"Oh?"

"Yes. She's thinking about not going to college next year. She says she wants to work a year—you know, be on her own for a while—then go to college after that."

The mother's friend became serious; her face was set in a disapproving frown. "Don't let her do it," was all she said.

"No, I won't," said the mother.

"These kids today," said the friend, "I wonder where they get all their crazy ideas."

The mother nodded her head in sympathy with the question.

And I thought: *Are they kidding?* Does the friend really believe she has the "right answer" for how a girl she doesn't even know should live her life? Does the mother really

believe that forbidding her daughter to make an important
decision will help the girl learn to make important decisions
in her life? Can they both be serious in summing up a
generation's turmoil as "crazy ideas" and thereby
dismissing it all?

Why did the girl want to take a year off? In what ways did
she want to be more independent? What were some of her
plans for the year off? What were some of the advantages and
disadvantages that she, the girl, perceived in her plan? What
made her realize she wanted to take the year off? It never
occurred to the friend to ask the mother these questions.
Perhaps it never occurred to the mother to ask the daughter.

These women were not malicious. Undoubtedly, they
sincerely wanted the girl to be happy, to live a satisfying,
fruitful life. Yet to me, their conversation symbolized one of
the main problems adults have in respect to the "younger
generation." *We don't listen to them.* I mean *really* listen
to them.

Listening is a skill, one of the hardest communication skills
to learn. It involves more than concentration. It demands the
ability to suspend one's own value judgments, the ability to
put oneself in the other person's shoes and see the world
through his eyes, the ability to sense fully the music—the
feelings—behind the words. In my work with parents and
teachers in many parts of the country, I find that one of the
hardest things for adults to learn is that *we do not have the
answers* to the serious values questions our youth are raising,
both through their words and their actions. The women on
the train were not atypical.

But as I look back on the two women's conversation now,
I feel less judgmental. They were in their mid-forties. One
was white, the other black. They rode the early commuter
train every day of the work week into center city
Philadelphia. For how many years have they done so? How
did their experiences in life—during the Depression and the
war years, for example—color their world view and value
systems? What struggles had they and their families gone
through so they could live in a nice part of the city and
send their children to college?

It's an old story—the generation gap—but Jesse Unruh
in *Saturday Review* speaks of it eloquently and sensitively
in describing his own inability to see the world through
the eyes of the young.

Much of the time, this sense of threat from the young does not bear rational scrutiny. I confess to a feeling of disgust at the sight of barefoot flower children quite apart from their philosophical convictions or the forms of their social criticism. What repels me, frankly, is the memory of my youth on a tenant farm in Texas where three of us in my family shared one pair of shoes—where to be barefoot in public was to be ashamed. My disgust with bare feet is irrational and perhaps even unworthy, but these kinds of memories die hard.

I have had a similar problem with the hairstyles of the young. For the first fifteen years of my life, my mother cut my hair, and angel that she was, barber she was not. So in my early teens, I let my hair grow as long as possible before facing the inevitable butchering job by her dull scissors. Today, long shaggy hair bothers me. Even some of my own sons annoy me; when able to afford haircuts, they let their hair grow long.

Many of my generation are annoyed by and even resentful of the freedom of our young people from economic concerns. A secure nine-to-five job, a house in the suburbs, two cars— these were distant, almost impossible goals for so many people for so many years that they became obsessive. It is incomprehensible to many of my generation that today's youth are not similarly obsessed. With our backgrounds of economic uncertainty still haunting us, it is difficult to remain calm as we see thousands of our children turning their backs on our hard-won affluence, sneering at their parents' insistence on the moral value of work, and willfully adopting life-styles reminiscent of the shame of poverty.

Understandably, parents do not understand.

To understand *why* it is difficult for us to understand does not free us from the obligation to try. If, as parents and teachers, we hope to be helpful to our children and students, then we *must* understand them. If we want to share a meaningful part of their lives, we must make the effort to listen. For if we do not listen to them, obviously, they will not listen to us.

The following two listening exercises are designed to help people learn more fully to understand and experience one another. They can be used as structured experiences in classrooms and families, or they can be applied informally in any situation where they might prove helpful. They are deceptively simple exercises, but usually very meaningful and very powerful for the participants.

Rogerian Listening

Dr. Carl Rogers popularized a form of psychotherapy known as "client-centered therapy" or "nondirective counseling." At its core is the ability of the therapist or counselor really to listen to the client. Good listening, according to Rogers, involves:

1. Not only hearing the words of the speaker, but hearing the feelings behind the words as well.

2. *Empathizing* with the speaker, that is, feeling his feelings and seeing the world through the speaker's eyes.

3. Suspending one's *own* value judgments so as to understand the speaker's thoughts and feelings as he himself experiences them.

This listening exercise can be done with three or more participants. One person serves as monitor, the others as discussants. The monitor helps the discussants find a subject of mutual interest, but one on which the discussants have different views or feelings. Once such a topic has been identified and agreed upon, one discussant begins the discussion by stating his position on the issue.

Normally, when discussions take place, we are so concerned with what we are going to say next, or so involved with planning our response, that we often tune out or miss the full meaning of what is being said. In this exercise, before another discussant can offer his own point of view, he must restate the essence of the previous speaker's statement, so that the previous speaker honestly feels his statement has been understood. It is the monitor's role to see that this process takes place. Here is an example:

Speaker 1: ...and that's why I'm in favor of a guaranteed, minimum annual income.

Speaker 2: OK. You're saying you favor the guaranteed income because you think it will break the cycle of people staying on welfare and because it will put more money in circulation and thus create more jobs. Is that right?

Speaker 1: You got it.

Speaker 2: OK. But I think just the opposite would happen. You'd have people knowing they'd get a decent wage if they didn't work, so...

Speaker 3: But that's ridiculous. Why would...

Monitor: Hold it, Fran. Hold it. First of all, Jerry didn't finish his point. Second, you didn't repeat it before responding.

Speaker 3: Sorry.

Speaker 2: Well, my point was, if somebody thinks he doesn't have to work and he'll get paid anyway, then why should he work?

Speaker 3: Well, I'll tell you. He'll work because...

Monitor: Hold it again. What did Jerry say?

Speaker 3: Oh, yeah. Jerry's worried this won't work. But I think...

Monitor: Wait a minute. Jerry, are you satisfied that Fran understands your argument?

Speaker 2: No.

Monitor: Fran, do you want to try it again? Or would you like Jerry to repeat his point?

And so goes the conversation. It's slow, meticulous, and sometimes frustrating. But it's a real learning experience. Participants see how communication is a two-way street, how difficult it is really to listen to another person (especially if you disagree with him), and through contrast, how much of normal conversation is really talking *at* rather than *with* one another.

When tempers flare, when tension rises, when parents and children, students and teachers, blacks and whites, or any group of people stop listening to one another, this listening exercise can reduce conflict and facilitate communication.

The Free-Choice Game

We frequently are in situations in which another person shares with us a choice in his life that he is considering:

"I'm thinking about buying a new car."

"I can't decide whether to cut my hair or not."

"I have a really good job offer, but I have mixed feelings about accepting it."

"I don't know how to make up with my friend after our fight."

"I think I'd like to work for a year—you know, be on my own for a while—before going to college."

At the beginning of this article, an example was given of an unhelpful way of responding to such a situation. If the decision the person finally makes is to be of value to him, if it is to be a viable decision which he can be comfortable with and carry out, it must be one that he has freely chosen after thoughtful consideration of the alternatives. People who moralize, grind their own ax, impose their own value judgments, plead their own causes, or justify their own lives are not the kinds of "helpers" who can help the person make *his* own choice.

Dr. Merrill Harmin of Southern Illinois University has developed a formal game to help people learn more productive ways of dealing with these "choice" situations. The game can be played with three or more people; five or six in a group is usually maximally productive. One person is the focus person, one is the monitor, and the rest are the helpers.

The focus person is a volunteer who has a choice in his life that he would like to discuss with a small group of good listeners. Although his choice may pose a problem for him or be related to a personality problem he has, the focal point of the game is on *an actual choice* the focus person faces. This is an important distinction. If the focus person raises a problem per se (lack of confidence, guilt feelings about a parental relationship, dislike of one's physical appearance, etc.), then the helpers are put in the position of being psychoanalysts, for which they are not equipped. But if the focus presents a *choice* situation (whether or not to ask her for a date, how much to spend on a parent's birthday present, whether or not to dye her hair, etc.), then the group can play a meaningful role.

The helpers' goal is to help the focus person make *his own best choice*. They do this by asking questions; they may not make a statement unless they first ask permission of the focus person. Generally, their questions follow a five-step progression:

1. *Understanding.* They ask questions to gain enough information so they feel they have a good understanding of the focus person's choice dilemma.

2. *Clarifying.* They ask thought-provoking questions to test out some of their own hypotheses and to help the focus person think more deeply about his situation.

3. *Exploring Alternatives.* They inquire about what alternatives the focus person sees open to him. With permission, they suggest other alternatives the focus person might want to consider.   ·

4. *Exploring Consequences.* They ask questions which get

the focus person to explore the consequences of the alternatives open to him.

5. They ask questions which encourage the focus person to explore his feelings about the alternatives and consequences and to think about what choice he is leaning toward at that point.

This format is not inflexible. Groups will naturally jump back and forth among the five stages of decision making. But, in general, this structure proves helpful. When the focus person feels he is understood, for example, he will be more open to clarifying questions. And when choosing comes before all the alternatives have been explored, the choice is likely to suffer.

The focus person is in control. He can end the game at any time. He can and should tell the helpers when he feels uncomfortable about their questions – for example, when he feels they are trying to persuade him toward a given choice.

The monitor's job is to encourage the group to follow the five-step process when he senses they are putting the cart before the horse. ("I think we are exploring alternatives before fully understanding the choice situation. Focus person, are you satisfied that we understand your dilemma?") The monitor also steps in if he senses people are making statements disguised as questions (e.g., "Don't you feel it would be wiser to...."). The game goes on for about a half hour to forty minutes. At any time, the monitor might ask the focus person if he feels the helpers are mostly being helpful or mostly trying to impose their views on him. At the end, he asks the focus person if he would like to share any insights he got with the group, or whether he is any closer to a choice.

Participants in The Free-Choice Game often experience, in a profound and meaningful way, what a helping relationship can mean. Simultaneously, they are sharpening their own ability to listen fully to another person.

Both the Rogerian Listening exercise and The Free-Choice Game are highly structured experiences. But the listening and communication skills that can be derived from them can be used in numerous situations in everyday life. Whenever people are involved in an exchange of ideas, whenever a person tells us about a choice he is considering for his life – this is a time for listening. Only by really listening to young people (or older people), can we ever hope to have any meaningful communication with them.

Other Applications for Values Clarification

INTRODUCTION

During the past several years, the values-clarification approach has been adapted and used in an increasing number and variety of situations. The previous sections have dealt with applications of this approach to school subjects, religion, and the family. In this section, we include a selection of writings which describe the use of values clarification in many different settings and contexts.

—in a black and Puerto Rican junior high school in New York City

—in a freshman college dormitory in Massachusetts

—in a values-clarification workshop in Massachusetts, a suburban elementary school in Maryland, and an inner city school in Philadelphia

—in a national women's organization business meeting in Iowa

—in Girl Scout programs all over the country

—in nutrition classes

—in a large public school system-wide training program.

The section closes with an article by Leland Howe, exploring the group dynamics implications of values clarification.

Values Clarification in Junior High School

by Mildred W. Abramowitz and Claudia Macari

From *Educational Leadership*, April 1972. Reprinted with pe mission of the Association for Supervision and Curriculum Development and the authors. Copyright © 1972 by the Association for Supervision and Curriculum Development.

Do I have to go to the streets to get changes?

Does it make any difference to our government what I do?

Does religion have any meaning for me?

Should I follow what my parents do in religion?

How can I make school more meaningful?

How can I make better use of weekends?

How do I know where to draw the line on a date?

What is there to talk about in my family?

Jack was a close friend. Now we pass each other without a word to say. What happened?

How can I get money to work for me instead of my working for it?

What should I believe about drugs? Diet? Eggs? Meat? Mercury?

How should I wear my hair? Should I grow a beard?

These are just a few of the questions young people are asking today, and, of course, they are not just for the young but for all of us.

If young people were to come to you for help with these questions, could you answer them?

They are the big questions in our lives, and only we can answer them for ourselves. Schools have not been very

helpful. They have not given us the tools to answer them.
The values-clarification approach is one attempt to give
young people the tools to answer — a chance to shape
their lives.

The Key Questions

Adolescents are living in a very confusing world where they
must continually make choices regarding their attitudes
and actions in politics, religion, work, school, leisure, love and
sex, family, friends, spending of money, health, and personal
taste. These are all areas of confusion and conflict for them,
because things are changing so fast that they have great
difficulty in looking to the past for the "proper" way to
behave. They have few established models. They are asking
questions; and as they weigh what their parents say and do,
what their friends say and do, and what their teachers
say and do, they find uncertainty, inconsistency, and even
no answers at all to the key questions of their lives. They
flounder for answers by themselves, and our schools have
not been very helpful in developing the processes to help
them get the answers.

Traditionally, schools have tried to impose values, or they
have tried to ignore the whole problem, or they have said
that it is not an area of their concern but that of parents and
the church. Yet in this day of rapid change, adolescents are
confronted with many different points of view, and they are
then left to sort them out. The purpose of the values-
clarification approach is to give pupils experience in valuing
to enable them to answer the questions that really concern
them. It is important to pupils that schools are concerned
with what they regard as personally important to them,
as well as with their traditional role of passing on the
achievements of the past.

Values are not readily transmitted, but they can be learned.
If one accepts the idea that values cannot effectively be
taught, but that they can be learned, one moves from
moralizing and inculcating toward a process of values
clarification. Values clarification involves a series of strategies
which are not guilty of forcing one set of right values down
the throats of all students. Instead, the process tends to raise
issues, to confront the student with inconsistencies, and to
get him to sort out his own values, in his own way, and at his

own pace. The practice of this approach and the theory on which it is based have been developed over a number of years by Louis Raths, Merrill Harmin, and Sidney Simon. A full presentation can be found in the book *Values and Teaching*.

In our school we are interested in values-clarification teaching as one way to help our pupils know what they feel about what happens to them in the course of a day. We believe that thinking is accompanied by feeling, and we would like to experiment with ways of taking advantage of this so that pupils can be helped to answer the questions: Who am I? Where am I going? What do I care about? Is this what I want to do? What alternatives do I have? Which choice is wisest for me? We think that being able to answer such questions would make life more meaningful to our boys and girls, and in the process would help to make school a place where they would grow and where their lives would be affected.

Sidney Simon says that "it turns out that most people have very few values."[1] Values-clarification teaching is based on the seven criteria for the determination of a value developed by Louis Raths. Raths' contribution was unique in that he was not interested so much in the content of the value (whether materialistic or spiritual) but was interested in the process whereby a value came about. He said a value started with a belief you were proud of and were willing to affirm, where you had chosen it from alternatives with regard to possible consequences and free from outside pressure to choose any particular thing, and where you had taken action on this belief other than to talk about it and had done this in a regular pattern, not just at sporadic times. Value indicators are people's beliefs, attitudes, morals, activities, interests, feelings, goals, and aspirations; but they are not values unless they meet the seven criteria. We may have many value indicators, which are certainly good things to have, but very few values.

The theory further states that people with very few values tend to be conforming, apathetic, inconsistent, and often very ambivalent; all of which seems quite sad when one realizes the extent to which values should guide a person's life. This argues strongly for the school's taking a more active part in the clarification of values. There are few areas in the affective domain about which there is so much talk and so

little action as there is with values. The valuing process
weaves together critical thinking and affective education
in a functional and relevant program.

Our ideas, methods, and inspiration were given to us by
Sidney Simon of the University of Massachusetts and his
colleague, Howard Kirschenbaum, the director of the
Adirondack Mountain Humanistic Education Center. We
attended several of their workshops and worked with five
classes and ten members of our faculty during the school
year 1970-71. This current school year (1971-72) we are
conducting a teachers' workshop in our own school during
the school day, and we are also working with three classes
for demonstration and practice purposes. One of these classes
was with us last year, and we are planning to continue with
this class for a third year.

William W. Niles Junior High School is located in a
disadvantaged area in the Bronx. The student body is 60
percent Puerto Rican and 40 percent black, and the pupils
are familiar with the problems of perpetual mobility,
broken homes, absent fathers, drugs, and violence in the
streets and in the home. Achievement is low in reading,
writing, and oral expression. Admissions and discharges
result in a one-third turnover in the course of a school year.
Literacy in any language is a problem. The boys and girls
are, on the average, more than two and a half years retarded
in reading and in mathematics when they come to us from
elementary school. The school is well thought of and well
liked in the community because it has a concerned faculty
that works hard at teaching and at establishing warm
relationships with children and parents, and it fosters
self-discipline so that teachers can concentrate on teaching.

Specific structured techniques have been designed to
accomplish the goals of values-clarification teaching. Some
of these are described here.

Strategies

The strategies which were presented to our students were
employed for the purpose of stimulating thinking and of
making them aware of the processes of values clarification.
Students were encouraged to take a stand on what they
believed, declare it publicly, make their choice freely, and
act upon it. However, the right of the student to "pass"

on any strategy was respected and protected. It is necessary
to have the right not to say anything. Whatever was said by
the student was accepted with no sign of condemnation,
rejection, or ridicule. The task of not commenting or of
controlling one's facial expressions is the most difficult of all.
It is only in a free and relaxed atmosphere of mutual respect
and acceptance that the pupils can express themselves and
think about where they stand and how they feel and how they
will act upon issues that affect their lives.

The following strategies are some examples of those used
in our classes:

Twenty Things You Love to Do. Students were asked to write
twenty things they love to do. (Incidentally, all written work
is absolutely private and is only shared with others if the
student wants to share it.)

The procedure that followed was:

1. Star the five things you love to do best of all.
2. Place a check after the things you love to do alone.
3. Place a cross after the things you love to do with other
   people.
4. Circle the things that cost you less than three dollars to do.
5. Write the date of the last time you did each of these
   twenty things.

This strategy gives the student some insight into what is
important to him. It reveals his needs for companionship or
his lack of it, pleasures which may cost very little, and helps
him to evaluate the way he spends his time.

Alternative Action Search. There are times when our
students are stymied and frustrated by situations and
incidents in their lives. They are overwhelmed by the feeling
that they do not know where to go or how to act and that
they inevitably have to bow to circumstances or fight
without direction or reason. Students must be trained to
examine a situation and consider all possible alternatives.

For example, the following problem is given to the students
as a strategy for alternative search:

*You are walking home, and as you approach the building in
which you live, you see a man and woman standing in a
doorway. They are arguing loudly and violently. Suddenly
the man pulls the woman by the hair, slaps her face, and
punches her in the eye. She screams again and again and
calls for help.*

Directions: Form a group of three people. Each person will say in turn one action he would take in this situation. One person will record what is being said. All answers are to be accepted without comment or criticism no matter how ridiculous or impossible they may seem. This is a way of brainstorming. Do not judge or evaluate the ideas given in this search for alternatives.

After this is done, we ask the person who has recorded the alternatives to share with us what has been said by the trio.

It is through this that students realize that people may think and act in the same manner, or that there are many different ways to try to resolve a problem, or that there are always possible solutions to every problem if we consider alternatives. It will also indicate to what extent a person will allow himself to become involved with other people and what feelings and ideas he is protecting.

Values Voting. This is a strategy that allows a student to indicate his feelings and thoughts publicly on any questions asked of him and to see how others feel about the same things. It emphasizes that people differ. This is a time when he can give an answer without being told that he is right or wrong. His opinion on an issue is respected. The value of this strategy in the development of self-confidence is immeasurable.

Directions: The teacher explains that a vote will be taken on ten questions and each student will show how he feels or thinks about the subject by doing the following: positive answer—raise hand; negative answer—thumb down; neutral or pass—fold arms.

If the student feels strongly about the subject, he may shake his hand vigorously up or down as the case may be.

All questions must begin with "How many of you...?" Some examples of questions are:

1. How many of you follow a religion?
2. How many of you are happy in school?
3. How many of you are honest all the time?
4. How many of you have a best friend?
5. How many of you are in favor of war?
6. How many of you choose your own clothes?
7. How many of you feel loved?
8. How many of you think sex education should be taught in school?

9. How many of you would like to live the rest of your life where you are living now?

10. How many of you think a family should be limited in size?

After the questions have been asked, the teacher can ask several students to share their feelings about a particular question and give reasons for voting as they did. This, of course, is on a voluntary basis. This strategy is a learning experience for the teacher because he is in close contact with feelings and ideas and values that his students are revealing. It is also a form of public affirmation of what he prizes or cherishes. It is up to the teacher to incorporate these in his teaching. Those questions where big differences occur can lead to good class discussions. After the first session, students are encouraged to bring in their own questions to have the class vote on them.

Values Continuum. The continuum is another device to get our students to examine how they stand or feel about issues at a particular moment in time. This shows how people are the same or differ and that there are many different positions on an issue. The position a student chooses on a continuum is not fixed. A student may change his mind due to certain experiences and reexamination of his feelings. In that case he will change his position on the continuum.

Directions: A line is drawn and two opposite ideas are put on each end of the line. Pupils take a position on this line which represents where they stand on the issue at that moment. They may not use the center—this is reserved for "compulsive moderates."

For example, if the subject is school marks, the continuum may appear as follows:

Mable Marks|————————————————|Gradeless George

The student is told to put his mark at the place he stands on this line.

Continuum on the draft:

Dodger Dan|————————————————|Eager Egbert

Continuum on medicine:

Pillbox Paul|————————————————|Natural Nell

Students are encouraged to think about their answers and to make any changes in position they wish to at subsequent sessions. They are made to feel free to change their position as they weigh more evidence. The value here is that students may see how their peers think and feel. Sharing

the same experience draws the group together and gives it
the comforting feeling of not being alone. This strategy
can be the forerunner of exciting discussions.

Rank Order. This strategy involves decision making,
evaluating, weighing consequences, and judging in a very
realistic way. The student has to become totally involved in the
problem at hand because he has important choices to make.

Directions: The student is given three statements, and he
must choose which would be hardest for him to do or
tolerate as a first choice; second choice, less hard; third
choice, easiest.

1. Three "things" that some men do that people do not like:
   a. A man who always interrupts his wife, finishes her
   story, contradicts her.
   b. A man who lies around watching TV all day.
   c. A man who smokes a pack of cigarettes a day.
2. You are on a Congressional Committee in Washington,
D.C. Ten million dollars has been given for three worthy
causes. Which would you do first, second, third? You must
spend all the money on one thing.
   a. Use the money to clean up rivers, garbage,
   sewage, pollution.
   b. Train those who do not have jobs.
   c. Divide the money among ten thousand needy families.
3. Which would you find hardest to do?
   a. Drop a bomb on Vietnam?
   b. Electrocute a man who has been judged to die
   in the electric chair?
   c. Run over someone who is threatening you with harm
   while you are driving your car?

This strategy allows the student to compare his thinking
with that of his classmates. If they feel as he does, he feels
reinforced. If the thinking is different from his, he can
examine the issue and reevaluate his own thinking if necessary.

A variation of this strategy is to have the students list
what they think might be other types of behavior that men
practice that they do not like; or to list other worthy causes
on which to spend ten million dollars. Any of the Rank
Order strategies might be the takeoff point for a social
studies lesson, a science lesson, or an English lesson.

The few strategies we have used for demonstration purposes
are just a sample of the many that have been developed. It is

through these devices that our students learn to think
critically in deciding what their values are. They learn to
accept them, and, at the same time, to respect and tolerate
other people's values.

A Better Rapport

We have been working with the values-clarification approach
for only nine months, and yet we see many benefits for
pupils, teachers, and administrators. Pupils have felt warmth
and there has been evidence of the development of mutual
trust. Students like the personal attention, the relaxation,
the period of "fun," the freedom to express their ideas and
feelings. Discipline problems seem to disappear. Pupils feel
important and they see their teachers and administrators as
human beings with the usual "ups" and "downs" of human
beings. They hear that other pupils have the same problems
and confusions and conflicts that they do. They hear their
ideas and thoughts being accepted without either praise
or condemnation.

Teachers and administrators have experienced a better
understanding and a better rapport with each other and with
pupils whom they can see as fellow humans. They have
shared experiences with each other and with pupils and have
become more aware of each other. Teachers have many
opportunities to really "listen" to each other and to pupils
and to build a group feeling among themselves and pupils.

Our main problem has been to contend with "killer"
statements — efforts by some pupils to put each other down by
ridicule, laughter, or jeering. Since we are living in a
"put-down" society where all of us find it difficult to speak
openly and freely of a person's strong points, we have really
had to do much thinking about how to stop this at least
during class time. We are also living with a society that has
had the biblical ethic that "pride goeth before a fall"
ingrained in it, so that all of us think that to be proud of
something will hurt us; and even if we do feel proud, we keep
it to ourselves. We are working on how to handle this and
have seen enough success to encourage us. "Put-down"
remarks and lack of self-esteem are both very characteristic
of the kind of children we are working with, and this,
of course, intensifies the problem.

There are authorities who doubt that values-clarification

work can be done with ghetto children at all. The feeling
is that until basic emotional needs are met, pupils will not be
able to look at their values. We understand this point of view,
but we feel we have seen enough success of the type
described in the previous paragraph to continue our
experimentation with enthusiasm. Perhaps we will not be
able to go as far with our youngsters as we could with
middle-class children, but we will have begun the difficult
process of getting pupils to decide for themselves what they
value and take steps to live the lives they would like to live.

NOTE

1. Sidney Simon, "Promoting the Search for Values," *Educational
Opportunity Forum* 1, no. 4 (Fall 1969): 84. Special issue on Psychological
Humanistic Education (Albany: New York State Education Department).

Value Clarification: Meeting a Challenge in Education

by Joel Goodman and Laurie Hawkins

From *Colloquy*, May 1972. Used by permission.

For the undergraduate, the college years are a transitional period, with the no-man's land between home security on one side, and "going out into the real world" on the other. It is a time when many students face conflict and confusion in their values. It is a time when they are trying to make sense out of how to live their lives.

Unfortunately, many universities and colleges have not found ways to help students deal effectively with the conflict which rages all around us in 1972. The challenge presents itself: How can we help students with their values-related concerns? Indeed, can there be a "higher education" than helping students to discover for themselves their own values and meaningful life-styles?

We offered an eight-week "course" which tried to meet this challenge. The course was called "Value Clarification." It met in a dormitory setting for two and one-half hours on Tuesday nights during the spring of 1971.

During this course, we had the opportunity to: 1) examine our values (guides to behavior) in many potential areas of conflict and confusion (sex, friends, money, politics, religion, war, drugs, death, race, leisure, work, grades, time, and self-appraisal); 2) learn value-clarification *processes* that we could apply to our own lives (learn *ways* of valuing, not *what* to value); 3) strengthen the values of our own choosing; and 4) learn in our immediate living environment – the dorm – with our dormmates.

THE FIRST SESSION

As facilitators, we went into the first session of the course excited and full of butterflies. Here's how the first session went.

Introduction

We shared our excitement about the potential of values clarification for helping people to shape their lives in a meaningful way and to develop congruency among their thoughts, feelings, and behaviors. After explaining our expectations for the course, we set out the agenda for this session (which was posted on newsprint for the students to see). During the course, we stressed: 1) the students have the responsibility and opportunity to suggest how and what they want to learn; 2) the facilitators are not "answer-men" – we will not tell the students what to value – but, rather, will provide processes through which the students can begin to generate their own answers; 3) through sharing in a supportive atmosphere, students will have a chance to get to know each other better; 4) the learner himself – his thoughts, feelings, behaviors, and values – are a valid and highly relevant subject matter; 5) people learn best if they feel good about themselves and are in an honest, uniqueness-encouraging atmosphere; 6) experiential learning can be very effective, especially when coupled with a cognitive evaluation of the experience; and 7) the course structure and curriculum must be flexible to meet the needs of the students.

Get To Know Each Other

As a first step in building trust and support, we suggested ways for all of us to share with each other.

– *ing Name Tags*. The participants each made up a name tag on a 4 x 6 card. We suggested that each person write six words ending in "-ing" on the card. These "-ing" words were to describe each person as he saw himself. For example, one person saw himself as loving, feeling, listening, understanding, jam-packed-living, and sportsing. After we had completed and put on our name tags, we nonverbally milled around the room and told each other about ourselves through our name tags.

As one person commented later in her evaluation, "I liked the name tagging way of getting to know people. It was fresh and uninhibiting." Another student said, "I learned some aspects of my personality that I desire to bring out when meeting people by marking them on a name tag."

Three Questions. After breaking into groups of three, we had the opportunity to focus further on ourselves and to share our positive feelings about ourselves in small groups. We posed three questions (one at a time): 1) What was the high point of your week? 2) What have you done to celebrate winter? 3) What was one success you had before the age of ten? The triads spent about five minutes sharing ideas on each question. Then each student individually (in a private, ongoing class journal) took time to inventory his reactions to this sharing.

Here and Now Wheel. This inventory was done through a quick Here and Now Wheel, which helps a student to identify and focus on his feelings. (We are indebted to Gerald Weinstein, director of the Center for Humanistic Education at the University of Massachusetts, for his pioneering work in the areas of humanistic and affective education.)

Each of us drew a circle with four spokes. After "getting in touch" with what he was feeling at the time, the student put a different word at each of the spokes to represent these feelings. We circled the most significant of the four words, and then wrote, in a few sentences, what that feeling meant to us.

Whole-Group Sharing. We then had a chance, in a whole-group circle, to express feelings and reactions to the three-question sharing. This sharing was the beginning of a community of people who supported and learned with each other. Responses that were shared in the whole group, and later in the "Dear Me" letter, included:

"I especially enjoyed talking about the three questions. It's amazing how much I learned about people I didn't know."

"I felt a feeling of excitement in discussing the very simple but personal ideas in the get-to-know session."

"I learned that I have a lot of good memories that somehow get hidden away in my mind by other not so pleasant thoughts and also shared them with others."

"I really enjoyed the beginning of thinking of pleasant or high-point situations of the near and distant past. It was a positive experience. I also enjoy writing my personal reactions to things as the class goes on. This allows no important, or even unimportant, thoughts to escape."

Generating Concerns

In order to make this course helpful and relevant, it was important to provide an opportunity for us to generate our concerns. Throughout the course, we designed and presented values-clarification strategies to speak to these concerns.

To begin, each participant individually wrote a list of his concerns (in his journal) in fifteen areas that often involve values conflict and confusion (sex, friends, money, etc.). We then springboarded from their own journals and continued to brainstorm their concerns in the fifteen areas on sheets of newsprint on the walls (one sheet for each concern area). In addition to being an excellent diagnostic tool, this concerns-brainstorming provided other learning payoffs, as a number of students excitedly revealed:

"I learned that I am not the only person who has the same questions about life."

"I got in touch with a lot of problems, concerns, and feelings—things I have been pushing out, turning off, turning down."

"I wonder how it is that people who seem so different outside to me can be so similar inside. Also, it was good just writing anonymous comments (on the concerns-brainstorming newsprint) and getting no flak."

"I began a thinking process tonight where I saw some of my needs becoming apparent."

Break

We took a short break at this point. During the break, we continued to brainstorm and generate our values-related concerns on newsprint. In addition to the aforementioned questions related to sex, family, and drugs, the students expressed such concerns as:

Race: "I wonder in what little, hidden ways I am prejudiced, not just to blacks, but to anyone who is different than I am." "Why do I worry about making a mistake socially concerning people of other races?"

Friends: "What is the difference between friends and lovers —what happens when they overlap?" "What is a true friend? Can I put all my confidence in a friend?"

Self-appraisal: "I'm confused as to what to value in myself, what goals are worth pursuing, how to accept my failure to come up to my standards, and how to consider myself likable and worthwhile." "How can I be helpful to others, instead of using people for my pleasures?"

Sample Values-Clarification Strategies

For this introductory session, we facilitators thought it important to share with the group our ideas of the exciting potential of values-clarification. To do this, we chose two from among the hundreds of available values-clarification strategies to sample. These strategies also served as means for us to generate data about ourselves, our lives, values, feelings, and patterns. (Sidney Simon, professor in the Center for Humanistic Education, has created and inspired many of these strategies.)

Alligator River. For college students, the area of "sex" is one that is just chock-full of concern, confusion, and interest. The Alligator River story provides a provocative and energizing way for students to examine their values in this area.

The facilitators related the Alligator River story to the whole group:

As most stories begin . . . Once upon a time, their was a river that was practically overflowing with alligators. As you may have guessed, it was called Alligator River. A girl named Abigail lived on the west bank of the river. Her boyfriend, Greg, lived on the opposite bank. Abigail and Greg were very much in love with each other and wanted very much to see each other. One slight complication: no boat, and an alligator-filled river stood between them.

Abigail decided to seek help so that she could see her boyfriend, Greg. She approached Sinbad the Sailor, who, as his name might indicate, owned a boat. Now this was very fortunate for Abigail, because Sinbad's boat was exactly what she needed to get across the river. She explained her situation to Sinbad and asked if she could borrow his boat. Sinbad thought for a moment and then replied: "Sure, you can borrow my boat, but only under one condition. The condition is that you sleep with me tonight."

Now this startled Abigail, because she didn't want to sleep with Sinbad—she just wanted to borrow his boat so she could see Greg.

After Abigail had told Sinbad "no deal," she wandered down the road until she came upon Ivan the Uninvolved. Abigail explained her plight (her desire to see Greg, Sinbad's response) to Ivan, who, as his name indicates, didn't give a darn. Ivan told Abigail: "Hey, don't bother me. That's not my concern, I don't care what happens. Take off." A despondent Abigail, her options exhausted, finally decided to go back to Sinbad. She slept with him that night. The next morning, Sinbad, true to his word, loaned his boat to Abigail.

Abigail sailed across the river and saw her beloved Greg. After spending a few delightful hours together, Abigail felt compelled to tell Greg what had happened. After she had related her whole story, Greg completely blew up: "You what? I can't believe you did that. I-I can't believe you slept with him! That's it—it's all over—just forget the relationship— get out of my life!"

Distraught, Abigail wandered off. She came upon Stan the Schlemiel. Borrowing his shoulder to shed her tears, Abigail related her tale to Stan. Stan then went looking for Greg (with Abigail close behind). Stan found Greg and proceeded to beat the stuffing out of him, with Abigail gleefully and laughingly applauding the bloody pummeling.

That's the end of the story.

We then suggested to our shocked and bubbling audience that each student individually (in his journal) rank the five characters in the story from the most to least despicable. Following this, the students formed groups of five or six. Each group faced the challenge of coming up with a consensus Rank Order. In the lively (to put it mildly) discussion of values and criteria for ranking that ensued, students *experienced* many of the valuing criteria posited by Louis Raths, Merrill Harmin, and Sidney Simon in their book *Values and Teaching:* 1) that each individual be entitled to

choose freely his own values; 2) that the individual seek
alternatives when making values choices; 3) that the
individual be aware of the possible consequences of his
choices; 4) that the individual feel good about his choices
and values; 5) that the individual be willing to affirm his
choices publicly; 6) that the individual act on his choices;
and 7) that the individual act on his choices repeatedly,
so as to form a pattern in his life.

Following the small-group consensus discussions, we wrote
our reactions to the strategy in our journals. Clarifying
questions from the facilitators helped students focus on
learning and feelings. For example, what values were you
protecting in your individual Rank Order? Did you compromise
on any of the characters? Was there any character on whom
you would not change your mind? Did you identify with any
of the characters? How many people were usually talking
at once in the small group? Did you feel others were
listening to you during the discussion? Did you listen
to others?

Some responses to Alligator River were:

"This was fun, and it was interesting to see the way
different people go about making judgments."

"I thought that dividing the class into small groups was
helpful, because I know I feel more at ease talking among
a small number of people."

"I learned that I have a lot of values I didn't realize were
there from the Alligator River game."

"Alligator River was especially successful since it brought
to the surface vital and sensitive values. I'd like to see
more of this."

"The Alligator River is a unique and creative strategy,
and one that I will probably use in the future as a teacher."

Pattern Search. At the foundation of this "course" was
the belief that the individual has responsibility for and
control over his own life. Like other values-clarification
strategies, the Saturday night Pattern Search seeks to have
students examine their own lives. How we spend our time
tells a great deal about what we value, perhaps even more
than what we say we value.

Each of us sat back and tried to remember what we had
done the last five or six Saturday nights (which seems to be
an important night in the life of a college student). After

recording this in our journals, we responded to such
clarifying questions as: Do you see a pattern? Do you like
what you see? What alternatives are there for you in the
way you spend your Saturday nights?

Homework

At the end of each session, we suggested "homework,"
which would be followed up in the next class. This homework
often provided a way for students to "practice"
the skills they had learned in class, and also provided
for continuity between sessions.

At the end of the first session, we suggested that we each:
1) add to our brainstormed lists of concerns in values areas;
2) make a list of twenty things we love to do; 3) make a
collage that represents us – what we find important in life
and what we value.

Dear Me Letter

Each session closed with each participant writing a Dear
Me, a letter to himself (and to the facilitators through use of
carbon paper) about what had happened to him during
the evening. This letter serves the dual purpose of: 1) helping
the student tie up and make meaningful his experiences, and
2) providing the means for effective, ongoing recognition
of students' concerns, as well as feedback for the facilitators.

We found it helpful to respond to such statements and
questions as: I learned...; I felt...; I wonder....What about
the facilitators' behavior did I like/dislike? What about my
behavior did I like/dislike? How did I respond to specific
values-clarification strategies?

The highly positive feedback from these first Dear Me
letters (note the students' quotes on the previous pages)
encouraged us. This first session provided the initial
momentum for what was to be a stimulating eight-week
exploration.

A QUICK LOOK AT THE REST OF THE COURSE

In later weeks, we learned values-clarification skills and
strategies that helped us examine and confront values-
related issues. Through following up the initial Saturday
night Pattern Search, students – individually and in groups –

generated alternatives to their patterns in many areas.
(For example, how shall I spend Saturday nights? How open
am I with my roommate? How do I negotiate using/not
using drugs? How honest am I/do I want to be with my
family? What is a meaningful physical relationship for me?)
In each area, if one or more of these alternatives was
attractive, we encouraged anyone to make self-contracts
to try it. In so doing, each of us expanded his repertoire —
expanded his range of drawing from life's big banquet table.
This pattern search, alternative generation, self-contracting
sequence helped us assume responsibility for our own behavior
and helped provide us with a process for enriching our
lives. We shared some of the significant changes in our
lives in a supportive and often tender atmosphere.

The participants speak:

"This course has been extremely meaningful for me. It has
put me up against some aspects of my life that I had not
seriously confronted before, specifically my relationships
with others. I have done a lot of thinking about my parents
and family. I realize more than before what is happening
and why. I am also more aware of what I should do in order
to maintain the beauty of our lives together."

"I was surprised at how much time I put into the course,
but I guess the reason it was so easy to do was that I didn't
think of it as work. How can one's own growth and
self-improvement be considered work?"

"Analyzing patterns in my life really hit home. There are
patterns in my life that I don't value too much that I'm
trying to change. I like getting high, but I was doing it
too often, and now I'm succeeding in getting more work done
and only getting high when I can afford it."

"This is the type of course that doesn't have a definite
terminating date. I'll be following this course up for the
rest of my life."

"Next year, I will be a steering board member in the dorm.
I can use some of these strategies to evaluate my actions
and can apply some to counseling problems if they
should arise."

"Many times people think of education as a preparation for
a job or occupation, but I think it should prepare us for
more than that; I think education should help us to understand
the whole process of life, because life is a lot more than

just a job. That is why I think the values course is
so important."

The applications of values-clarification are endless. First,
think of the potential for the training of heads of residences,
or dorm counselors. Think of the tremendous impact a
values-clarification-centered freshman orientation program
could have. Then there are the possibilities for applying
value clarification to campus (drug) drop-in centers, to
draft-counseling services, to campus abortion and birth-control
agencies. It could be a vital force for confronting both
individual and institutional racism on our campuses.

All these issues are really values issues. All of them are
problems in which students face conflict and confusion.
But absurd as it may seem, there is no organized center at
most colleges where students can grapple with making
sense out of chaos.

The challenge is here. We must help each other deal with
the basic questions: Who am I? Where am I going? How am I
to live my life with passion and tenderness and love and
purpose? Values clarification, we have found, meets
this challenge.

Doing Something About Values

by Farnum Gray

On the first day of school in Rockville, Maryland, a teacher calls the attention of the children in her class to the long bulletin board at the back of the room. A line stretches the length of the board, and large letters spell out "Sad Sam" at one end and "Happy Harry" at the other.

Each child has made a paper emblem representing himself. Pin your emblem, asks the teacher, where your feelings are – all-the-way happy, all-the-way sad, or anyplace between.

As the days go by and moods change, the teacher encourages the children to move their emblems accordingly.

To the north, in central Philadelphia, a teacher tells his seventh graders: "All right, we've taken a minute to think about what we did this week that we're proud of. Now, let's whip around the room and tell about it. You may pass if you choose, but try to give something to the rest of us that you are proud of."

The smallest boy in the class starts it: "I'm proud I finally got on top of our human pyramid. I was really scared the first few times I tried."

"I'm proud I got Wendell for my frien'."

"I'm proud our family got a new TV."

"I'm proud of the film I made."

"I'm proud I ain't lost a fight this week."

Both teachers are providing their students opportunities to develop personal values through an approach called values clarification. Engendered by Louis Raths, values clarification avóids indoctrination of students and seeks instead to help them learn processes for creating their own values.

Fortunately for teachers who decide to try the values-clarification approach, the repertoire of activities is versatile and inexhaustible. The developers call these activities "strategies," and a recently published book, *Values Clarification: A Handbook of Practical Strategies* by Sidney B. Simon, Leland W. Howe, and Howard Kirschenbaum, details seventy-nine of them. The Rockville teacher was using a strategy called a Values Continuum, and the Philadelphia teacher was using a Proud Whip.

To grasp both how these strategies facilitate development of values and the importance of schools helping students to develop values, Raths' theories on *what* values are and *how* they develop must be understood.

Out of our experiences grow personal guides. Only when these guides become fully developed, Raths says, do they become values. These values give direction to life, help us relate to our world and take purposeful action.

Raths defines a seven-part valuing process. To create a value, a person must experience it in all seven ways. It must be *prized and cherished, publicly affirmed, chosen from alternatives, chosen after considering consequences, chosen freely, consistently linked to other values, and acted upon.*

The values-clarification strategies stimulate students to experience these seven parts of the process, thus increasing the likelihood that they will develop clear values. The valuing process combines cognitive activity (such as choosing) and emotion (such as cherishing). Indoctrination violates the requirement that a value must be chosen freely. Thus, according to the Raths theory, values cannot be inculcated in one person by another (although the example of one person's life can influence the values that another will develop). Here, the Raths theory offers one explanation of why attempts to instill values in schools have not succeeded, of why people tend not to act in accord with what they were taught to believe.

Beliefs, according to Raths, are not values but *value indicators*. These are guides that have met only some of the seven criteria of the valuing process. Value indicators include attitudes, opinions, feelings, morals, thoughts, ethics, goals, aspirations, and worries. As these value indicators are taken through all seven parts of the valuing process — with classroom strategies or other experiences in life — they are likely either to be modified or to become values.

According to *Values and Teaching* by Raths, Harmin, and Simon, people who have values — giving them a clear view of their relation to society — tend to be positive, enthusiastic, and proud. Value indicators do not accomplish that. They are ineffectual in giving people clarity about their relation to the world and the direction of their lives.

Raths also identifies eight behavior patterns of people who do not have clear values and are therefore confused about how to relate their lives to their surroundings. These values-confused people might be apathetic, flighty, inconsistent, drifting, overconforming, overdissenting, or posturing. They might have these characteristics in varying degrees and combinations.

Raths, Harmin, and Simon see an epidemic of values confusion in the United States. They assert that if children are helped to use the valuing process, "they will behave in ways that are less apathetic, confused, and irrational and in ways that are more positive, purposeful, and enthusiastic." They note, however, that before much progress can be made in developing clear values, the emotional needs of students must be satisfied. Students will not profit from values-clarification experiences if they have very little feeling of being lovable and capable.

In employing these strategies in the classroom, the teacher draws from the areas of conflict and confusion in people's lives. Some typical areas of confusion and conflict are politics, religion, work, leisure time, school, love and sex, family, material possessions, culture (art, music, literature), personal tastes (clothes, hair style), friends, money, aging and death, health, race, war and peace, rules and authority.

To better understand how this values construct is implemented, I visited a workshop conducted by Dr. Sidney Simon at Groton, Massachusetts. The workshop is structured much as a class with students might be. The fifty teachers who are present gain experience in clarifying their own values as well as learn ways to help their students develop values.

Simon, easily identified by his gray beard and pixie nose,

greets the workshop participants in the Groton High School gymnasium. He begins the session by asking the participants to make special name tags. Following Simon's instructions, each of us writes his name in large letters in the middle of a sheet of paper. In one corner go the names of four people, other than relatives, who have had a significant impact on his life. In another corner go the names of four geographical locations where he underwent dramatic changes. In a third corner go three years: "a year in which you were deliciously happy for at least five consecutive days; the year of your most intense love affair; and the year you did the most good for other people's children."

In the fourth corner goes a Rank Order, a useful old standby in the values-clarification repertoire. We're given three abilities and asked to rank them in accordance with our desire for personal improvement: "to have my anger the same on the outside as on the inside and to be able to use my anger as a disciplined tool; always to be able to admit when I am wrong; to be able to ask boldly for affection."

Finally, each of us writes on the paper at least six words applying to himself with "-able" added as a suffix (reason*able*, break*able*, mean*able*, teach*able*). As we write, Simon expresses "an important theory plank: Whatever is a value of yours, you must be willing to publicly affirm." He also makes out his own name tag. What Simon says, Simon does.

Following Simon's instructions, we pin the name tags to our chests, and without talking, mill about the room and find partners. We read the data on each other's chests and try to communicate nonverbally. On signals from Simon at one-minute intervals, we move on to new partners.

That done, we break into groups of three—preferably three who don't know each other well. This is called a *focusing session*, and each participant takes a turn at being the focus of the other two in his group for five minutes. The focus person talks about any of the four people on his name tag and how that person influenced him. Simon explains that it is important to allow "a choice of entrypoints." A person might "feel menaced" if he were told exactly which person to talk about. For example, one of the young women in my group tells of how she was influenced by Carl Rogers when she took a course given by him at the University of Wisconsin. Rogers might be a safer choice for her than someone whose relationship with her was more personal.

In my turn, I tell about a person I am surprised at having put on my list. I never before realized that this fellow—something of an eccentric mountaineer—had such an impact on my life. The other young lady in my group, amazed, exclaims, "How could you have been influenced by someone like *that*? Weird!" It was an honest reaction but the kind that could cause some people to draw back, and after the first round Simon provides focusing rules to prevent responses that provoke caution:

1. *Focus*. Members of the group should maintain eye contact with the focus person. They may ask him only those questions that do not shift the focus away from him.

2. *Accept*. Listeners should be warmly interested and understanding, and their facial expressions and postures should reflect it.

3. *Draw out*. Listeners should try to understand the focus person's position and beliefs. They ask questions to clarify the reasons for his beliefs and feelings and avoid questions that reveal negative feelings.

Simon warns against such "fogging" questions as:

"Don't you think that...?"

"Wouldn't you agree...?" (Which means, "Wouldn't you agree with me?")

"Aren't you saying that...?" (Which isn't what you're saying at all.)

The rules are scrupulously observed in the second round. Having formed new groups, we each tell what happened in one of the years on our name tags.

Simon notes that exercises with time limits are likely to leave some matters unresolved. He advises us to finish up such "unfinished business" in our free time.

Focusing can be a useful part of almost any activity that includes small-group discussion. A topic recommended to introduce students to focusing is: "I feel best (worst) when I am in a group of people who...."

"I really urge you to teach this to kids," Simon says. "I think they need it desperately. One of my colleagues says there are kids who have never in their entire lives had five minutes of focused attention." Simon then asks participants to volunteer some I Learned Statements, based on what we have done that morning. This same technique

can be used in the classroom by posting a chart with
stems such as:

"I learned that I...."

"I relearned that I...."

"I discovered to my surprise (dismay, joy)...."

Completing the appropriate stem normally becomes an
incisive windup. When I Learned Statements are made orally,
the listeners often gain new insights into the activity. It is
a far healthier way for students to take stock of what they
have learned than competitive grading, which Simon
outspokenly detests.

Here is a sampling of I Learned Statements heard at the
Groton workshop. From a woman volunteer: "I learned that I
don't allow women to influence my life as much as I do men."

From a male principal: "I learned that I'm opening up
and relaxing, but I still have my inhibitions. I'm very
appreciative of these techniques."

Another woman offers: "I learned that the five days I was
happiest were also in the year that I was most effective
with children."

A fourth participant: "I relearned that I get a very nice
high from sharing parts of my life with other people and
hearing about theirs."

And a fifth: "I learned that I've changed more in the last
few years than I did in many years before."

This segment of the workshop shows how a full
values-clarification lesson plan might work, with each activity
building on those preceding it and leading into the next.
The strategies are also effective for spot use in classes. An
alert teacher who understands many values strategies
can pick up on cues in classroom action and extemporaneously
bring in strategies.

Recently, for example, a middle school class was talking
spiritedly about poems related to war and man's inhumanity
to man —"Flander's Field," "The Hollow Men," "Death of
the Ball Turret Gunner" and others. From there, the dialogue
ranged through the draft, the Vietnam War, and human
meanness. Eventually the students deadlocked on the question
of whether soldiers who killed civilians under orders in
Vietnam are murderers.

At this point, the teacher called for a vote: "Are you least
opposed to 1) killing someone in civilian life, 2) killing

someone in war, or 3) committing suicide?" The youngsters
decided they were least opposed to killing in war, and
their discussion of the different reasons they had for voting
the same way brought new life into the conversation.

Values Voting and Rank Order are among the strategies
that are good for getting a class off to a fast start.

Values Voting is a quick and simple way to allow students to
express themselves on a string of issues. Those answering
affirmatively raise their hands; negative answers are
thumbs down; the undecided fold their arms; and those
wishing to pass do nothing.

If the teacher has prepared a list of ten to twenty good
questions and pops them in a brisk rhythm, children often
become excited and start to call out questions they want to be
asked. For a mixed-bag approach, some sample questions
relating to areas of confusion and conflict are:

"How many of you have a dog?"

"How many of you like to ride a bicycle?"

"How many of you have all the friends you want to have?"

"How many of you daydream sometimes?"

"How many of you think it's OK for boys to play with dolls?"

"How many of you are afraid of the principal?"

Values Voting can also be used to initiate exploration of a
topic such as ecology. "How many of you throw trash out the
car window? How many of you would sort your garbage
each day for the recycling center? How many of you would
want your family to have a slower car if it discharged less
exhaust? How many of you would swim in a river that
smelled bad?"

In any activity calling on students to make statements, the
student always has the right to pass.

How about the teacher? The conflict over whether a teacher
should state his opinions on controversial matters seems
never to die. But the values-clarification advocates are clear
in their answer. The teacher should state his opinions and
take part in exercises, but only by reserving his statement
until after most of the students have given their views, can
the teacher minimize any tendency for the students to
feel pressured towards his point of view.

An exciting strategy, one that Simon uses in the afternoon,
is the Public Interview. This strategy involves a single
student answering questions in an interview of five to ten

minutes. Simon fires questions from the back of the room while the subject stands up front. "A little showbiz is useful to a teacher," Simon comments. The subject must be completely honest with each answer, but he has the right to pass. When time is up, the subject can ask the teacher any question that he answered, but the teacher *cannot* pass. The teacher should be careful to gauge the questions to the individual subject so that he is challenged but not threatened. Some subjects would be upset by questions that others would thrive on.

In this session Simon demonstrates two forms of interview questions. After the first interview, in which he uses normal fire power, he says, "I think that with Farnum, our friend from *Learning*, I can show you a different procedure." He does.

He asks me to name all of my past loves and tell how many dropped me and how many I dropped. Then: "What are *Learning* magazine's chances of failure? Give me numerical odds. Would you be hurt financially if it fails? Would you be hurt personally? Has any organization you worked for gone down? How did it happen? Are you and your wife comfortable with the idea of an open marriage in which you are both free to have sexual relations with other people? Are you jealous?"

The strategies, of course, are only part of what the teacher can do to help students process values. An effective way of conversing with students that encourages them to apply the valuing process to what they do and think is described in "The Clarifying Response," Chapter Five of *Values and Teaching*, a chapter which rewards repeated readings.

In the foreword to that book, Kimball Wiles recalls his first experience with clarifying responses.

"Years ago when I was in graduate school, Louis Raths intrigued me with his reactions to my comments. As far as I could detect he never really approved any statement I made. He would ask a question, make a noncommital observation, test my assertion by supplying additional data, ask if I had considered a different alternative.

"The experience was disconcerting to me. My previous educational experience had led me to expect to use the teacher as a means of determining the correctness of my answers. He was the person who knew and his role was to keep me informed of my progress in the search for truth...."

And this teacher did not! I expected positive affirmation and support. And I received more questions and the expectation that I would continue to probe."

In making clarifying responses, the teacher asks questions that stimulate students to go through parts of the valuing process. "Are you proud of this piece of work? Did you choose your opinion freely? What other conclusions could you have reached? Is this a personal preference or do you think most other people should believe that? Have you done anything about that idea?"

The general climate of a school does much to help or retard values development. Simon sprawls shirtless in the New England sun at the lunch break and discusses the subject. "There really needs to be a sense of positive acceptance and an elimination of grades, punishments, and rewards. There has to be an absence of a right-answer syndrome. That's one of the most destructive ideas—a single right answer that we all have to arrive at. Put the focus on process, search, inquiry. I think this morning what you experienced was a damn good sample of the climate and tone." For the most part, he said, it was "a beautiful, sweet, sensuous morning— weaving in and out of people's lives."

How should a teacher new to values work prepare himself? Simon feels that "no one should use a strategy with students unless he has used it to examine his own material." He suggests that a teacher could read about values clarification, then work through strategies himself before using them with kids. Going to a workshop such as the one at Groton is good preparation, but a teacher who cannot do so can work on his own. Teachers can also form their own Support Groups (strategy number seventy-nine in *Values-Clarification: A Handbook of Practical Strategies*). Group members might take turns leading their colleagues while testing the different strategies, much as the workshop participants are doing. He warns that teachers must be alert to keep "moralizing crap" out of their work with values.

Values work, according to Simon, has been successfully offered both by entire schools and by individual teachers working alone. In some cases "an individual principal with courage has said, 'Come train my entire faculty.'" Dr. Dick Davis, principal of the English Manor Elementary School in Rockville, did that some years ago. The teachers have

been using values strategies with children and are working
to integrate values development with academic studies.
Davis has found attendance up, vandalism down, parent
satisfaction higher, and the morale of teachers enhanced.

Teachers working in schools that are not ready to unify in
such an undertaking, Simon explains, have had "major
success by closing their doors and doing things that they
believe in." Values strategies can be used in virtually any
class. Simon says that when he was teaching at Temple
University, "I always bootlegged the values stuff under other
titles. I was assigned to teach Social Studies in the Elementary
School, and I taught values clarification. I was assigned
Current Trends in American Education, and I taught
my trend."

Simon's closed-door policy brought teaching success without
controversy. But several years ago, just as he was up for
tenure at Temple University, he quit playing the grading
game. That had to be noticed, and tenure was denied.
Demonstrations were staged by students acting on *their* values.

It seemed obvious to Simon that when a man teaches that
grading is pernicious and that acting on one's beliefs has
great psychological benefit, he has no logical choice but to
stop grading. True to the Raths theory, the stand made him
feel "alive, purposeful, and proud." The demonstrating
students eventually prevailed, and the tenure decision
was reversed.

Now a professor at the Center for Humanistic Education at
the University of Massachusetts Graduate School of
Education, Simon has a strong sense of destiny about his work.

"Values-clarification work is going to grow dramatically
in the next few years because of the unrest in schools,"
he says. "Something has to be done for the kids. They're
hurting as much as us adults."

Values Clarification in an Organizational Setting

by Howard Kirschenbaum

Used by permission of the author and the Adirondack Mountain
Humanistic Education Center, Upper Jay, New York 12987.

*The following letter was written by Howard Kirschenbaum
in preparation for the United Presbyterian Women's National
Business Meeting. A segment of their program was to be
a values-clarification workshop which Merrill Harmin
would lead.*

*This letter outlines a program design which Dr. Harmin and
the UPW Planning Committee were asked to react to and
illustrates how values-clarification strategies can be used
in the pursuit of specific organizational goals.*

Dear Merrill,

The UPW has set for their theme for the coming three
years (1973-1976) The Fullness of Life for All. In addition
to that theme, the United Presbyterian Church has
developed what they call the Nine More Urgent Concerns.
They are: 1) committed and equipped Christians;
2) communicating our faith; 3) combatting racism; 4) youth;
5) family life; 6) world peace; 7) justice and human
development; 8) women; 9) unity of the church. These have
been elaborated upon with an impressive list of Objectives.

The National Business Meeting is a time when leaders of
the various UPW groups from all over the country gather

to discuss and vote upon goals for the organization in
addition to typical business matters. The following are the
goals they set for the meeting:

1. To help women discover how their lives relate to the
biblical concept, Fullness of Life for All.

2. To help women explore and experience the meaning and
implications of Fullness of Life for All so they might
help others to have fullness of life.

3. To help women explore the theme in terms of the Nine
More Urgent Concerns of the church.

4. To help women explore the theme in terms of its
meaning for UPW as an organization.

5. In light of the Urgent Concerns of the church and their
implications for UPW, the discovery, exploration, and
experience of the theme will come through worship,
business, program.

We are to provide a program which utilizes values-
clarification strategies with this two-fold purpose: 1) to help
the women at the conference become clearer about their own
values and priorities in general and to see how these values
and priorities specifically relate to the Urgent Concerns;
and 2) to have the women at the conference experience a
model or method which they in turn can use with their own
regional groups in a way that will help *their* members
become clearer about what their values and priorities are.

The UPW leaders agree that effective local programs can
come about only if the women perceive the meanings of the
Urgent Concerns in relation to their own value system.
The National Business Meeting program would begin
that process.

There will be about four hundred women at the meeting.
We will begin by working with the entire group, then
quickly divide into about nine subgroups for most of the time,
and end with the entire group together again. Of the
eleven hours involved in the values-clarification part of the
meeting, only the first hour and a half and the last hour
will be spent as a whole group.

UPW leaders will group the women according to regions.
The number of women and the number of areas represented
in each subgroup will vary, but women from the same
geographical area will be together whenever possible. The
rationale behind grouping the women geographically is this:

Women in the same general areas can establish loose or
formal support systems, joint projects in their own regions,
communications networks, and so on—if these seem desirable.

The UPW can help the process of subgroup formation
by coding the name tags according to geographical region.
This will facilitate forming subgroups more quickly when
the women are asked to do so.

Each subgroup will be facilitated by one woman who will be
trained for the task. (This will be explained more fully later.)

We have five time blocks to work with on the program:

Wednesday afternoon	3 hours
Wednesday evening	2 hours
Thursday morning	2 hours
Thursday evening	2 hours
Friday evening	2 hours

Here is my proposed design for the program. At times I
have been quite specific. At other times, where the design is
adaptable, you or the UPW planning committee may wish
to modify it.

WEDNESDAY AFTERNOON

First Half

The entire group of women will be together.

1. *Introductions.* You may wish to ask voting questions
of the whole group to put people at ease, establish climate, etc.
Perhaps questions related to the Nine More Urgent Concerns.
This might be followed by an introductory strategy such
as Values Name Tags, with milling. A choice of one stranger-
partner to sit with for a brief exchange on a name-tag related
topic will further help people to loosen up and will create
an accepting climate. This strategy will also begin to turn the
corner toward the meeting concerns. I would suggest that
some of the name-tag items be church related, for example:
Give the name of the person living today whom you regard
as the most ideal Christian.

2. *Forced Choice Ladder on Nine Concerns.* People remain
seated where they are and on a full sheet of paper draw
a nine-step ladder. At this point a Resource Person is
introduced. He/she is someone the UPW has invited because
of a particular knowledge of the Nine Concerns. The
Resource Person will be available throughout the conference.

The strategy should be explained to the group. The Resource Person then describes one of the Nine Concerns that is not religion-oriented. (The women will receive a copy of the Nine Concerns later.) The Resource Person conveys the concern in no more than two minutes. You ask the women to place the key word of the concern high or low on their ladder to indicate its relative priority for them. Then the Resource Person introduces a second concern, again, for no more than two minutes. You instruct the women to put it on another step. The strategy continues in this fashion.

3. Once all Nine Concerns have been presented and the women have completed their ladders, there should be a sharing strategy.

4. Conclude this part of the afternoon by briefly acknowledging the differences in values, legitimizing people's feelings about the Nine More Urgent Concerns, pointing out that local programs need support based on the values of the members, discussing the difficulty in maintaining clear values in our society, and emphasizing the need for values clarification.

5. The design for the next four and a half sessions will be reviewed and people oriented to their groups.

Second Half

This half will be conducted by the subgroup leaders in rooms designated for their subgroups.

1. An introductory strategy should begin the subgroup session. The session might begin by milling and looking at the Values Name Tags again, which takes only a few minutes and is nonthreatening. The women could also sit in groups of fifteen and do the Values Name Game. (First person says, "My name is ... and I value ...." Second person says, "Her name is ... and she values .... My name is ... and I value ...." and so on.) It's funny, relaxing, and people actually remember a lot of the names and what people value.

Much of this might have to be modified before the meeting or even on the spot due to personnel or scheduling changes.

2. There are two other strategies that are positive, low-threat experiences for almost everyone. They are Twenty Things You Love to Do and I Learned Statements. They would give the women and the leaders a productive, successful start. Then, by the time the group undertakes the more difficult strategies, the leader and group will have established a good rapport. I would suggest that one or two

of the codings on the Twenty Things You Love to Do relate
to the matter at hand, e.g., "How many of the items on
your list relate to the Nine Concerns?"

WEDNESDAY EVENING (In subgroups)

1. Hand out the following unfinished sentences (related to
the Nine Concerns), and have each woman, individually,
complete them.
>   **a.** A Christian...
>   **b.** The church should...
>   **c.** I wish young people...
>   **d.** Blacks and whites...
>   **e.** Poverty...
>   **f.** My family...
>   **g.** As a woman, I...
>   **h.** War will...
>   **i.** Church unity might...

2. Arrange people in groups of four. Explain rules of the
Values Focus Game to them:
>   **a.** rule of focus
>   **b.** rule of accepting
>   **c.** rule of drawing out

3. Each woman in the group takes a turn as focus person
(of course she may pass). The focus person reads her
completed sentences to the group. She may omit reading
any which she does not wish to share. The other three in the
group follow the rules of focus. Focus lasts five to ten
minutes. Then the next person becomes focus.

Either before or after this sequence (1-3), or for perhaps
one or two minutes before *and* after, the leader explains
that this activity is designed to help explore a bit more
deeply some feelings on the Nine Concerns. (Subgroup
leaders should be trained in the most effective use of
these strategies.)

4. *A Three Dimensional Values Continuum.* Have the group
picture a triangle. At one point is "Ritual, Prayer, Focus on
God." At the second point is "Charity." At the third point is
"Social Change." Describe these three possible orientations
toward religion and ask people to put themselves somewhere
on the triangle to represent their own emphases. (This might
also be done as a Rank Order.)

5. *A Proud Whip on the Nine More Urgent Concerns.* Leaders

ask two groups or three groups of four to combine, making groups of eight or twelve. Each person takes a turn: "I'm proud, pleased, etc., with..." (completing the sentence with something she's done on any of the Concerns). Anyone may pass.

6. Close the session by having someone from each bigger group retell something they heard in their Proud Whip which they would like to share with the entire group of fifty or so.

THURSDAY MORNING (In subgroups)

1. Have each woman individually re-rank the Nine More Urgent Concerns in order of importance to her. Then have them go to a part of the room designated for the Concern which they would like to work on for the next two sessions. It may or may not be their top item. There they should break up into work groups of three, four, or five. Thus the work groups will share a common interest in one of the Nine Concerns. (If there aren't enough to form a group around a given Concern, ask that person to choose her second or another Concern.)

2. Each group takes about ten to fifteen minutes to share why it chose this Concern to concentrate on.

3. Group members should then read the Objectives which the church has spelled out for each Concern. Then, using their chosen concern as a focus, they should spend about ten minutes discussing objectives they would delete, which they would add, and which they regard as most important.

4. The leader should explain the brainstorming process and rules and give them a topic of interest to brainstorm on for five minutes.

5. The leader then asks them to brainstorm, in their work groups, all the possible ways they can think of to implement the Objectives they have for their Concern. Every member of the group should record all the suggestions.

6. Leader then has each person code her brainstormed list by putting:

    a. the letter I or G next to each item, based on whether this would be done best by an individual or a group. (IG if it could be done equally well by individual or group.)

    b. a dollar sign next to any of the alternatives that involve a significant outlay of money.

c. an R next to those she regards as realistic, either for an individual or a group.

d. a Y, N, or M based on whether her reaction to the alternative is "Yes, I think this is something my chapter or I would like to do"; "No, this is not something I as an individual or my chapter as a group would want to do"; or "Maybe I or my chapter would want to do this—it deserves more consideration."

7. Each woman chooses the three alternatives on her list that she likes best. Then the work-group members combine their three favorites to try to find the one alternative that the work group as a whole likes best and would be willing to work with during the next session.

THURSDAY EVENING (In subgroups)

Each work group, using the action alternative it has identified as being the one most favored by the group, goes through a series of three strategies aimed at putting the alternative into action.

1. *Force Field Analysis.* In this strategy the women list all the forces back home that will help them or their chapter put the alternative into practice and all the obstacles or forces that will get in their way.

2. *Removing Barriers to Action.* Here they find ways to lessen or eliminate the hindering forces. This will allow the helping forces proceed toward their goal.

3. *First Steps.* This strategy asks them to take the previous analysis and put it into a series of concrete action steps which they or their group can do back home. These should be attainable steps. If they have time, they should list steps their local chapters can take to begin the process of change. They should also list first steps which they, the leaders, must take in order to start the group working on *its* first steps. Each first step should have a realistic date for completion.

The leaders should be flexible in helping each work group adapt these strategies to fit the concern, objectives, and alternatives they are working with. It is important to note that the alternative they are working with or the specific helping and hindering forces will not be the same in the back-home situation of each work-group member. Nevertheless, by going through the process together,

they can help each other learn it. Later they can apply it to
their specific goals and back-home realities.

FRIDAY EVENING

First Part (In subgroups)

1. *Self-Contracts.* Each woman writes some self-contracts
for what she will consider doing independently when she gets
home. Again, these contracts should be believable and
achievable. They may merely be first steps in a long series
of actions, but they are to be concrete first steps.

2. Leader asks the women to sign any self-contracts to
which they are willing to commit themselves when they
return home.

3. Leader asks for five volunteers to read their
self-contracts aloud to the group.

4. Time and structure should be provided for organizing
back-home regional support or communication systems even
though not every woman will want to take part in such
a group.

5. Subgroup session closes with I Learned Statements, and
depending on the feeling of the group, the leader asks for
volunteers to stand and say their I Learned Statement or
asks for people to pass their I Learned Statements to the
front and reads thirty or so aloud. The first is preferable if
it seems that individuals are willing to share their statements
aloud. They may very well be.

Leader talks for ten minutes or so, reviewing the series
of experiences and raising some implications as to different
priorities and values. It is natural for groups to have different
priorities as well as some common values which make them
a group; therefore, no group has to always be working on the
same thing all the time. The various UPW chapters may
want to focus on different Concerns to work on, and
subgroups of the same chapter likewise can work on different
Concerns. Finally, the leader asks "Will you fulfill the
contracts you signed? Will you sign some you didn't sign?
Will you make new ones?" and gives encouragement for the
fulfillment of the contracts.

Close on the I Wonder Statements — usually a very
powerful ending. If you want to build in a feedback device,

the feedback could go at the beginning of this
part, at the very end, or the next day if the Planning
Committee wants feedback on the entire meeting.

This design may be modified in light of the realities of the
situation, meetings with the group leaders, and so on. It may
also be further modified as I talk with the UPW Planning
Group to see if the design meets their needs. I will advise you
of any changes.

Now to the question of group leaders:

The UPW will select a group of women to serve as leaders
of the subgroups. I'm not sure what their criteria for
selection will be, but they appreciate the type of workshop it
will be, so I'm sure the selection will be as informed as
possible. As a necessary condition for their serving as leaders,
these women will each attend one of the values-clarification
workshops set up throughout the country this spring.
Therefore, you will probably meet some of them ahead of
time. It is also understood that leaders will read *Values and
Teaching, Values Clarification: A Handbook of Practical
Strategies*, and selected articles we designate or that might
interest them. I would suggest "Values," "Values-Clarification
vs. Indoctrination," and "Three Ways to Teach Church School."

You, the leaders, and some of the UPW staff members will
arrive for the meeting early. Ideally, you should have time to
do a run-through of the entire program with them, allowing
time for questions, practice, etc. To accomplish this
thoroughly would take two to three entire days, but there
will not be quite that much time. The UPW Planning Group
was not positive about the time and money they could devote
to this training part of the program, and I will clarify that
after speaking with them. Hopefully, we will have most of
Monday and Tuesday. The training will be in your hands.
You'll decide how to use the time in light of the objectives, the
proposed design, and the women (leaders) themselves.

I am also proposing that you remain after the Wednesday
afternoon session to meet with the leaders and help them
process how their first small group session went. I would think
you'll surely be done by 6 P.M. on Wednesday. You'll have
three pretty full days cut out for you.

I'll keep you informed.

—Howie

Teaching Values

by Sidney B. Simon, Geri Curwin, and Marie Hartwell

Reprinted by permission from the June 1972 issue of the *Girl Scout Leader* Magazine.

The girl growing up in this decade faces increasingly difficult decisions concerning her identity, her choice of companions, and the directions she chooses to take.

The Girl Scouts, my two co-authors and I feel, can and should provide a program where this girl can develop and practice the personal skills she needs to deal with these challenges. Values clarification – a process of weighing alternatives to decide just what's important to you – is an approach that leaders can incorporate into already existing programs for just this purpose. Ideal for group settings and activities, the values-clarification process is beneficial to those involved and – believe it or not – it's also fun to do!

Values clarification takes people through a series of exercises, called strategies, designed to help them sort through their thoughts and make a conscious effort to determine where they stand and why – to help them discover, examine, and utilize their own value system. It is a process that focuses on awareness and personal management. It does not promote a single value system, but allows for individual differences.

Numerous values-clarification strategies exist. Some can be used as is; others can be adapted to meet the specific needs of the individual girls involved. It's not difficult to learn to use these strategies, and then once you get into the spirit of values clarification, to go on to developing some strategies of your own.

Strategies can be as simple as an examination of a song with a values focus or as complex as a contrived model of a real-life situation. They can be as public as a vote by a show of hands or as private as an unshared fantasy. But each of these strategies follows certain ground rules:

1. It is an exercise in sharing and caring as well as discovery.

2. It is a time for girls to find their own values, but not to impose them on others.

3. It is the leader's responsibility to provide an open and nonjudgmental atmosphere to foster questioning and exploration, but not unthinking acceptance of others' standards and values.

Values clarification is a new approach to an old concern: helping girls develop a considered and strong set of standards with which to meet the challenges of a confusing world.

Do you really believe in what you sing? The song, "When E'er You Make a Promise," has been sung by Scouts for many years. An examination of the lyrics provides questions worth exploring.

> When e'er you make a promise
> Consider well its importance
> And when made, engrave it upon your heart.

Questions:
>   1. Do you think that promises should always be kept?
>   2. Can you think of anytime in your own life that it was better to break a promise than keep it?
>   3. When was the last time you made a promise that made you feel uncomfortable?
>   4. Do you think that all promises are of equal importance?

Dealing with questions like these (which focus on the girls' own lives and feelings) will help girls develop the awareness they need to take charge of their own lives.

Life Inventory Surprises

Some strategies involve asking an individual to inventory a part of her life and then to examine the data gathered for patterns. Patterns are often an indication of values.

One of the major concerns of girl scouting is helping others. Ask the girls to keep a record in the next week of all the things they do to help other people. At the end of the week ask the girls to note beside each entry:

a. which were voluntary; which required

b. which they enjoyed; which they resented doing

c. which they received appreciation for doing; which went unnoticed

d. whether the people helped were friends, family, strangers, others

Each girl is then asked to really look at the information about herself that she has collected. Do any patterns emerge? If so, is she happy with the patterns she sees? Are there any patterns she would like to change? If so, what is the first step she can take to make that change a reality? Girls may share their patterns if they wish to, and those who want to make changes might make verbal contracts with each other.

Unfinished Sentences

Ask the girls to form groups of four. Privately, each girl should complete the sentence, "Frustration is..." or any other open-ended sentence such as: "On Saturdays I...; If I had a million dollars...; The hardest thing for me...; If I were a teacher I would...." Girls who are willing may share and expand one of their sentences in the group. It is extremely important in an exercise of this nature that the right to pass, or decline to share, be legitimized and supported by the leader. Often shy individuals need to hear others discuss such issues before they feel comfortable taking part.

Positive Points

Again, groups of four are formed, and girls are asked to share, on a voluntary basis, such items as:

1. The high point of our last camping trip was....
2. The best thing about scouting for me is....
3. The happiest day of my life was....
4. The best surprise I ever had....

This exercise is excellent for fostering positive and high self-concepts. It also provides a vehicle for girls to get to know each other on another level. The idea that the things we like best are often reflections of our values can be included in the subsequent discussion of the exercise.

Fantasy Seeds

Fantasies are another means of approaching the values area. Some fantasy seeds for discussion are:

      1. If you were guaranteed success at any endeavor you might choose during the next year, what would you choose to do?

      2. What is your greatest wish?

      3. If you could do one thing to change scouting, what would you do?

Again, the above can be shared and expanded upon in groups. How do your fantasies reflect your values? What can you do to make your fantasies realities?

These last three strategies all involve the examination and sharing of personal experiences and expectations that reflect values issues. Such sharing provides support for dealing with values and raises the awareness that most values problems are not unique.

Teaching Nutrition with a
Focus on Values

by Jack D. Osman

Reprinted from *Nutrition News*, April 1973, Courtesy, National Dairy
Council.

Nutrition educators have done a commendable job in
sorting out the reliable research and transmitting that
information to their students. Some nutrition educators
erroneously believe that since they have presented the
facts of nutrition (especially if they have presented
controversial points of view), they have fulfilled their
didactic duties.

An emphasis on the scientific-factual-research approach
tends to minimize the psycho-social-humanistic aspects of
nutrition education. As trite as it may sound, educators must
remember that their goal is to produce well-adjusted,
rational people who can think as well as relate and feel, not
just nonlinear, calculating computers.

One of the ultimate objectives of education is to be able to
make intelligent decisions based upon the best knowledge
available, to live in congruence with what a person knows.
Syllogistic reasoning would suggest that those who know the
most should behave the best. Yet the world is filled with
persons who know much better than they do. The overweight
dietitian knows that excessive weight is harmful to her
health, but she still leads an underactive, high-calorie life.
Such behavior could hardly be described as rational or

intelligent or as the kind of behavior that characterizes truly educated people.[1] Perhaps knowledge is not as simplistically related to attitudes and behavior as educators once thought. We need to go beyond just disseminating knowledge. Even the Basic Four and conceptual approaches have recently been criticized as being "inadequate to accomplish the desired results in nutrition education."[2]

Facts and concepts can still leave students cold, abstract, and impersonal. What is needed is a personal, "you-centered" approach based, in part, on the here and now of reality. The scientific approach needs to be tempered with a values-level application of the specific facts and general concepts. The values level is characterized by lifting and transforming both information and concepts to a personal, "you-centered" level. This level adds meaning and relevancy to the facts, thereby increasing the possibility of their application to the student's life.

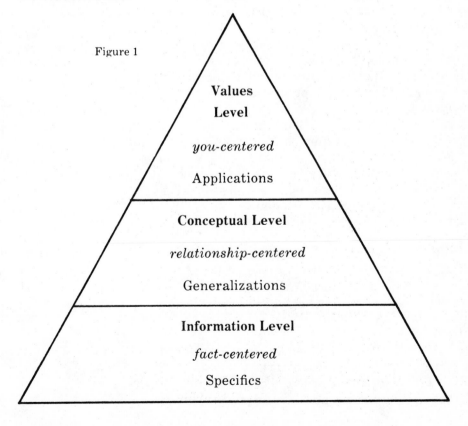

Figure 1

Values
Level

you-centered

Applications

Conceptual Level

relationship-centered

Generalizations

Information Level

fact-centered

Specifics

We need to assist students in clarifying what all the content and concepts mean to them at this point in their lives. As Figure 1 suggests, facts and concepts provide a base for effective thinking, but it is our values, in the final analysis, that ultimately determine our behavior. In short, facts are needed to inform our values.[3]

Values are like stars that guide our lives. Some people freely choose to follow certain values, others choose different values (life patterns) that have meaning for their lives at that point in time.

Students should be educated as to the alternative nutritional values open to them. Students need to choose freely those nutritional values which have meaning for them at that point in their lives. Some educators, however, feel that the only values worth mentioning in a classroom are the ones that can be stamped in, indoctrinated, moralized, inculcated, or rammed down kids' throats.[4]

Often in life, things (situations, circumstances, problems, conflicts) obfuscate or cloud our vision of the choices open to us. We can no longer see clearly those values that guide our lives. At times like this we need someone to blow away the clouds. Instead of teaching his own values, the teacher should assist students in the process of seeing and following their own values.

Within this values-clarification process, the educator acts as a facilitator, not a dictator. This involves going through a well-thought-out series of steps and teaching strategies which confront, clarify, and challenge students to put into practice what they have learned. A seven-step process of valuing defines values clarification and collectively characterizes the person who uses his values to guide his life.

Choosing: 1) freely; 2) from alternatives; 3) after thoughtful consideration of the consequences of each alternative. *Prizing:* 4) cherishing, being happy with the choice; 5) willing to affirm the choice publicly. *Acting:* 6) doing something with the choice; 7) repeatedly, in some pattern of life.[5]

A series of teaching strategies has been developed to assist the student through each of the seven steps of valuing. Several nutrition-oriented examples follow; they are adaptable for various age or information levels.

Nutrition and Weight Dual Continuum

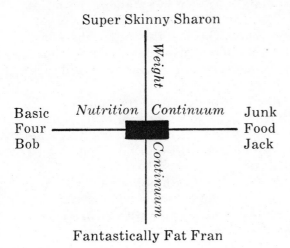

Figure 2

A self-image evaluation strategy (diagramed in Figure 2) sets up extremes in an attempt to help students identify other alternatives. They are asked to mark their position but to avoid the middle of the road. The teacher should explain each continuum as follows: Basic Four Bob refuses to eat anything unless the meal has been balanced by at least one food from each of the four groups. Pizza with meat or pepperoni would be acceptable; so would a cold cut and cheese submarine sandwich. Junk Food Jack is oblivious to any sound dietary practice; food selection is based on the sweet-tooth syndrome. Jack refuses to eat a balanced meal because all those foods and nutrients at the same time would play havoc with his digestive process.

On the vertical Weight Continuum, Super Skinny Sharon would be the classic 1-1-7 ectomorph who almost disappears when she turns sideways. Fantastically Fat Fran is the female counterpart of Bill Cosby's "Fat Albert," a pure 7-1-1 endomorph.

Adequate class time should be given students to follow these directions:

    1. Mark the horizontal line with an X at the spot which best approximates your food selection practices. Do the same for

the vertical line in reference to your present weight. Plot
your position on this dual continuum by extending both Xs
until they meet.

2. Find someone else in class who is in the same general area
(quadrant) as you are. Talk to him about his food selection
practices. Ask him to honestly evaluate your build and rate
your weight.

3. Where would you like to be on this dual continuum?
Mark that spot with an O. Is there a significant difference
between where you are now and where you would like to be?

4. If you are not happy/satisfied with your diet/weight, what
do you plan to do about it?

5. Contract with yourself, in writing, how you plan to make
a concerted effort to improve your nutritional behavior. Sign
and date the contract. Share its meaning with someone in
the class.

Ten Foods You Love to Eat and Drink

Have the students list their ten favorite foods on paper.
Explain that the following coding is only a means of
self-evaluation.

1. Circle the food you could most easily do without for
one year.

2. Mark a plus next to each food that's relatively high in
nutrients.

3. Indicate with a dash those foods high in calories and low
in nutrients.

4. Star those foods low in calories.

5. Use a check mark to code those foods you eat too much of
or too often.

6. Put the number 5 by the foods that would *not* have been
on your list five years ago.

7. Put an X next to junk foods.

Ask students to write answers to the following three
questions on the back of their paper after they objectively
study their codings:

1. What did the Ten Foods exercise reveal to you about
your food selection?

2. Are all of the food groups represented? In balanced
amounts?

3. What, if anything, do you plan to do as a result of
the exercise?

As is customary in values-clarification strategies, the students' papers are shared with no one (including the teacher) unless a student so chooses. In this way they are more likely to be honest with themselves. Some students may be anxious to share something they have learned about their food selection from the Ten Foods exercise. Therefore a good follow-up is the I Learned Statements strategy. Following an exercise like the one above, students voluntarily complete statements in a three-to-five-minute time period.

Values Voting

This strategy helps elicit responses from the entire class. It encourages students to take a stand on what they believe is right at the same time it reveals pertinent information about what students know and do not know. The voter has five alternatives: 1) A raised arm with the thumb up indicates being in favor of the idea. 2) Thumb down reveals opposition. 3) If you don't know, don't care to reveal your answer, or if you're not sure, you indicate *any* of the three by folding your arms. 4) If you're really in favor of the idea, wave your raised arm with thumb up. 5) To register strong disapproval, move your thumb up and down. Here are some sample voting questions:

1. How many here take therapeutic doses of vitamin C to prevent or cure colds?
2. How many here drink at least three glasses of milk a day? Four?
3. How many here feel increased activity is very beneficial in weight reduction programs?
4. How many here believe that excessive sucrose may lead to heart disease?
5. How many here regularly follow the Basic Four food groups?
6. How many here think pizza is a junk food?
7. How many here consciously limit your cholesterol intake?
8. How many here strive for 50 percent of your fats to come from polyunsaturated sources?
9. How many here believe potatoes are fattening?
10. How many here feel you have a weight problem?
11. How many here eat potato chips regularly?
12. How many here drink at least one sugar-containing soft drink a day? Two? More?

13. How many here drink skim or 2 percent milk?

14. How many here believe that you suffer from lactose intolerance?

15. How many here think your nutritional patterns will change as a result of this course?

After reading about five questions aloud to the class it's advisable to ask, "Does anyone want to ask anyone else why he voted a particular way?" Teachers should join in the voting fun but with a brief delay so as not to sway students who are easily influenced.

Rank Order

Ranking gets at priorities. Priorities reveal values. Value discussions often bring out inconsistencies, faulty reasoning, misinformation, or new information. Ask students to rank order three or four items. The variations in answers create interesting discussion.

1. Rank as most nutritious:
   a. instant breakfast with water
   b. salted peanuts
   c. pizza with pepperoni
   d. orange drink with a B-complex pill

2. Rank food with most calories first:
   a. medium-sized baked potato
   b. nine potato chips
   c. extra large apple
   d. ten celery stalks

3. Rank drink with most calories first:
   a. beer, 8 oz.
   b. whole milk, 8 oz.
   c. skim milk, 8 oz.
   d. cola drink, 8 oz.

4. Rank as most reliable source of weight control information:
   a. dietitian
   b. magazine ad
   c. pharmacist

Many more values-clarifying strategies can be easily adapted for use within nutrition courses.[6] I have used the above strategies, and feedback from students indicates that these are efficient, effective, and satisfying teaching techniques.

NOTES

1. J. R. Frymier, "Learning and Life – Some Answers Must Be Questioned," *Theory Into Practice* 8, no. 1 (February 1969): 37-38.
2. M. A. Poolton, "Predicting Application of Nutrition Education," *Journal of Nutrition Education*, Summer 1972, pp. 110-113.
3. Sidney B. Simon and Merrill Harmin, "Subject Matter with a Focus on Values," *Educational Leadership* 26 (October 1968): 34-39.
4. Sidney B. Simon, "Promoting the Search for Values," *School Health Review* 2 (February 1971): 21.
5. Louis E. Raths, Merrill Harmin, and Sidney B. Simon, *Values and Teaching* (Columbus, Ohio: Charles Merrill Publishing Co., 1966), p. 30.
6. Sidney B. Simon, Leland W. Howe, and Howard Kirschenbaum, *Values Clarification: A Handbook of Practical Strategies for Teachers and Students* (New York: Hart Publishing Company, Inc., 1972).

Training a Large Public School System in Values Clarification

by Diane Greene, Pat Stewart, and Howard Kirschenbaum

Values clarification came to Akron, Ohio, because the Assistant Superintendent of Curriculum and Instruction felt the need to give teachers some new methods to use in teaching values to children. Several programs were evaluated. In 1969, the Akron City Schools and the Akron Council of Churches joined to send eight people to a values-clarification workshop in East Rochester, New York. This was the beginning of a professional relationship with Dr. Merrill Harmin, Dr. Sidney Simon, and Howard Kirschenbaum.

Upon their return, the eight served as staff members for a workshop conducted by Dr. Simon and Mr. Kirschenbaum in August 1969. Sixty-two teachers, approximately one from every school in Akron, attended this first workshop. For five days, from 9:00 A.M. to 3:30 P.M., the teachers were introduced to these new methods. They returned to their buildings in September, highly motivated to use the strategies in their instructional program for the coming year. An important outcome of the first workshop was *Values Clarification: A Teacher's Guide*. A compilation of the ideas generated by teachers in the workshop, the book was developed through the joint efforts of the Akron Public School

Curriculum Committee on Moral and Ethical Values and an Akron Council of Churches Committee on Religion and Public Education. The first copies were distributed to members of the workshop.

The First Year

Ongoing activities the first year included an in-service meeting — a demonstration of values-clarification techniques — conducted by Dr. Sidney Simon and Howard Kirschenbaum for over one thousand teachers, the majority of the professional staff. At this time, teachers who were interested in further training submitted forms indicating their interest. In late spring of 1970, several evening in-service meetings in values clarification were held, using teachers from the previous summer workshop as resource people. These meetings were a prerequisite to being considered for the summer program and were attended voluntarily by about 250 teachers, with no stipend. Following the completion of these sessions, all interested teachers were given an opportunity to apply for the summer workshop. The plan was to give priority to the schools having at least three teachers apply for the workshop. These teachers would form the nucleus of a team which could present the strategies to other members of their staff during the next school year.

The Second Year

Harmin and Kirschenbaum were the leaders for the workshop in August 1970. Eight Akron teachers who had been to an advanced values-clarification workshop in Canandaigua, New York, a week prior to this, served as discussion leaders. Seventy-five teachers, representing a number of schools, attended. The workshop was coordinated by two secondary resource supervisors who had been involved in planning the original workshop. The stipend in this workshop as in all other summer workshops was fifteen dollars per day. In the fall of 1970, Kirschenbaum returned for a weekend follow-up workshop, attended voluntarily by about fifty of the seventy-five summer participants. The teachers received no stipend for any of the follow-up workshops. Early in 1971, teachers who had attended previous workshops were asked to submit samples of work or

examples of lessons using values clarification, identifying
successes and failures to the Office of Curriculum and
Instruction. This material was read and forwarded to
Kirschenbaum and Harmin. The plan at this time was to train
a team of Akron teachers to assume some of the responsibility
for workshop leadership. Ten teachers were selected and sent
to the Adirondack Mountain Humanistic Education Center,
in August of 1971, for advanced training. Upon returning,
the team assisted Harmin in conducting the workshop.

The Third Year

Approximately three hundred teachers attended this third
summer workshop. The ten team members worked as
assistants to Harmin in large group sessions during the
morning. In afternoon sessions, the team worked as
facilitators for smaller, grade level or subject matter groups.
In the fall of 1971, Harmin and Kirschenbaum returned for the
follow-up weekend workshop. Kirschenbaum remained in
Akron the following week visiting the classrooms of the
team and meeting with administrators. A meeting was also
held with the team, administrators, and Kirschenbaum to
discuss the future role of values clarification in Akron.
A plan for 1) values-oriented curriculum development; 2) a
newsletter for the four to five hundred Akron teachers who
had been in a summer values-clarification workshop; 3) the
formation of a demonstration school staffed by volunteer
teachers from the summer workshops; and 4) further
transferring of training responsibilities from the outside
consultants to the Akron team of specialists was
enthusiastically endorsed by the consultants, the team,
and to a large extent by the administration. Due to
administrative problems and delays, however, the first
three proposals never were actualized. In Kirschenbaum's
opinion, this inability to move beyond the workshop stage to
more concerted efforts on the part of the values-clarification
"community" within Akron represented a major
disappointment to, and a serious limitation of, the program.

On the other hand, the fourth proposal, the increasing
responsibility for training undertaken by the Akron team,
went ahead very successfully. The members were asked to
submit a written personal evaluation of their strengths and
weaknesses and their desire for future involvement with

values clarification as specialists. In the spring of 1972,
four of them (two elementary and two secondary teachers)
were selected to serve as specialists for a beginning workshop
in the coming summer. A week was spent at the Adirondack
Mountain Humanistic Education Center, with
Kirschenbaum and Harmin planning the workshop.

The Fourth Year

For the first time, the workshop was divided into two
groups based on prior involvement. A beginning workshop
for approximately two hundred teachers was conducted by
the four specialists, assisted by the other team members.
Harmin conducted an advanced workshop for fifty teachers
who had attended a beginning workshop in previous years.
He also served as consultant to the specialists. The two
workshops ran simultaneously in separate buildings.

Physical Plant for Workshops

Each year the summer workshop has been in a different
school. Among the factors considered important in
selecting the site were: 1) accessibility; 2) rooms for large
and small group activities; and 3) movable furniture.
Materials were kept at a minimum—chart paper, magic
markers, and index cards. Some audiovisual equipment was
used. In addition to the stipend, each teacher was
allocated a sum of money to purchase books and materials
on values clarification from the Adirondack Mountain
Humanistic Education Center.

Evaluation

At the end of the summer workshops of 1971 and 1972, the
participants were asked to fill out an evaluation. In 1971, 209
teachers responded. In the overall rating of the workshop,
97.1 percent indicated that the workshop was "good" or
"excellent." Over 94 percent indicated that they would welcome
further training; 78 percent of this group indicated that
they would be interested even without a stipend. In 1972, 239
teachers responded. There were about the same number
of teachers from outer city schools as there were from inner
city schools. The totals showed that almost all felt the
workshop was "good" or "excellent." Ninety-five percent
indicated they were interested in further training, and most

of them said they would attend without a stipend. In both years, 99 percent indicated they would use the strategies they had learned in their classrooms. The Summary and Conclusions for both 1971 and 1972 showed these comments:

"All respondents viewed the Values-Clarification Workshop as extremely worthwhile."

"Workshops should be offered even if stipends were not available."

"Workshops should include representation of professional staff personnel (teachers, counselors, principals, and central office staff)."

"All teachers should attend a workshop on values clarification."

Comments also frequently mentioned were:

"In-service sessions throughout a school year should have the main theme: Values Clarification."

"More time should be spent working on grade levels, subject areas, and special areas, i.e., art, gym, music, etc."

Classroom Involvement

The impact made by the first group of teachers who attended a values-clarification workshop was subtle and appeared to lack impetus. A closer appraisal indicated, as with any pioneer effort, that slowly but surely progress was made in interesting other teachers in values clarification. The first efforts resulted in teachers in isolated situations using the strategies. As other teachers in their buildings listened and observed them, they became interested enough to ask questions. In the spring of that year, Simon and Kirschenbaum returned to do an in service for most of the district's professional staff. Since that time there has been a substantial increase each year in the number of teachers who have attended workshops. The pattern can be characterized as being "each one teach one."

Teachers at every grade level and from all sections of the city report enthusiastically about their use of values clarification in the classroom. In the early stages they found it difficult to make it a part of the regular classroom activities. Often, the strategies were presented as an activity to stimulate thinking in a very general way. As teachers became more skilled at using the strategies, a greater degree of sophistication emerged. Teachers are now able to work with subject matter on three levels: 1) the facts level; 2) the concepts level; and 3) the values level. In many classrooms the experienced teacher has integrated values clarification with curriculum to such an extent that students no longer see strategies as isolated activities. A few examples may be useful.

One teacher was being cautioned by colleagues about a student he had received as a disciplinary transfer from an inner city high school. The teacher was told "never to turn his back on the student." By the time the teacher received these warnings, the student had been attending his classes for over a week. When he first came into class, the other students automatically included him in their groups. One particular strategy, Validation, was very effective in making him feel a part of the group. After a few days, he told the teacher that this was the first time anyone had ever paid any attention to what he did that was good. When slower students reach high school, many are afraid to respond because they have been "put down" so often by teachers. Students who have not been successful with traditional educational approaches see values clarification as giving them an equal place in the classroom. They find that working with teachers and students in such a humanistic way develops an awareness of being capable, yes, lovable too.

A high school boy who was "flicking" classes made an effort to regularly attend his English class. The teacher had developed a feeling of trust among her students using values strategies. In one Values Sheet which he completed, he told of stealing a TV set from a friend. Later he reported his part in the theft to the authorities. Many teachers report that students became more accepting of each other. Values clarification also gives students an opportunity to see the human side of teachers. When a student becomes aware of the conflicts in a teacher's life, it legitimatizes his feelings about his own conflicts and gives him some support as he seeks solutions.

The classroom environment becomes more dynamic when values clarification is used. Teachers report a more mobile and flexible program is developed. Students move from large group arrangements to small groups as the need arises. Often a discussion period becomes more meaningful and open when three or four people share with one another.

In one situation where a teacher was observing a Support Group discussion, she noticed one child who rarely said anything. Using a clarifying response, the teacher asked the child about this. The reply was: "I like to listen." This little girl was well on her way to developing a very important communication skill.

During a Class Circle meeting, a teacher was using strategies to clarify conflicts that were of concern to the students. The school counselor was also a part of the group. As the children became more aware and involved with the interaction taking place, one little girl directed a question to the counselor: "Are you learning things from us?" A simple sentence revealing the insight of a young child who felt comfortable in asking an adult if he was clarifying his values.

An awareness of the group process following a class project was revealed to a third grade through some Unfinished Sentences. Children completed the phrase "Working in groups I . . . ." Here are some responses.

"Working in groups I learned to get along."

"Working in groups I learned a lot about other people."

"Working in groups I learned that if I want to work, I can."

"Working in groups I learned working in groups is OK, but I like working by myself."

A kindergarten teacher draws faces that express moods, that is, sad face, happy face, angry face, etc., on individual discs. She then uses an Unfinished Sentence, and the children turn up the face that expresses their feeling. If she says, "Snowy days make me . . . ," then each child turns up a disc reflecting his feeling about snowy days. They are given an opportunity to state the complete sentence, building verbal skills as well as affective understanding. As the year progresses, she includes sentences that confront issues very real to the small child. When children don't want their feelings known, they cover their faces after they turn them up. Others are quite open and check to see who is in agreement with them and who differs. At other times she asks the children not to use their discs, but to use their own faces to express feelings — more of a role-playing situation.

A counselor at the junior high school level uses values-clarification strategies when counseling groups of students who have been referred to him for disciplinary action. He helps them explore alternatives to the actions which got them in

trouble and the consequences of each. Also, he gives the
students the alternatives he has for dealing with them as
offenders. They seek other possible alternatives and rank
order the realistic ones. Each student makes a choice based
upon his understanding of the total process.

A secondary resource supervisor visits classrooms and
observes the lessons for possible uses of values-clarification
strategies. In a conference with the teacher she shows how
the strategies might have been used. Hopefully, she has
aroused the teacher's interest and a desire to attend
a future workshop.

Since values clarification has been introduced to teachers
in the Akron schools, special curricular areas have included
the technique in their programs. Probably, the most extensive
project is a new career education program. It includes
every grade level, kindergarten to twelve. Values clarification
is used by the teachers and counselors in the program to
make the students aware of careers, work, and themselves.

A new course in behavioral science at the high school level
is being taught using values clarification and other
humanistic education techniques. In the fall of 1972, one of
the junior high schools was changed to a middle school. The
teachers assigned to the school attended a values-clarification
workshop. They report that using values-clarification
strategies is an important part of lesson planning. An
urban-rural project which works with two inner city junior
high schools presented a beginning workshop to the staffs
of those schools. This will be followed by an advanced
workshop in the summer of 1973.

Another project, "Friends Across the City," involved two
elementary classes from an inner city and outer city school
who visited one another each month for a year. They spent
a whole day getting to know one another. The teachers used
values-clarification strategies to bring about an awareness
of themselves that destroyed many of the racial myths
and prejudices.

Specialists' Activities

Values clarification has spread from workshops and
classrooms into many other areas. Akron values-clarification
specialists have been called on to demonstrate strategies for
college classes and to talk to student teacher seminars.

The specialists and team members have done in-service
programs within their own buildings and also for teachers
in other buildings. As a part of the Trend project, an
adult-education program in Akron, members of the team
have taught mini-courses in values clarification to parents
desiring it. Other school districts within the state have had
in-service programs and workshops facilitated by the
specialists. The specialists' involvement has also extended to
workshops out of the state. Teachers, principals, and
counselors from both in-state and out-of-state schools have
come to observe values clarification in action in classrooms.
College professors and church administrators have asked
for and received permission to attend summer values-
clarification workshops being taught in Akron. Presentations
have been made to the Akron Board of Education, church
groups, an honorary teacher's sorority, a group of
administrators, counselors, supervisors, and school
psychologists from northeast Ohio, and other interested
community groups. Teachers as well as specialists have
pretested materials to be published in the values-clarification
area for Dr. Harmin.

Strengths

From the evaluations come these statements:

"Values clarification teaches children how to think,
make decisions, choose from among alternatives, get along
with others, and understand themselves and their
world better."

"Values clarification brings out the importance of
listening."

"I now realize that living together happily depends on our
listening and actively trying to understand people, and this is
as important as teaching subject matter."

"I think I can teach my subject better through values
clarification because it humanizes education and also
humanizes the teacher."

"The strategies are easy to use and are very flexible."

"The strategies expose children to ideas in ways that are
new and interesting to them."

Weaknesses

Weaknesses expressed by teachers were:

"No set curriculum or study guides."

"Not enough representation of principals, counselors, resource teachers, and central office staff (administrators)."

"Vagueness of role of specialists in planning past, present, future."

"More techniques should be demonstrated for teachers of special areas, that is, art, music, gym, etc."

"Groups should be smaller."

Conclusion

Values clarification has received strong support from the Central Office Administration and the School Board. It was the beginning of a trend to include more humanistic approaches to education in Akron. Changes in attitudes and student participation can be seen by visiting teachers in classrooms where values clarification is being used.

Since its beginning in 1969, 651 teachers have attended at least one week-long summer values-clarification workshop. Many of these teachers have attended two or more workshops. These teachers have also attended weekend follow-up sessions with Harmin and Kirschenbaum on their own time with no pay, which indicates their degree of commitment.

In the future, Akron plans to continue involving teachers in beginning and advanced values-clarification workshops. This year, many programs are being offered without stipends because funds are short in Akron as in many other cities. The story of values clarification in Akron doesn't end "and they lived happily ever after." The opposition to its use has been heard from some parents and teachers. But the professional manner in which it has been handled at all levels is the primary reason for the satisfaction expressed by many. Some of the weaknesses cited by teachers have been corrected. There have been many audiovisual materials and books on values-clarification strategies added to professional libraries.

Principals are becoming more interested because they see the positive changes in students and teachers. The supervision and follow-up in individual classrooms at this time is not available.

In-service meetings for special subject areas have been held to show how values clarification can be a part of the regular, instructional program.

As the interest in humanistic education grows and teachers continue to develop this interest, the use of values clarification will continue to grow in Akron, Ohio.

Group Dynamics and Value Clarification

by Leland W. Howe

Reprinted from *Penney's Forum*, Spring/Summer 1972. Used with permission.

How do group dynamics in a classroom affect the process of values clarification? Why is it, for example, that one type of group arrangement in the classroom facilitates discussion of value issues while another inhibits communication?

The group dynamics in a classroom are often very complex. In such a brief article as this, one cannot hope to develop any real expertise in group dynamics; participation in university group dynamics courses or human relations labs can provide this kind of training. However, with just a little knowledge of some of the simpler dynamics, the teacher can improve the quality of interaction that occurs during the values-clarifying process.

One of the most common group dynamics problems teachers encounter in helping students clarify their values is selecting the appropriate group arrangement to facilitate student discussion and involvement. Teachers who do not realize the importance of the classroom seating arrangement often continue to use a didactic seating pattern. (See Figure 1.) This works well for presenting material with the purpose of informing; however, it is hardly appropriate to the values-clarifying approach.

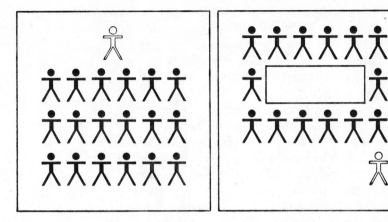

Figure 1 – Didactic Arrangement

Figure 2 – Discursive Arrangement
Around Tables

One of the problems in the didactic arrangement is that students, arranged in rows facing the front of the room, are forced to speak to each other's backs or turn in their seats to talk to one another during a values discussion. As a result, much of the nonverbal communication expressed in the face and body is lost. In addition, should the teacher remain in front of the class, as many do, the very fact that all eyes face forward tends to put the teacher in control of the discussion whether she likes it or not. Of course, the teacher may feel comfortable in this role, but it does little to encourage students to feel that *they and the teacher* are searching together as equals for the best values; instead, it is likely to foster the image that *only* the teacher knows what are the true, right, and wrong values that should be held. This, of course, violates one of the basic tenets of values clarification – that the student must, of his own free choice, arrive at his own values.

Of those teachers who do realize the importance that group arrangement has on a values discussion, some of them attempt to improve the situation by providing tables around which students are seated in a discursive type group. This is, indeed, an improvement over the didactic arrangement. However, there are still some problems to be encountered. For example, if students are seated around rectangular tables (see Figure 2), those at the ends, unless they are the

group leader(s) or the teacher, are likely to find that the focus
of the discussion centers *in the middle* of the table and they
are left out. Or, on the other hand, if the teacher or a strong
leader is seated at one end of the table, he or she is likely
to command the group's attention, as "the head of the table,"
and dominate the discussion.

One way to correct this, of course, is to provide round
tables. However, the tables themselves often create a
psychological barrier to the value-clarifying process. It is as
if people use the tables to hide behind so as not to reveal
personal information about themselves. During the early
stages of values clarification, as students are learning to
trust one another, the tables may help to create a climate of
psychological safety; but once a trusting climate has
developed in the classroom, the tables may well keep students
apart who, in fact, desire to be more personally involved
with one another in the search for values. When the tables
begin to act as barriers, they should go.

Figure 3 — Discursive Arrangement   Figure 4 — Maieutic Arrangement
     Without Tables

Figure 3 represents one of the most effective seating
arrangements for a group discussion of value issues. In this
arrangement, students pull their chairs into a circle so that
each is an equal member of the group. As simple as it sounds,
the teacher may have to help students see that those who
do not pull their chairs fully into the circle are usually not full

members of the group; their participation is likely to
be minimal—a fact that students, once it is pointed out, can
observe for themselves. The same thing tends to hold true
even in the smallest groupings of pairs or trios. For example,
students often sit side by side in a diad instead of facing each
other, or in a trio, swinging their chairs around so that each
is an equal member of the group. When this happens, the
teacher should help students develop more appropriate
spatial relationships.

Note that the teacher in Figure 3 has not joined the group,
but instead, makes her contributions from outside. By not
joining the group she is nonverbally communicating her
desire that students learn to carry the weight of the
discussion and not be dependent upon the teacher to do all
the clarifying. Of course, she may also verbalize this
expectation, but the important thing is that she *acts* to
encourage students to begin developing the clarifying skills
which she is modeling.

However, it would be a mistake for the teacher to always
remain outside the group. Once the group is able to function
on its own and no longer looks to the teacher for complete
guidance or total clarification, the teacher should attempt to
join the circle (see Figure 4) as simply another group
member (as much as this is possible). To remain outside the
group after it is functioning on its own may well communicate
to students, again nonverbally, that the teacher cannot
benefit from an ongoing search for better values—that,
perhaps, the teacher has already *arrived* at her values and
no longer needs to examine them. The point is, that if we are
to teach students that values clarification is a lifelong
process, as the theory holds, we teachers must be willing to
participate actively, as one human being with another,
in the search for values.

An Annotated Bibliography

INTRODUCTION

There have been several heroic efforts to pull together the vast number of publications dealing with attitudes, opinions, beliefs, morals — and *values.*

In 1959, E. M. Albert and C. Kluckhohn compiled their "Selected Bibliography on Values, Ethics, and Esthetics" (New York: The Free Press), containing nearly two hundred references. In 1966, Louis Raths, Merrill Harmin, and Sidney Simon (in *Values and Teaching,* Columbus, Ohio: Charles E. Merrill Publishing Co., pp. 263-267) listed a hundred sources which contributed to the formulation of their values-clarification approach. In 1967, Walter Thomas' "Comprehensive Bibliography on the Value Concept" (Project on Student Values, 3869 Plainfield, N.E., Grand Rapids, Michigan 49505) cited some eight hundred articles and books dealing with values, mostly appearing after 1945.

The bibliography which follows is less ambitious and more specialized.

With the publication of *Values and Teaching,* in 1966, there began a significant growth and interest in the educational approach that has come to be known as "values clarification." This bibliography is devoted entirely to the sources which fall directly in that values-clarification tradition. Criteria for inclusion were: 1) The item was written in 1965 or later, i.e., during and after the publication of *Values and Teaching.* 2) The author mentioned Raths' seven criteria or processes of valuing as being central to his discussion, *or* the author referred to the basic works or key names in values clarification as the basis for his discussion, *or* the author utilized much of the language, concepts, or methods of values clarification. 3) The writing presented an accurate picture of what values clarification is, even if to criticize it. In other words, writings that misrepresent values clarification were not included.

Clearly, these criteria do not encompass many excellent writings on the subject of values, including scores of articles and books that are entirely consistent with the goals and methods of values clarification even though they do not use its terminology. Nevertheless, we think there is value in a focused bibliography such as this one.

First, we hope to call attention to the significant number of writings on values clarification which have been published in the last several years. Secondly, the bibliography, hopefully, will be helpful in demonstrating that values clarification is not just the product of a few individuals, but that many educators and students have been furthering the work in this field. Implicit in this second reason is a third, and the most important, reason for this bibliography. We hope that others, by gaining a perspective on what has already been done in values clarification, will see new directions for carrying the work further — applying values clarification in new fields, modifying older values-clarification theories and practices, and applying the rigors of research to the values-clarification approach.

One final word. Undoubtedly, we have omitted many items which should be in this bibliography. Others that were included could not be annotated because we did not have a copy of the article by press time. Finally, new writings are appearing every month which are worthy of inclusion. We plan to up-date this bibliography periodically. Therefore, we welcome copies of any articles or other writings (tapes, films, etc.) which readers think should be included in the values-clarification bibliography. These may be sent to the authors at the Adirondack Mountain Humanistic Education Center, Upper Jay, N.Y. 12987.

An Annotated Bibliography On Values Clarification

by Howard Glaser-Kirschenbaum and Barbara Glaser-Kirschenbaum

Reprinted by permission of the authors and the Adirondack Mountain Humanistic Education Center, Upper Jay, New York 12987.

1965

Harmin, Merrill, and Simon, Sidney B. "The Subject Matter Controversy Re-Visited." *Peabody Journal of Education* 42, no. 4 (January 1965):194-205.

This article introduces the three levels of subject matter — the fact-oriented, generalization-oriented, and value-oriented levels — and applies them to the Pilgrim story, the Shakespeare play *Macbeth*, and Newton's laws of motion. It suggests that schools move from a focus on facts to a greater emphasis on the second and third levels as a means of making learning more exciting and meaningful.

Lieberman, Phyllis, and Simon, Sidney B. "Values and Student Writing." *Educational Leadership* 22 (March 1965):414.

This is the fullest discussion of the Value Cards strategy in the values-clarification literature. It includes many examples of students' Value Cards, an extended rationale for their use, many variations on the basic strategy, and helpful suggestions for the teacher.

Simon, Sidney B., and Lieberman, Phyllis. "Current Events and Values." *Social Education* 29 (December 1965):523-533.

Advocating that values-clarification strategies be an integral part of current events curricula, the writers provide examples of Value Sheets, with their controversial statements, followed by clarifying questions. Value Sheets included are: 1) a quote from Pastor Niemoller entitled "Speak Up"; 2) an article by C. A. Walls entitled "The Price of Peace"; and 3) an excerpt from *Core-later* entitled "Long Island Pickets."

1966

Harmin, Merrill. "Values in the Classroom: An Alternative to Moralizing." *Inservice Training for Teachers of the Gifted.* Edited by William Rogge and G. Edward Stormer. Champaign, Ill.. Stipes Publishing Co., 1966

A variety of strategies are presented to provide teachers with some classroom methods for helping children develop their own values. Examples included are: Value Sheets dealing with the areas of financial priorities and public affirmation of beliefs; the Devil's Advocate strategy exploring the topic of space travel; Thought Sheet; and several Values Continuums.

Raths, Louis E.; Harmin, Merrill; and Simon, Sidney B. *Values and Teaching.* Columbus, Ohio: Charles E. Merrill Publishing Co., 1966.

This was the first major book on values clarification. The first part of the book is a theoretical section with chapters on "The Difficulty of Developing Values," "Values and Valuing," and "Teaching for Value Clarity." The second part has chapters on "The Clarifying Response," "The Value Sheet," and a chapter that briefly discusses eighteen other strategies. The third section focuses on applying the value theory, with chapters on "Getting Started: Guidelines and Problems," "Emotional Needs, Thinking, and Valuing," and "Research Completed and Needed."

1967

Harmin, Merrill, and Simon, Sidney B. "Values and Teaching: A Humane Process." *Educational Leadership*

24 (March 1967):517-525.

Included in this article are examples of several strategies:
1) Clarifying Questions; 2) Value Sheets on the issues of
financial priorities and public affirmation of beliefs; 3) Values
Continuums on the topics of personal freedom, seat belts,
and military service; and 4) Thought Sheets.

Harmin, Merrill, and Simon, Sidney B. "Working with
Values in the Classroom." *Scholastic Teacher* 89
(6 January 1967):16.

This article provides an introduction to values clarification
for classroom teachers along with examples of Value Sheets,
Values Continuums, Devil's Advocate, and Zig-Zag Lesson.

1968

Clegg, Ambrose A., Jr., and Hills, James L. "A Strategy for
Exploring Values and Valuing in the Social Studies."
The College of Education Record, pp. 67-68. Seattle: University
of Washington, May 1968.

Contending that the schools constitute a major influence
in shaping children's values, the authors urge teachers
to adopt instructional materials designed to help students
explore value issues. They present an instructional model in
which they attempt to integrate Taba's approach to cognitive
tasks with Raths' valuing processes. A pilot study is
described in which this teaching strategy is applied to a fifth
grade social studies curriculum.

Harmin, Merrill, and Simon, Sidney B. "Using the
Humanities for Value Clarification." *Impact,* Journal of New
York State ASCD 8, no. 3 (Spring 1968):27-30.

The authors propose that in addition to teaching the factual
and conceptual levels of humanities subject matter, the
values level should be emphasized. Examples of these three
levels of teaching are given for the story of the Pilgrims in
America and for Shakespeare's *Macbeth.*

1969

Harmin, Merrill; Kirschenbaum, Howard; and Simon,
Sidney B. "Teaching History with a Focus on Values."
Social Education 33 (May 1969):568-570.

Using the three-levels concept of subject matter (facts, concepts, and values), the authors show how lessons on the United States Constitution and the topic of war might be taught with a focus on the students' values.

Harmin, Merrill; Nisenholtz, Bernard; and Simon, Sidney B. "Teaching for Value Clarity." *Changing Education* 4, no. 1 (Spring 1969):20-22.
The authors consider the values confusion of the urban slum child and his struggles; for example, the disparity between his desires and the social and economic realities he often must confront. The authors urge that educators teach the valuing process as a means of helping students sort through many of the conflicting issues and desires they must deal with. A variety of action-oriented projects are surveyed as a means of assisting students to act upon their values and perceive themselves as capable of effecting changes in their lives.

Kirschenbaum, Howard, and Simon, Sidney B. "Teaching English with a Focus on Values." *The English Journal* 58 (October 1969):1071.
The entire article is devoted to using the Value Sheet strategy in the English classroom. Examples are given to show how teachers can use the Value Sheet to help teach literature, poetry, composition, and discussion with a focus on values.

Raths, Louis; Harmin, Merrill; and Simon, Sidney B. "Helping Children Clarify Values." *Today's Education* 56, no. 7 (October 1969):12-15.
In light of rapid social change and the changing desirability of particular values, the authors offer teachers the "seven valuing processes" as an alternative to traditional methods of teaching values. A detailed description and explanation of the Clarifying Response is provided, and the Value Sheet strategy is presented briefly.

Simon, Sidney B. "Promoting the Search for Values." *Educational Opportunity Forum* 1, no. 4 (Fall 1969):75-84.
Following a brief introduction describing the need for values clarification, the author presents several strategies designed to help students develop their own values. Included

are: Weekly Reaction Sheets, Weekly Value Cards, an
Autobiographical Questionnaire, Time Diary, Confrontation
Questions, Value Sheets, and a description of a Values
Confrontation experience.

Simon, Sidney B., and Carnes, Alice. "Teaching Afro-
American History with a Focus on Values." *Educational
Leadership* 27, no. 3 (December 1969):222-224.
After a brief discussion of the need for values clarification,
the following strategies are discussed in connection with the
subject matter: Rank Order, Values Continuum, Devil's
Advocate, Open-Ended Question, Role-Playing, and the
Value Sheet.

Simon, Sidney B., and Harmin, Merrill. "Subject Matter
with a Focus on Values." *Educational Leadership* 26, no. 1
(October 1968): 34-39. [Reprinted as "Focus on Values for
More Relevant Schools." *NJEA Review* 43, no. 2 (October 1969).]
The authors present the three-level theory of subject
matter (facts, concepts, values) with examples from the study
of the United States Constitution and Shakespeare's *Hamlet.*

1970
Harmin, Merrill; Kirschenbaum, Howard; and Simon,
Sidney B. "The Search for Values with a Focus on Math."
Teaching Mathematics in the Elementary School, pp. 81-89.
Washington, D. C.: National Association of Elementary
School Principals and National Council of Teachers of
Mathematics, 1970.
The authors show how teaching mathematics and values-
clarification fit together. Examples of numerous math
problems, projects, and assignments that can be taught with
a focus on values are provided.

Harmin, Merrill; Kirschenbaum, Howard; and Simon,
Sidney B. "Teaching Science with a Focus on Values." *The
Science Teacher* 37, no. 1 (January 1970):16-20.
The authors point out that teaching science can and should
help students clarify their own values and the values
implications of the subject matter. Using the three-level
conception of subject matter (facts, concepts, and values)
they provide numerous examples of values-level teaching with

units on Newton's laws of motion, the earth's crust, electricity, weather, dissecting a frog, and a dozen other science topics.

Kirschenbaum, Howard. "The Listening Game." *Colloquy,* October 1970, pp. 12-15.
Reflections on a conversation between two women, overheard on a train, lead the author to thoughts on inter-generation communication and how we help young people make their own decisions. Two strategies for better communication and decision-making are then described — Rogerian Listening and The Free Choice Game.

Kirschenbaum, Howard. "Sensitivity Modules." *Media and Methods,* February 1970, p. 36.
This article includes a full discussion of the Sensitivity Module strategy, its purposes and risks. Examples of Sensitivity Modules are given on the theme of race and poverty. There are also examples of modules to use with young children and some in relation to subject matter.

Rees, Floyd D. "Teaching the Valuing Process in Sex Education." *School Health Review* 1, no. 1 (February 1970):14-17.
The author eloquently describes the need for sex education, the various approaches that educators have taken, the need for young people to formulate their own values regarding sexuality, a five-step valuing process, and many classroom activities to implement the process.

Schindler-Rainman, Eva. "Are Values Out of Style?" *Journal of NAWDC* (National Association of Women Deans and Counselors), Fall 1970, pp. 18-22.
Dr. Schindler presents three ways of looking at values, three types of value dilemmas, three stances for the value educators, a value dilemma exercise, and a somewhat novel section (with respect to this bibliography) on the characteristics of a value educator.

Simon, Sidney B. "Sensitizing Modules: A Cure for 'Senioritis.'" *Scholastic Teacher,* 21 September 1970, p. 28.
In an effort to vitalize twelfth grade curriculum and assuage senior restlessness, the author proposes a variety of experiential activities designed to increase students' social awareness and to confront them with real values

issues and concerns. Examples of twenty-five such Sensitivity Modules on the issues of race and poverty are described.

Simon, Sidney B. "Three Ways to Teach Church School." *Colloquy* 3, no. 1 (January 1970):37-38.
The author discusses the three levels of teaching (facts, concepts, and values) and gives examples of three-level teaching as applied to the story of Jesus' triumphant entrance into Jerusalem and the life of Saint Francis of Assisi.

Simon, Sidney B. "Your Values Are Showing." *Colloquy* 3, no. 1 (January 1970):20-32.
This article provides descriptions and examples of numerous values-clarification strategies: 1) Value Sheets, on the topics of football, migrant harvesters, and international peace; 2) Weekly Value Cards; 3) Values Continuums, on the military and on racial conflict; 4) Confrontation Questions, using the "Who Comes to Your House?" example; 5) Rank Orders, on famous civil rights leaders and on means to eliminate slums; 6) Time Diary; 7) Autobiographical Questionnaires; 8) Weekly Reaction Sheets; 9) list of Sensitivity Modules; and 10) Action Projects.

Westerhoff, John H. III. "How Can We Teach Values?" *Colloquy* 3, no. 1 (January 1970):17-19.
The editor of *Colloquy* reviews the Raths, Harmin, and Simon book *Values and Teaching*. In doing so, he puts together his own essay, discussing the need for values clarification and for teaching the valuing process. He concludes by suggesting the application of this approach to religious education.

Values Systems Techniques, 28 min, b&w, 16mm. Produced by Hamilton Wright. Available from ROA's Films, 1696 North Astor Street, Milwaukee, WI 53202.
This is a film showing Dr. Sidney Simon leading a panel of senior high school students in a demonstration of four values-clarification strategies: Values Voting, Rank Order, Proud Whip, and Public Interview.

1971

Harmin, Merrill, and Simon, Sidney B. "Values." *Teacher's Handbook*. Edited by Dwight Allen and Eli Seifman, pp.

690-698. Glenview, Ill.: Scott Foresman & Company, 1971.
   Three major alternatives for dealing with values are
carefully examined: 1) to do nothing about values; 2) to
"transmit" values using various approaches such as modeling,
reward and punishment, manipulation, etc.; and 3) to
"clarify values" using the "clarifying liberal arts approach"
and the "values skills approach." Critical consideration is
given to the issues and implications presented by each of
these orientations. A good, short bibliography of value
approaches is included.

   Kirschenbaum, Howard. "Clarifying Values at the Family
Table." Upper Jay, New York: Adirondack Mountain
Humanistic Education Center, 1971.
   This article is a description of and rationale for the Family
Circle strategy — a variation of the Values Whips. Fifty-two
Family Circle topics are given, with special examples of
circle topics for holidays, vacations, and guests.

   Kirschenbaum, Howard. "Teaching Home Economics with
a Focus on Values." Upper Jay, New York: Adirondack
Mountain Humanistic Education Center, 1971.
   Using examples created and used by home economics
teachers in their classrooms, this article shows how five
values-clarification strategies can be applied to home
economics issues. The strategies are: Unfinished Sentences;
Sensitivity Modules; Rank Order; Proud Whip; and Chairs,
or Dialogue with Self.

   Kirschenbaum, Howard, and Bacher, Robert. "Clarifying
Our Values." In *Community Communication and Communion
for Tenth Grade*, a Listening Post Program. Minneapolis:
Augsburg Publishing House, 1971.
   This article details instructions for conducting a ninety-
minute values-clarification session with students of high
school age. Strategies included are: Strongly Agree/Strongly
Disagree, the Values Grid, Rank Order, and Proud Line (Whip).

   Osman, Jack D. "The Feasibility of Using Selected
Value-Clarifying Strategies in a Health Education Course for
Future Teachers." Doctoral dissertation, Ohio State
University, 1971.

This is the full study summarized in Dr. Osman's article "The Use of Selected Value-Clarifying Strategies in Health Education," in the *Journal of School Health*, 1973. The dissertation is available through the University of Oregon Health and Physical Education Microcards at a minimal cost.

Simon, Sidney B. "Dinner Table Learning." *Colloquy*, December 1971, pp. 34-37.
To help make the evening meal an interesting and provocative learning experience, a variety of values strategies are presented with guidelines for their use. Included are examples of: Family Coat of Arms, Rank Order, Twenty Things You Love to Do, Family Circle topics, and Value Sheets.

Simon, Sidney B. "The Search for Values." *Edvance* 1, no. 3:1.
Not available to us for annotation at press time.

Simon, Sidney B. "Two Newer Strategies for Value Clarification." *Edvance* 2, no. 1 (September/October 1971):6.
Two values-clarification strategies – Twenty Things You Love to Do and I Learned Statements – are described.

Simon, Sidney B. "Values Clarification vs. Indoctrination." *Social Education*, December 1971, p. 902.
The values-clarification approach to values education is offered as an alternative to indoctrination, moralizing, or the denial of values issues. Five strategies are briefly described: Twenty Things You Love to Do, I Learned Statements, Baker's Dozen, I Urge Telegrams, and Personal Coat of Arms.

Simon, Sidney B.; Daitch, Patricia; and Hartwell, Marie. "Value Clarification: New Mission for Religious Education." *Catechist* 5, no. 1 (September 1971):8.
This article is the first of three designed to help religious educators assist children to develop a sense of worth and identity and to increase their ability to make choices and confront moral dilemmas. Strategies to accomplish these goals, provided in the article, are: Clarifying Questions, Twenty Things You Love to Do, I Learned Statements, High Point Identification, and Value Cards.

Simon, Sidney B.; Daitch, Patricia; and Hartwell, Marie. "Value Clarification: Part II." *Catechist* 5, no. 2 (October 1971):36-38.

This is the second article in a three-part series designed to help religious educators assist children in developing the valuing process. The values theory is briefly presented, and the following strategies are introduced: Values Grid, Personal Coat of Arms, Alligator River, and Hair Biography.

Simon, Sidney B.; Daitch, Patricia; and Hartwell, Marie. "Value Clarification: Part III." *Catechist* 5, no. 3. (November 1971):28-29.

This is the final article in a three-part series introducing values clarification to religious educators. The authors present the person of Jesus as one who had a clear set of values which he publicly affirmed and acted in accordance with. They urge teachers to serve as similar models of the Christian life. Contending that beliefs are prerequisites to the valuing criterion of affirmation and action, they offer four more strategies designed to help students examine their beliefs: Time Diary, Fall-Out Shelter Problem, I Urge Telegrams, and People Like Me.

Simon, Sidney B., and Hartwell, Marie. "Personal Growth Through Advertising." *Colloquy* 4, no. 11 (December 1971):34-37.

Not available to us for annotation at press time.

Simon, Sidney B., and Sparago, Edie. "Values: Clarification and Action." *Momentum* 2, no. 4 (December 1971):4-9.

This article seems to be several articles in one. It begins with a religious-existential discussion, asserting the importance of self-exploration and the determination of one's own values. Then, two examples of three-level teaching are described, using Jesus' triumphant entry into Jerusalem and the life of Saint Francis of Assisi. Then, five values-clarification strategies are presented: Twenty Things You Love to Do, Values Statements, Confrontation Questions, Values Continuums, and Rank Order. Dr. Simon concludes the article by discussing the values on which his own actions are based and the consequences of these actions.

Workshop on Values Clarification. New York: Seabury
Press. Complete reference not available to us at press time.
    This is a design for a ten-hour workshop on values
clarification.

1972

    Abramowitz, Mildred, and Macari, Claudia. "Values
Clarification in Junior High School." *Educational
Leadership* 29, no. 7 (April 1972): 621-626.
    This article is a comprehensive discussion of the need for
values clarification in the black and Puerto Rican high school
where the authors are administrators. Examples of five
strategies are provided: Twenty Things You Love to Do,
Alternatives Search, Values Voting, Values Continuum,
and Rank Order.

    "An Exchange of Opinion Between Kohlberg and Simon."
Learning 1, no. 2 (December 1972) :19.
    This brief article is introduced with the statement:
"Kohlberg and Simon talked with *Learning* about each other's
work and how it relates to his own. Their exchange of
opinions should help the teacher who wants to choose
between the constructs or create his own synthesis of
the two."

    Curwin, Gerri. "Pages from My Autobiography." *Trend* 8,
no. 1, Spring 1972.
    Not available to us for annotation at press time.

    Curwin, Gerri; Curwin, Rick; Kramer, Rose Marie;
Simmons, Mary Jane; and Walsh, Karen. *Search for Values.*
Villa Maria, Pa.: The Center for Learning, Inc., 1972.
    Search for Values is a unique collection of seven structured
units designed to assist junior and senior high school
students in personally exploring their values on the topics of
time, competition, authority, personal space, commitment,
relationships, and images. The package consists of an
instructor's manual and seven envelopes (one for each unit)
containing a total of seventy-seven spirit masters of
various strategy sheets.

Goodman, Joel, and Hawkins, Laurie. "Value Clarification: Meeting a Challenge in Education." *Colloquy* 5, no. 5 (May 1972):18-22.

This article provides a detailed description of the first session of an eight-week values-clarification course offered by two graduate students to a group of undergraduates in a college dormitory. Strategies described include -ing Name Tags, Here and Now Wheel, Alligator River, Pattern Search, Dear Me Letters, and brief descriptions of several others.

Gray, Farnum. "Doing Something About Values." *Learning* 1, no. 2 (December 1972):15-18.

The author describes his experiences in a two-day values-clarification workshop conducted by Dr. Sidney B. Simon. Interspersed are the author's observations of values clarification as it is used in several schools and excerpts of his interview with Dr. Simon.

Hawley, Robert C. "Values in the Classroom." *Independent School Bulletin* 32, no. 1 (October 1972):19-23.

The author discusses the need for values clarification, reviews Raths' seven valuing processes, and describes the open-accept-stimulate sequence of values clarification in a classroom. He gives examples of eight strategies: Values Voting, Rank Order, Values Whips, Value Cards, I Learned Statements, Here and Now Wheel, and forced choice games which include The Fall-Out Shelter Problem and Alligator River.

Howe, Leland. "Group Dynamics and Value Clarification." *Penney's Forum*, Spring/Summer 1972, p. 12.

This article examines several student seating arrangements, considers the group dynamics facilitated by each seating arrangement, and discusses how these group dynamics would affect the use of values-clarification strategies.

Kelley, Paul, and Conroy, Gladys. "A Promotive Health Plan Preventing Alcohol and Drug Abuse in the Schools." *Arizona Medicine*, January 1972.

This is a brief article in which the authors state that drug abuse is merely a symptom which must be cured by building a healthy psychological foundation. This foundation consists of a positive self-concept (the "IALAC" concept is described) and an effective "valuing process."

Kirschenbaum, Howard. "The Free Choice English Curriculum." Upper Jay, New York: Adirondack Mountain Humanistic Education Center, 1972.
This article shows how a junior or senior high school English department can help students develop both their own values and a better appreciation of literature and writing. In the "free choice" curriculum, students choose their English course from a variety of English department offerings. Many examples are provided, and the realities of changing to such a curriculum are discussed.

Knapp, Clifford E. "Attitudes and Values in Environmental Education." *The Journal of Environmental Education* 3, no. 4 (Summer 1972):22-29.
This paper briefly defines "attitudes" and "values," discusses the role of teachers and schools in teaching attitudes and values, and examines some of the research in environmental attitudes.

Knapp, Clifford E. "The Environment: Children Explore Their Values." *Instructor* 81, no. 7 (March 1972):116-118.
The author discusses the need for values clarification in the environmental area and presents many strategies to help students explore their environmental values. This article was later expanded into "Teaching Environmental Education with a Focus on Values."

Knapp, Clifford E. "Teaching Environmental Education with a Focus on Values." Upper Jay, New York: Adirondack Mountain Humanistic Education Center, 1972.
After discussing how the seven valuing processes relate to environmental education, the author shows how to apply the valuing strategies to the subject. Strategies presented are: Value Sheets, Pictures without Captions, Role-Playing, Contrived Incidents, Devil's Advocate, Values Continuum, Open-Ended Questions, Time Diary, Autobiographical Questionnaire, Values Voting, Rank Order, and other class activities.

Simon, Sidney B. "Election Year and Dinner Table Learning." *Colloquy* 5, no. 9 (October 1972):23-25.
Focusing on election-year topics, this paper describes several values-clarification strategies for use with children during the evening meal. Examples include: Values Voting topics, Rank Order, Designing Buttons, I Urge Telegrams, Pictures without Captions, If Situations, Where Do You Draw the Line?, and Value Sheets.

Simon, Sidney B. "The Teacher Educator in Value Development." *Phi Delta Kappan* 52, no. 10 (June 1972):649-651.
A brief introduction and summary emphasize the need for values clarification as a part of teacher training. The bulk of the article describes six strategies for doing this: Twenty Things You Love to Do, I Learned Statements, Personal Coat of Arms, Baker's Dozen, Opposite Quadrants, and a sample Value Sheet entitled "We're Really Getting It Together, Man."

Simon, Sidney B. "Values Clarification and Shalom." *Colloquy* 5, no. 7 (July/August 1972):18-21.
The concept of "shalom" is examined through the use of eight values-clarification strategies: What You Know and What You Don't Know, Unfinished Sentences, Priority Ladder (Forced Choice Ladder), Rank Order, Significant Others in Your Life, Where Do You Draw the Line?, Values Sheet, and Composition for Personal Growth.

Simon, Sidney B. "What Do You Value?" *Penneys Forum*, Spring/Summer 1972, pp. 4-5.
This article consists of instructions for the use of three values-clarification strategies: Twenty Things You Love to Do, Personal Coat of Arms, and Baker's Dozen.

Simon, Sidney B.; Curwin, Gerri; and Hartwell, Marie. "Teaching Values." *Girl Scout Leader* 14, no. 4 (June 1972) :12.
After a brief introduction to values clarification, the authors present various values strategies focusing on Girl Scout interests and materials. Exercises include: a Girl Scout song lyric used as a Value Sheet, Inventory Surprises, Unfinished Sentences, Positive Points, and Fantasy Seeds.

Simon, Sidney B.; Howe, Leland W.; and Kirschenbaum, Howard. *Values Clarification: A Handbook of Practical Strategies for Teachers and Students.* New York: Hart Publishing Company, Inc., 1972.

This book is the second major work on values clarification, pulling together much of the developmental work completed after the publication of *Values and Teaching.* After an overview of the values-clarification approach and a chapter on the use of the handbook, the bulk of the volume is devoted to describing seventy-nine strategies for values clarification. Each strategy includes a section for: Purpose, Procedure, Examples, Variations, and To the Teacher. Hundreds of examples of the basic strategies such as Values Voting, Rank Order, etc., are provided, often distinguishing questions appropriate for different age levels.

Simon, Sidney B.; Kirschenbaum, Howard; and Fuhrmann, Barbara. *An Introduction to Values Clarification.* New York: J. C. Penney Company, 1972.

This is a packaged seven-session teaching unit. For each session, there is a folder containing instructions to the teacher as well as wall charts, overhead transparencies, Value Sheets, etc. All seven folders and an Introduction folder are boxed. The whole kit may be borrowed, at no cost, from the Consumer Relations Department of any J. C. Penney Store.

Simon, Sidney B.; Howe, Leland W.; and Kirschenbaum, Howard. "Strategies for Value Clarification." *Penneys Forum,* Spring/Summer 1972, pp. 8-11.

After a brief introduction to the seven valuing processes and the guidelines for using values-clarification exercises, three strategies are presented: What's in Your Wallet?, Unfinished Sentences, and Chairs, or Dialogue with Self.

Values. A game by Colin Proudman. Cincinnati: Friendship Press, Distribution Office, P.O. Box 37844, 1972.

This is a board game for about three to six players. Depending on where the spinner stops, players choose from one of four piles of cards. Each card has a values topic or problem. Depending on some other game variables, the player answers one question on the topic from each player, makes a statement on the topic, chooses to be interviewed on one of the areas of confusion and conflict, or is challenged by another player.

1973

Harmin, Merrill; Kirschenbaum, Howard; and Simon, Sidney B. *Clarifying Values Through Subject Matter: Applications for the Classroom.* Minneapolis: Winston Press, Inc., 1973.

This book draws together and amplifies all the previous work by the authors and their colleagues in combining values clarification with the teaching of subject matter. The three-level conception of subject matter receives its fullest discussion to date. Examples of three-level teaching are provided for every subject in the school curriculum. Other approaches to teaching subject matter with a focus on values are suggested.

Howe, Leland; Wolfe, David; and Keating, Marianne. "Teaching Foreign Language with a Focus on Values." *Hispania,* Journal of the American Association of Teachers of Spanish and Portugese 5b, March 1973.

Not yet available for annotation at the time of this writing.

Kirschenbaum, Howard. "Beyond Values Clarification." In this work, pp. 92 -110.

The author critiques Raths' seven criteria for a value; advocates the elimination of "criteria" in favor of "processes of valuing"; relates the processes of valuing to other process goals of humanistic education; and, using a new concept of the "life processes" or "life skills," recommends the integration of various humanistic approaches.

Kirschenbaum, Howard. "Values Clarification in an Organizational Setting." In this work, pp. 327-335.

In a planning letter to his colleague Merrill Harmin, the author describes a developmental sequence of strategies to help a national organization clarify its values, goals, and program directions.

Kirschenbaum, Howard, and Simon, Sidney B. "Values and the Futures Movement in Education." *Education for*

Tomorrow. Edited by Alvin Toffler. New York: Random House, Inc., 1973, in press.

The startling increase in knowledge has forced subject matter education to move from the learning of facts to "learning how to learn." Similarly, the threat of "future shock" demands that values education change from "teaching values" to teaching a "process of valuing." The values-clarification approach is examined in detail in a historical context.

Osman, Jack D. "A Rationale for Using Value Clarification in Health Education." *Journal of School Health*, May 1973.

The author summarizes the major aspects of values clarification—the need for it, the seven processes of valuing, the three levels of teaching, the strategies—and advocates the use of values clarification in the health education curriculum. He concludes with a listing of the "student advantages" and "teacher advantages" of values clarification.

Osman, Jack D. "Teaching Nutrition with a Focus on Values." *Nutrition News* 36, no. 2, (April 1973):5.

Using the three levels of teaching concept and the seven processes of valuing, the author argues for the use of values clarification in nutrition education. He describes four values strategies for doing this: a Dual Continuum on the subjects of nutrition and weight; an ingenious adaptation of Twenty Things You Love to Do called "Ten Foods You Love to Eat and Drink"; Values Voting; and Rank Order.

Osman, Jack D. "The Use of Selected Value-Clarifying Strategies in Health Education." *Journal of School Health*, October 1973.

Dr. Osman summarizes his doctoral research, in which he measured the effects of values clarification on several groups of education students. He presents many examples of Value Sheets and Thought Cards to illustrate two of the twenty valuing strategies the students experienced and discusses the measures and tests he used and what the results were.

Simon, Sidney B., and Hartwell, Marie. "Values Clarification, a Heritage of Wisdom." *Curriculum Trends*, January 1973.

The amount of time that children spend watching TV (they average 350,000 commercials by age seventeen) points up the need to help young people sort out all their inputs, i.e., the need for values clarification. Several methods of doing this are described: three-level teaching, using *Macbeth* as an example; the Values Continuum, using the issue of seat belts as an example; and Value Sheets, using the example entitled "Ecology and Its Implications."

Simon, Sidney B.; Hawley, Robert; and Britton, David. *Composition for Personal Growth: Values Clarification through Writing.* Amherst, Mass.: Education Research Associates, 1971. New York: Hart Publishing Company, Inc., in press.

A large number of values-clarification and personal growth activities are suggested to encourage students to begin writing about themselves, their feelings, their thoughts and opinions, and their values. The activities are designed to make writing a comfortable, enjoyable, and successful experience that will lead to more effective written communication. Some rationale and theoretical background for the teacher is provided.